The Incomplete
Traveler

The Incomplete Traveler

Diaries of a Cuban Exile

Andrea Bermúdez

Copyright © 2010 by Andrea Bermúdez.

Library of Congress Control Number:		2010914313
ISBN:	Hardcover	978-1-4535-8650-1
	Softcover	978-1-4535-8649-5
	Ebook	978-1-4535-8651-8

All rights reserved. No part of this book may be reproduced or transmitted in any form or by any means, electronic or mechanical, including photocopying, recording, or by any information storage and retrieval system, without permission in writing from the copyright owner.

This book was printed in the United States of America.

To order additional copies of this book, contact:
Xlibris Corporation
1-888-795-4274
www.Xlibris.com
Orders@Xlibris.com
85344

CONTENTS

Part VI—Surviving the Odds

DEDICATION

To María Rodríguez (Tata) whose memory inspires me every day, and to my grandchildren John Paul, Katherine, Julianne, Peter, Andrea, and Max for whom this book was written.

ACKNOWLEDGMENTS

THERE ARE MANY people who deserve acknowledgment. I want to thank my partner, Dr. Deborah Shaw, for her support and encouragement and for having acted as *un diccionario ambulante* (a walking dictionary). My appreciation also goes to my daughter Flori Oross for sharing her high tech skills in photo editing and website design. I am also grateful to Saroj Baxter and Lynn deMartin for their invaluable comments and suggestions.

Special gratitude is extended to Hilda Rush, my young-at-heart ninety-eight-year-old friend, for her enthusiasm about the premise and contents of this book. She understands well the grief of losing a homeland and the need to reinvent yourself to cope with a new environment.

I am specially appreciative of my children, Flori and James Oross and Julie and E. J. Bermúdez, who showed an interest in my past as part of their future, and of the ever-present memory of my son Peter (1962-1982).

I also want to thank my six grandchildren, my true inspirations, John Paul and Katherine Oross and Julianne, Peter, Andrea, and Max Bermúdez. They are the future.

It would have been so much easier to write this book without the help of our two dachshunds, Charlie and Lily, who chose my lap while I researched and wrote this narrative. However, their devotion is worth the aggravation of precariously balancing my laptop on my lap doxies.

PROLOGUE

Memory is a way of holding onto the things you love, the things you are, the things you never want to lose.

—From the television show, *The Wonder Years*

THE INCOMPLETE TRAVELER: Diaries of a Cuban Exile was conceived as a narrative to be shared with my grandchildren. Those who have suffered the loss of a homeland know that one of the most difficult realizations is the inability to pass on to the next generations the love and respect that are felt for the mother country. My children and grandchildren may never get to see the Cuba of their ancestry, and I wanted very much to portray this experience for them.

The book is divided into six parts following a chronological path as closely as the course of a complex life has allowed. The experiences have taken place as narrated with very few liberties taken. Most names of the individuals herein mentioned have been changed to protect their privacy.

Part 1, "Setting the Stage Leading Up to the Revolution," presents the history of events that preceded the arrival of Castro. The narrative is not intended to be a historical compendium, but I have done my best to compress such a rich and varied history into a few pages without glossing over important events.

The second part of the book, "Support Systems," describes the family as the axis from which all support and love must come. Family life and the circle of friends are included in what is intended to explain the complex role of the Cuban family before the Castro days.

"Understanding the Cuban Spirit," the third part, attempts to define what I see as the essence of being Cuban. Special attention is given to the role of language, religion, and music in the development of the Cuban psyche. A tour of Cuba, along with its flora and fauna, provides the context for getting to know the Cuba of yesteryear, my Cuba.

As a matter of historical background, part 4, "The Anatomy of a Revolution," discusses the historical events that gave rise to the communist takeover of the island. It provides chapters explaining how the change in the course of history affected us directly as a family.

Part 5, "In Search of a Homeland," presents the challenges to overcome in the new environment. After Bay of Pigs came the realization that we would not be returning to Cuba. Cultural adaptation vis-à-vis the American dream is the central thread of this section.

Lastly, part 6, "Surviving the Odds," talks about loss and survival and shows the main character, Elena, looking forward to her next step in life, just as her father did when he was approaching the end of his.

I hope that I have been fair in judging the events and people that destiny has placed along my way. It has been a long and productive journey with a few difficult bumps in the road. If there is one message I want to convey, it is to have the courage to accept life as it presents itself, understanding that every event in our lives serves a purpose.

ANDREA BERMÚDEZ

PART I

Setting the Stage Leading Up to the Revolution

CHAPTER 1

When the Past Becomes a Memory

*We live in a moment of history where change is so speeded up that we begin
to see the present only when it is already disappearing.*

—R. D. Laing

I T WAS AUGUST 5, 1960, in Havana, Cuba, at the Iglesia Corpus
Christi, an intricately decorated but surprisingly modern church. Its
massive stained-glass windows contradicted the small size of the chapel. It
would have felt cozy if it had not been for the excessive presence of gold
relics. A beautiful young bride and her proud father were making their way
down the aisle as guests smiled appreciatively at the pair.

Dr. Bernardo Vidal had made a name for himself as a family physician.
A devoted man, he was revered by his patients and his family. Dr. Vidal
and his wife, Sara, had been married for over thirty years. Together, they
had four children: Bernardo Jr. (Bernie), who had just finished his medical
degree; Alejandro (Alex), a fourth-year law student at the University of
Havana; Elena, who had attended the University of Havana; and David
(Davidsito), a recent high school graduate.

Tonight, Dr. Vidal was giving his daughter in marriage to Roberto
Medina, a young attorney from a distinguished Catholic family. The
Medinas were a large clan, and Roberto was the youngest. The father
was also an attorney well-known for his aggressive manner in court. Mrs.
Medina was devoted to the children. The eldest was a nun in the Order
of the Sacred Heart, and their second, a son, had been ordained as a Jesuit
priest. Their three other boys were in a successful auto parts business
together. Roberto had thought of following in his older brother's footsteps

but decided that he did not have the discipline required to become a priest. Although disappointed by Roberto's decision, the family seemed very pleased with the marriage.

As Elena and her father continued their stroll down the aisle, she was committing faces to memory, knowing that in two weeks the newlyweds would be leaving the country for an indefinite time. Elena looked at Pilar, Teresita, Ramiro, Mrs. López, their high school history teacher. They were all beaming with delight at the sight of their friend. Every face brought a pleasant memory, and that in itself made Elena realize that soon that would be all she had left of them.

Dr. Bernardo Vidal and his
daughter Elena on her wedding day, August 5, 1960.

There was Tata, Elena's lifelong nanny, who was not beaming. She was overwhelmed by the memory of her and Elena, then five, anxiously waiting for Dr. Vidal's blue sedan to arrive with a promised surprise for the little girl. Tata remembered a moment of perfect happiness when the little girl opened the big box to find a red and blue wooden *carriola* (scooter) already assembled. Elenita could not wait to get outside, so she did not hesitate to

ANDREA BERMÚDEZ

drive the scooter into the living room. It was slow, but the little girl thought it was special and enjoyed it until the toy was outgrown. The memory made Tata smile at the bride. It was a moment of perfect sadness.

Tata and Elena

It should have been a joyous day for Elena, but her heart was heavy. At a deeper level, she sensed that this moment could be the last time she ever saw her friends, and suddenly memories of happy times were overpowering. By the time Elena and her father reached the altar, she was wondering why everyone was smiling.

After a short ceremony, the wedding guests joined the family at their home to celebrate the event. Toasts to a happy future failed to give Elena confidence about their impending plans after the wedding. Suddenly a sharp knock at the door silenced the animated festivity. Mrs. Vidal opened the door to three armed militiamen who pushed their way into the living area. They informed her that they needed to conduct a *registro* (search) of the premises. Word had gotten to the officers that the former chief of police was hiding somewhere in the neighborhood. With no other alternative than to let them in, Mrs. Vidal took upon herself to follow two of the men as the third one stayed by the door, weapon drawn. The two men looked inside closets, inside drawers, under beds, Mrs. Vidal never failing to remind them that the former chief was too chubby to fit in the spaces they were searching.

To Dr. Vidal's relief, the three returned from the unexpected search. Sara was still in one piece despite her hostility toward the uninvited visitors. The men left empty-handed and as unapologetic as when they had come in. The party came to an abrupt end, and the signs were loud and clear that the new Cuba was no longer a welcoming place for the family.

In Cuba, it was customary for friends of the bride to decorate the hotel room where newlyweds would go before leaving on a honeymoon. Elena and Roberto had chosen the brand-new Havana Hilton, the tallest and most luxurious hotel at the time with first-class restaurants, casino, and rooftop swimming pool. Her best friends Ofelia, Xenia, and Pilar made it their mission to decorate the quarters, a fact that should have served as a warning sign to Elena. Suite 1517 was beautiful, sporting views of a city that, until then, "never slept." As Elena moved around admiring her friends' good taste, she started to find notes everywhere. Under a champagne bottle, she found "*maliciosa*" (bad girl); under her pillow, "*dale muchacha*" (go for it); under her beautifully handmade negligee, "Is this necessary?" Elena was so mortified. It was hard enough to meet her destiny without reminders of what was about to happen. She could have killed her friends who, as a "by the way," later told her that they were across the street sipping white wine, staring at suite 1517, and creating their own unleashed version of what was going on. Elena must not have been too upset with her buddies as she saved those notes as a reminder of all the fun times they had shared together.

With two weeks to spare before their travel date, Elena and Roberto took a weekend in world-renowned Varadero Beach for their honeymoon. Situated on a peninsula in the northern coast of Matanzas province, the beach was an exemplar of the immeasurable beauty only nature can create. Views from the Hotel Internacional highlighted the splendor and serenity of Varadero's turquoise seascape. As she looked at the incomparable view, she felt overwhelmed by the immensity of what she and Roberto were about to give up. "Are we sure we must leave?" she would ask her husband, knowing full well what the answer would be. The newlyweds held hands, and for the first time Elena saw Roberto cry. They walked down the miles and miles of powdery sand in silence, each saddened by the realization that their beloved homeland was to be no more. They walked until pain reminded them that they were alive. Their return to the hotel was nothing more than a farewell to the beauty of their island and a hopeful prayer that someday they would return.

August 20, the departure date for the young couple, was fast approaching. Elena was already having second thoughts about her plans

ANDREA BERMÚDEZ

for a new life. She realized that she had lived in a shell, protected. From what? From life itself. Domestic responsibilities had not been passed on to her. She had been raised to live in a world that no longer existed. Elena was now embarking on a journey that would place her into an unknown environment for which she was ill-prepared.

That very date, August 20, happened to commemorate the feast of Saint Bernard of Clairvaux, a twelfth-century French saint of noble parentage, after whom the two Bernardos had been named. This year, it would be a very different day for the Vidal family. Traditionally, August 20 was the only date the family celebrated. The festivities started early in the morning and would last till the wee hours. Hundreds of people —patients, friends, family— attended the open house. Mrs. Vidal's siblings and their help assisted in the preparation of the generous food and drinks that were served to the guests. Numerous gifts, too many to count, were brought for the good doctor. It was an incredible day! And so was the next when the presents were opened— hundreds of pens, ties, money clips, cigar boxes, what have you. It was enough to open a curio shop! Mrs. Vidal knew that this gathering would soon become another thing of the past.

As Elena prepared for her impending departure to the United States, she could not help but be overcome by early memories of growing up in Cuba. Born on Easter Sunday in 1941, she vividly remembered a brutal cyclone, later named the Havana Hurricane, which hit Cuba late in the 1944 season. Its force destroyed Havana harbor and caused in excess of three hundred deaths, mainly in the rural areas of Cuba. Early that day, she recalled walking down the street with her dad as the family was moving to a safer place, her aunt and uncle's home, which had a basement. Papi, as she affectionately called her father, was not a big man, but his stride forced Elena to be on her tippy toes running as fast as she could. Realizing that Elenita was panting, Papi had to adjust his pace, and it took them quite a while to walk the three blocks that separated the families.

The experience of a hurricane filled the little girl with horror. Only candlelights illuminated the dwelling, and the howling of the wind frightened her. Papi realized her anxiety and picked her up in his strong arms. Elena could now see through a small window big objects flying in the wind. Suddenly, all noise stopped, and an eerie silence engulfed the family. The eye of the hurricane was now passing over them. After that, she remembered lots of rain.

When the Vidals returned home the morning after the hurricane, they found their bedroom door blown away and Mrs. Vidal's closet emptied.

Days later, the cook came in doubled up in laughter, saying that people at the neighboring grocery store were poking fun at a woman's girdle hanging from an electric pole— probably Mrs. Vidal's. In future years, Elena and her friends would enjoy the aftermath of a hurricane, as schools would be out, and there would be plenty of downed trees to climb on. The innocence of childhood.

Elena had grown up living across the street from a long-standing political family who had five daughters, all named María— María Elena, María Cristina, María del Pilar, María de Lourdes, and María Dolores. Las cinco Marías, as they were dubbed, went by their middle names. Pilar had been one of her closest friends and Elena loved her like a sister. Extended families were composed of distant relatives and close friends who shared a special appreciation for the relationship. Since families in Cuba tended to live in the same place for years at a time, it was likely they would develop close and stable relationships with friends and neighbors. Elena grew up loving her "Aunt" Katia, for instance, who was not related to anyone in the family but was a good friend of her mom's.

Elena and Pilar had shared many enjoyable times throughout their long friendship. During the early times of the revolution, they also lived some anxious moments, which, fortunately for them, had no serious consequences. One of those incidents took place one evening in early 1960. The friends were driving brother Bernie's car when, as they crossed the Almendares River bridge, they came to a halt in traffic.

Almendares River bridge in Havana

ANDREA BERMÚDEZ

They continued their nonstop conversation when suddenly Elena realized that the military jeep in front of them had moved ahead and she needed to catch up. Cars behind them were getting annoyed and were honking impatiently, so Elena accelerated to get closer to the jeep. When Elena tried to stop, the brakes would not work. With little or no time to react, she took a chance that the right lane would be clear and, in the blink of an eye, maneuvered the car around the jeep. The militiamen stared at them, seemingly ready to follow. Elena turned right at the first opportunity, and the car eventually came to a halt. Pilar's purse had wedged itself under the brake pedal prompting the near miss. Their hearts were beating fast and loud rendering them unable to speak. It took a few minutes for nervous laughter to take over and give Elena the courage to drive on. Looking at the possibility of being followed, they meandered until they were assured the jeep full of militiamen was nowhere in sight. They had tempted fate one more time and gotten away with it.

Living with political turmoil had been a big part of Elena's growing-up years. Like hurricanes, revolutions disrupted people's lives, but in the end, coping mechanisms helped Cubans survive and adapt. During Elena's nineteen years in Cuba, she had lived through two major revolutions and numerous student demonstrations and armed conflicts. Both of her parents' experiences eclipsed Elena's as they had lived for most of their lives with political instability, military unrest, and revolution.

It was hard for Elena to accept that all that was familiar was going to be left behind only to be replaced by things unknown. She was not thinking only about humans, she was also thinking about her black horse, Onyx, and Lady, the family dog. Her eyes filled with tears at the memory of her Saturday outings with Cundo, the horse trainer, and her dad. Onyx was a Tennessee walker that had belonged to Bernie and now was her refuge. She was a fine specimen! On those Saturday rides, Elena seemed to forget the unsteadiness of the life around her. She remembered the Almendares River, the magnificent ceibas (silk cotton trees), the stately royal palms, and most importantly, her Papi by her side. Elena cherished the image of scratching behind Onyx's ear and feeling her gentle nuzzling as a gesture of affection for the rider.

It was also going to be tough leaving the family dog behind. Lady, an eight-year-old white and black pointer, had been a Christmas present from one of her father's patients. Lady's parents were both champions, so she came expecting the special attention guaranteed by her aristocratic lineage. She got it. Everyone loved her highness. After one of Bernie's trips to the United States, Lady was renamed. For years, the family unwittingly called Lady by her new name until Mrs. Vidal found out they had been using a vulgar English word Bernie had learned in the States. The infamous prankster had embarrassed his mom, and Lady was back to her old name. Only those individuals who love nature can truly appreciate how genuine friendship with animals really feels and how much it hurts to let them go.

Elena was going to miss her favorite restaurants, not to mention her much-loved Cuban cuisine. On her eighteenth birthday, Roberto, her husband-to-be, had invited her to the Floridita, a famous restaurant in Old Havana, not too far from the Cathedral. The restaurant, launched in 1817, had been a favorite of Ernest Hemingway. His stool was still reserved in his honor at the bar. In the 1950s, the place was considered one of the world's premier restaurants. The Floridita has also been celebrated for its daiquiri (rum, sugar, lemon juice), Hemingway's favorite drink. It gained the restaurant the nickname *cuna del daiquiri* (daiquiri's cradle). Elena and Roberto thoroughly enjoyed the legendary drink as well as the fabulous meal that lived up to the young couple's high expectations. Traditional Cuban music played by a trio of guitars added to the enjoyment of a memorable evening, which was played out in her mind many times over.

During her last days in Havana, Elena was going around memorizing faces and places. She had no idea when a return would be possible, so for now all she could do was to transform her life into memories. The idea of an imminent departure filled her with anxiety and fear, but was there an alternative? The answer was no. Living in fear was far worse.

ANDREA BERMÚDEZ

CHAPTER 2

Spanish Colonization

Each nation feels superior to other nations. That breeds patriotism— and wars.
—Dale Carnegie

As an avid student of her own history, Elena was captivated by pre-Colombian life in Cuba. She had been taught that the populations of Taíno (men of the good), Guanahatabeyes, and Ciboney peoples had been annihilated. She knew that this was not completely accurate as entire neighborhoods or *caseríos* in the eastern province of Oriente have claimed Taíno ancestry. Some *guajiros* (country people) in this area have shown racial similarities and common cultural practices still in vogue today. The aborigines had a secretive existence for most of their post-Colombian times for fear of persecution. However, Elena learned that many, who still practiced their customs, remained identified with their roots.

Stamp commemorating pre-Colombian cultures in Cuba

Although Cuban history has usually been told as beginning with the arrival of Columbus who "discovered" America, the aborigines already had a life there. Elena thought that the wiping out of a people was also achieved by deliberately marginalizing these people's contributions to the fabric of the culture through selective historical recording. If not by direct Spanish intervention, the ethnocentric way of recording history had indeed been successful in minimizing the role of the natives in the underpinnings of Cuban culture.

An estimated 200,000 Taíno and Ciboney Indians were on the island at the time the Spanish arrived. Taínos were a self-reliant tribe of mariners and farmers, known as *guajiros*, while the Ciboneyes favored living in isolated areas in western Cuba. It is probable that both tribes were descendants of the South American Arawakans. A third group, the Guanahatabeyes, had been on the island the longest and had been described as the least advanced technologically of the three ethnic groups. Elena wondered why this group had been described in her history books as backward savages and not as a tribe who lived the simple life in communion with nature. The Guanahatabeyes were nomadic cave dwellers, mostly hunters and gatherers, who also congregated in the westernmost part of the island. They were heading for extinction prior to the arrival of the Spanish.

The three indigenous tribes cohabited with relative peace, despite the fact that the Taínos were the dominant group who had displaced the other two. The aborigines' lives were disrupted by frequent raids of the more aggressive Carib Indians, a neighboring tribe from the Lesser Antilles. The Guanahatabeyes did not share the Arawakan heritage. They were thought to be descendants of native peoples from the Florida Keys.

It is difficult to deny Taíno modern-day presence as groups of descendants, some of the *guajiros* living in rural areas, claim their Taíno identity as they continue practicing old rituals. Ceremonial dances (*areítos*) have been passed down through the generations. Taínos left an imprint on the culture of the island. There are Taíno words still used in contemporary Cuban Spanish such as *jicara* (gourds), *manigua* (wilderness), *bohío* (thatch palm abode), and the geographic names of many places. *Guamo* (a type of shell) has been used in rural cemeteries in eastern Cuba to protect the deceased from evil spirits, and to call one another if at a distance. The *bohío* itself, square structures made from royal palms, has been the typical dwelling of the *guajiros* for centuries. The word *bohío* means "home" in Taíno language. If Elena were to be asked what the soul of a Cuban landscape would be, she most likely would say, "a bohío and palm trees."

Native bohío

When the Spanish arrived in the fifteenth century, there were several Taíno territories under the power of the *cacique* (chieftain). Tribes would support them by paying considerable tributes. Taíno day-to-day living was highly developed for the times. They were regarded for their complex social structure and religion, their building skills, and the development of a universal language. Their "green medicine," based on the benefits of herbal remedies (*cocimiento*), has been passed on to future generations of Cubans.

In 1492, Christopher Columbus arrived for the first time in Guanahaní, as Cuba was known then by the natives. He claimed the island for the Spanish Crown and renamed it San Salvador (Holy Savior). Generations of Cuban children have been taught that Columbus was in awe of its beauty and expressed this first impression by saying, "Es la isla más hermosa que ojos humanos vieron" (It is the most beautiful island ever seen by the human eye). The Taínos were first in greeting the explorer when he landed.

Columbus had aimed to discover a more direct route to Asia in hopes of participating in the lucrative trade of the time. Instead, he landed in the Caribbean. As a result of his miscalculation, he referred to the natives as Indians. A geographic error had named American natives for all future generations. In his first of four voyages, Columbus "discovered" America, the New World. Elena always struggled with the word *discovered* as it revealed to her the Eurocentric bias present in recorded Western history. She also was offended by the reference to this world as "new." She would tell her friends, "How would you like it if someone knocks on your door for the first time and claims to have 'discovered' you? Does that mean that the life you led before did not count?"

The relatively peaceful and simple life of the aborigines soon took a dramatic turn. On his second trip, Columbus started requiring that the Taínos pay him tribute under penalty of physical punishment if they refused. The relationship between Spaniards and natives began to crumble. By order of Pope Alexander VI, Spain had been charged with conquering and Christianizing the "pagans," and after replacing Columbus, Diego Velázquez was commissioned to do so. His welcome was not as hospitable as it had been earlier for his predecessor's first voyage. By instituting the *encomienda* system, which lasted approximately one hundred years, the Crown essentially established slavery in the Americas. Through this system, the conquistadores became trustees of the natives. The Spanish had granted them a number of aborigines as serfs to provide the labor for the colonial plantation economy. Sugar, tobacco, and citrus fruits were cultivated and exported to Spain. The slave-master relationship between the natives and colonizers led to abuse and torture. Spanish Friar Bartolomé de las Casas became an advocate for the natives' rights against the brutality of their masters. He chronicled their history of subjugation and ill-treatment.

Taíno chieftains, led by Hatuey, opposed the colonizers through a ten-year period of guerrilla warfare. Ultimately captured by the Spaniards in 1512, the chieftains were burned alive. When asked to choose between conversion to Christianity or death, Hatuey chose to die. Soon after, the Spanish were in complete control of the island, managing to establish settlements along the coast from which they could fulfill their mission. Within three centuries, these small settlements grew into an empire, which included Mexico, Central and South America, as well as parts of what later became the United States.

Brutal treatment and disease contributed to the decline of the Taíno and the annihilation of the Ciboneyes by the end of the sixteenth century. For over four hundred years, Spain would be the sole authority on the island, and its governor, appointed by the Catholic sovereigns, ruled with almost unlimited power. As the native population declined, Spaniards saw a need to import slaves to work the oxen-powered plantations. Early in the 1500s, the first African slaves were brought to the West Indies, and for three hundred years, slavery burgeoned in Cuba, one of the last colonies to free slaves. To protect the native population, Fray de las Casas had spoken on behalf of black slavery but withdrew his support when he witnessed the dreadful treatment slaves received from their masters. In 1528, the first

ANDREA BERMÚDEZ

black slave, Spanish-born Estevanico, arrived in colonial America as part of a plan the Crown had devised to conquer Florida. Devastating storms, fierce opposition from the natives, and desertions brought the voyage to a disastrous end. Estevanico and a few of the survivors managed to flee to Spanish-held territory only to be resold into slavery several years later. A violent encounter with the natives, believed to be Zuni, ended his life in what later became New Mexico.

Starting in the mid 1550s, and covering two centuries, pirates caused havoc in various parts of the world, including the Caribbean. Spanish ships were particularly vulnerable to these attacks, as they were transporting valuable cargo between the Caribbean colonies and Spain. French, Dutch, and English pirates attacked and captured several cities in Cuba, including Havana. Since communication at the time was mostly by sea, piracy was taking a toll on Spanish hegemony.

Several fortresses were built to defend the island from pirate attacks, which lasted well into the eighteenth century. Havana's Castillo del Morro (Morro Castle) was erected in 1589 to guard the entrance to the bay and to serve as a prison. Another fortress by the same name was built later in Santiago de Cuba, in the eastern province of Oriente. The Havana Morro was briefly captured by the British in 1762 during the Seven Years' War in Europe, in which Spain supported France against the British. The next year, El Morro was returned to Spain.

Morro Castle

Soon after, another fortress, La Cabaña, was built to keep these events from recurring.

A view of Havana and its bay from La Cabaña Fortress

After the British left Cuba under a peace treaty signed in Paris, slave trafficking to Cuba increased exponentially. From 1701 to 1714, the War of the Spanish Succession was fought by several countries to keep Spain and France from uniting under one kingdom. The situation became a serious political crisis in Europe as the balance of power was at stake. The war ignited a civil war and caused Spain to lose part of its empire. It also ensured that the king of Spain be removed from France's line of succession, further weakening aspirations of supremacy.

With the help of African slaves, Cuba's sugar industry had become a large-scale international operation by the early nineteenth century. As a result, work on the plantations became more demanding, and the ratio of black slaves to white masters continued to grow. Dissatisfaction led to insurrection, which became commonplace in the Caribbean colonies. There were a number of uprisings on sugar and coffee plantations, including in 1809 when hundreds of slaves rebelled in Havana and other provinces to protest their unfair conditions.

It was evident that the Spanish Empire had begun to erode since its pinnacle in 1492 during the reign of King Ferdinand and Queen Isabella.

By 1825, the Crown had lost most of its colonies in Central, North, and South America, but it maintained control over Puerto Rico and Cuba. The French occupation of Spain during the Napoleonic Wars weakened the empire further and paved the way for the independence of Cuba and Puerto Rico, after four hundred years of colonial imperialism.

CHAPTER 3

The World in Black and White

Have you ever wondered what is the color of one's soul? Blood is red for everyone. Why is it that the color of the skin matters so much?

—*Andrea Bermúdez*

E LENA ALWAYS THOUGHT that people who claim that they are "color-blind" are actually racist. She recognized that there is nothing more conspicuous than a person's skin color. So to her, pretending that this noticeable characteristic did not exist was an indication that the individual thought racial differentiations were a negative. She felt, instead, that diversity in color, like any other cultural difference, should be recognized and celebrated. Her Tata had taught her that and much more about the history and realities of race relations in Cuba.

The first slaves arrived on the island in the 1500s, but it took two hundred years for the Spanish to open the slave trade to Havana. As the plantation-based economy intensified in Cuba with the opening of the sugar markets to the rest of the world, the demand for slave labor increased, making a bad situation worse. Starting in 1790 and for the next three decades, the number of slaves brought to Cuba increased dramatically until the trade was officially abolished in 1820.

Cabildos (ethnic associations) were formed early on to provide entertainment for the slaves and alleviate the tensions created by the master-slave relations. The slaves could legally gather on holidays and practice their tribal dances and other traditions. The *cabildos* became a support center to help slaves in times of need or to provide an opportunity to practice their religious rituals. Afro-Cubans were diverse peoples united by the shared experience of slavery. The slaves represented a variety of African tribes—including Congo, Lucumi, Carabali, Arara, and Mandingas—with identities tied to their distinctive languages and customs. The ethnic associations protected slaves from losing contact with their African roots as each was named according to the place of origin. The various tribes left an imprint on Cuban folklore, language, music and religion, among other manifestations of culture. With the end of slavery, the prominence of *cabildos* in Afro-Cuban life declined.

Unfortunately, success in the sugar industry meant increased efforts to secure the free labor slaves provided. Some trade companies would disregard their obligation to return the laborers to their country of origin at the end of their one-year contract when the *zafra* (sugar harvest) had concluded. The practice of bringing slaves to Cuba did not stop with the abolition of slavery as smugglers preserved the system for decades more.

Between 1812 and 1843, Cuba witnessed numerous slave rebellions that were immediately stifled. A series of revolts, known as the Aponte Rebellion for their suspected connection to the free black militia leader, erupted across Cuba in 1812. Seeking social change, free people of color and slaves joined in protest of the injustices of the plantation economy. The Aponte Rebellion has been considered a very significant event in the road to emancipation. With the execution of Aponte and his followers, the revolts may have been suppressed, but their spirit remained alive to inspire future uprisings. The rebellions also served to increase the tensions already developing between Spain and the United States.

Almost three decades later, the Spanish schooner *Amistad* was taken over by fifty kidnapped Africans who had been illegally bought and sold as slaves by Portuguese traders. After killing the captain, the men requested that the ship return them to Africa. Off the New York coast, the navy apprehended the insurgents. An 1841 United States Supreme Court decision freed the men, arguing that since slavery had been abolished, the trade of these Africans was illegal and that the situation warranted their right to rebel. The surviving men went home, and the abolitionist cause was further advanced. The right of slaves to fight against injustice had been protected.

As time passed, slave rebellions in Cuba became more organized. Several sugar and coffee plantations witnessed uprisings during the next few years with railroad workers joining in the effort. Unfortunately, plans for a major slave rebellion were discovered by the Spaniards. The Conspiración de la Escalera (Ladder Conspiracy) referred to a series of insurrections during

1843 and 1844 aimed at destroying property and killing the abusive masters in the provinces of Havana and Matanzas. The term *escalera* symbolized the corporal punishment directed at slaves and free people of color who were tied to a ladder and lashed to obtain information. This form of injustice was not the only manner of repression used against blacks during this period of history, as other types of torture have been documented. The Escalera conspiracy was exposed by a woman slave in exchange for her freedom and monetary reward. This betrayal was responsible for the foiled insurrection that brutally punished a great number of slaves and free people of color. Several hundred were killed; others were incarcerated or expelled from Cuba to serve as exemplars of what would happen to those opposing the control of colonial Spain.

One of Elena's favorite operettas was *Cecilia Valdés*, which immortalized the intricacies of race relations during slavery. The plot described Cecilia, a beautiful light-skinned mulatto, who was the illegitimate daughter of an influential slave trader. Unknowingly, she fell in love with her white half brother and conceived his son. Her lover left her to marry an upper-class white woman but was killed by Pimienta, one of Cecilia's black admirers. Pimienta was later captured and executed, and Cecilia, the mastermind, was sent to prison. Although highly dramatized, the narrative described events that were far from unusual.

As a matter of fact, Tata's parental history followed a similar course. Her mother had been a slave in a sugar plantation in Las Villas. Tata never met her father who, she was told, was a white *capataz* (overseer of the estate). Her mother had been brought illegally to Cuba from Ghana in the mid 1800s when she was thirteen. Although Tata did not enjoy revisiting her past, she did share some glimpses of her mother's culture, particularly her language, rich in proverbs, and her polytheist religion.

Tata became a fervent Catholic, but her mother's beliefs in a variety of deities were superimposed. Every need called for a different saint, with whom Tata had developed a personal relationship as if the saints were living and breathing creatures. She made offerings to them so that they would miraculously intercede in her favor. One of her much loved sacred figures was La Virgen de la Caridad (Our Lady of Charity), who was made patroness of Cuba by Pope Benedict XVI in the early part of the 1900s. An Afro-Cuban herself, the statue of Our Lady shows also the image of three fishermen on a boat that she is protecting from a storm, one white, one black, and one Indian, signifying the three main ethnicities of Cuba.

Our Lady of Charity, Patroness of Cuba

Frequently, Tata spoke in proverbs. Elena would often hear her say, "Al mal tiempo buena cara" (Meet the bad times with a good face) or "Al que madruga Dios lo ayuda" (God helps he who wakes up early— better known as "the early bird catches the worm"). Tata was happy in her home environment at the Vidals' who treated her with the respect worthy of an important member of the family.

Race relations in Cuba were complex, and so was the definition of race itself. It was not a simple matter of black and white as each term was subdivided further in distinct groupings. For instance, the black race comprised several categories depending on the preponderance of white or black genes in the person's racial makeup. From darkest to lightest, a person can be *negro azul, prieto, moreno, mulatto, trigueño, jabao,* or *blanconaso*; and each has told a very different story of prejudice and rejection.

The eventual end of slavery did not bring racial equality to the island. The castelike system that emerged from the plantation society led to a history of segregation and prejudice. Color and ethnicity were two important factors that separated the people. Whites, at the top of the pyramid, were either Spanish or *criollos* and enjoyed social, political, and economic advantages. The free people of color, mostly illegitimate children of the colonizers, were notably involved in business and commerce. The least powerful of the three were former slaves, laborers without rights who depended on their masters for all their needs.

After emancipation, very few blacks could read or write, and despite the fact that segregation by race was not legal for the larger communities after 1880, some schools denied access to black children. Segregated schools appeared alongside private schools for white children, creating separate and unequal opportunities for blacks and whites.

Refusal of service in public places along with other discriminating practices, such as race requirements for certain jobs, kept a large number of blacks from attaining upward mobility in the new society. As a result, color societies were formed throughout the island, with a board that coordinated their activities and represented their interests. A parallel elite black society emerged, which threatened the ambitious colonists and created an antagonistic environment fueled by "fear of blacks."

Fear and mistrust led to prejudice and persecution. Cuba had gained independence, but uprisings were far from over. The Partido Independiente de Color (Independent Black Party) was formed in 1908 by members who had fought for Cuba's independence to claim a place for blacks in the New Republic. The party initiated the Guerrita de Color (Little War of Color) in 1912, which was waged in the easternmost province of Oriente. After the insurrection was destroyed, the party disbanded.

Historical accounts from a Eurocentric vantage point have had a significant responsibility in reinforcing prejudice. Blacks made significant contributions to the various attempts at independence from Spain. These efforts have gone largely unrecognized. The unsung heroes continued to take part in the common history of the country. For instance, on November 27, 1871, eight white medical students had received a death sentence following a false accusation of having desecrated the grave of a controversial Spanish journalist. Five black voices rose to protest the injustice and were also executed. The death of the white students, known historically as the Fusilamiento de

ANDREA BERMÚDEZ

los estudiantes, has been commemorated as a holiday every November 27, a date that has largely ignored the role of the brave black men in the shameful incident. Elena wondered why her history lessons had been selective in not acknowledging this aspect of the events, and why the monument erected in 1890 to memorialize the students did not include recognition of the black heroes. "History from whose perspective?" she pondered.

Monument commemorating the death of eight
medical students by firing squad in 1871.

Cuba had suffered from a fragmented social organization throughout its history, and to this day, race relations in Cuba remain unresolved. Even after the abolition of slavery in the 1880s, and despite the fact that Cubans, black and white, fought against Spain during the war for independence to attain racial equality, segregation had kept the races apart. Early claims by José Martí —who said, "Everything that divides men, everything that classifies, separates or shuts off men is a sin against humanity ... Man is more than white, more than mulatto, more than negro"— did not materialize. The seemingly "color-blind" Castro government has not been completely successful in attaining a balance among the races despite his hollow words in 1959: "Nobody can consider himself purebred and of superior race." The history of relations between black and white Cubans on the island and in exile has continued to be tarnished by segregation and racism.

In Castro's Cuba, little progress has been made toward racial equality. Discrimination and prejudice still run deep and discord among the races remains an issue. Music, rapping in particular, is suggestive of the racial tensions still existing in Cuba. Not always do musicians escape punishment, when their sometimes not-so-subtle criticisms land them in jail.

Castro had promised a society without racial boundaries, but the absence of a dialogue about race and refusal to recognize differing points of view have made it impossible for the revolution to resolve racial tensions. Social status and color still have an inverse relationship: the higher the incidence of black features, the lower the social status. There are few blacks in the top echelons of Castro's government. In contrast, there is a high incidence of blacks among dissidents and prisoners.

ANDREA BERMÚDEZ

CHAPTER 4

Fighting for Independence

And let us never forget that the greater the suffering, the greater the right to justice, and that the prejudices of men and social inequalities cannot prevail over the equality which nature has created.

—José Martí

E LENA HAD A keen interest in Cuban military history as two of her great-grandfathers had fought against each other during one of the many attempts for independence from Spain. The fact that Elena was genetically connected to this period of time gave her a sense of having directly participated in forging a free Cuba. Ironically, she had experienced very little of this freedom.

During Cuba's much anticipated respite from Spanish domination, the British occupation of 1762 opened the doors to commerce with colonial America. During the Seven Years' War in Europe, the British declared war on Spain. With the help of the thirteen colonies, two hundred British ships and fourteen thousand soldiers descended on Havana. The Morro Castle, a large military installation built by the king of Spain to protect the entrance to the bay, was taken by the British and Havana was bombarded. Surrendering was the only option after experiencing so much death and destruction. The reprieve from Spanish control was more a delay than a relief, as it did not last long enough to change the course of history. After eleven months of British occupation, Cuba was returned to Spain in exchange for Florida, and all signs of new prosperity were erased. However, dreams of total independence began to materialize.

By 1825, Cuba still remained a colony of Spain, although most of the others had already claimed independence. The plight of Cubans had been evidenced in several failed attempts at freedom. During the early part of the 1800s, there was evidence of a separatist movement that involved the upper-class *criollos* (Cuban-born Spanish) who declared Cuba independent from Spain and even drafted a constitution. Elena's ancestors on her father's side fought for a free Cuba but were sent back to Spain as prisoners of war after these efforts failed. This defeat did not stop separatist movements on the island.

The González side of Elena's family, her mother's side, remained loyal to the *peninsulares* (Spaniards in support of Spain's domination) while her father's side, having been Cuban for several generations, favored the *criollos*. Arguments made during family reunions tended to show this particular bias, nurtured by each family's role in the development of Cuban history. It was critical for Elena to understand both sides of the conflict, although she undoubtedly favored Cuban independence.

Elena's grandfathers Dr. Eloy Vidal and Máximo González

The first official war of independence was actually initiated in 1868 when a Cuban landowner freed his slaves and declared the beginning of *La Guerra de los Diez Años* (the Ten Years' War). The United States refused to support the efforts of the Cubans and, instead, sold weapons to Spain. Cubans counted on popular support, but without military capability, there was not much hope of success. Consequently, a guerrilla-type war ensued. In 1878, the war reached an impasse. Despite the superiority of Spanish

ANDREA BERMÚDEZ

forces, and the loss of key *criollo* figures, neither side could claim victory. A pact was signed ending the war and declaring amnesty for those who had participated. Slaves who fought on either side of the conflict were freed. The Ten Years' War had ended, but efforts to liberate Cuba went underground for almost two decades.

The fact that a significant number of the promises made by Spain did not materialize created tension between the separatists, in favor of independence, and the loyalists who supported Spain. An economic crisis added to the already stressed relationship. Cuban revolutionaries meeting in New York declared a manifesto against Spanish control of the island as well as a protest over broken promises, particularly along the lines of political reform. Between 1879 and 1880, La Guerra Chiquita (the Little War) was fought in an effort to finally separate Cuba from Spain. Although many lives were lost, the Cuban rebels were defeated. Lack of experienced leadership, insufficient weaponry, and war fatigue pressed the revolutionaries to surrender. However, the experience paved the way for the third and final war for independence. For over a hundred years, Cubans had dreamed of a free country. They would have to wait a little longer.

A third attempt to liberate Cuba came in 1895. During the first battle against Spain, Cuban patriot José Martí lost his life. Rather than squelching the revolutionary spirit, his death precipitated a surge in the nationalist movement. Despite the fact that Spain had superior forces to stifle the opposition, the Cubans managed to invade the western provinces traversing the island from the east. The United States was secretly supporting the Cuban forces since its relationship with Spain had deteriorated.

Spain, in an effort to subdue Cuban rebels, sent General Valeriano Weyler, better known as the Butcher, to govern the island. His drastic measures, including the use of concentration camps, caused the starvation and death of many Cubans. Antonio Maceo, *el Titán de Bronce* (the Bronze Titan), and other important leaders of the revolution fell victim to Weyler's tyranny. As with Martí's death earlier, the loss of these patriots inspired the Cubans. Spain was distracted. It was fighting a war in Cuba, and another in the Philippines, while Puerto Rico was threatening as well. The *criollos* were close to victory.

Lack of trust between the United States and Spain caused negotiations to sour. Riots erupted throughout the island, and the SS *Maine* was sent to protect American interests. In 1898, the battleship mysteriously exploded and capsized at the entrance of the Bay of Havana. The United States government did not blame Spain for the incident, but the American people were outraged. To pacify the island, the United States entered the war with the promise not to stay once the war was over. After four months, Spain conceded defeat in 1898, leaving Cuba devastated and in debt. The end of the Spanish-American War also gave the United States rights to Guam, the Philippines, and Puerto Rico. After this episode, the United States developed a new function in international affairs, an interventionist role in the political and economic affairs of other countries whenever the United States deemed it necessary.

The Cuban revolutionaries were concerned that the real interest of the United States was annexation of the island, so they felt that independence was nonnegotiable. Nevertheless, the Cuban flag did not replace Spain's. It was the American flag that was raised on December 10, 1898. Less than a month later, on January 1, 1899, Cuba passed into American hands, and the full-blown military intervention lasted until 1902. As a trade-off, Cuba committed itself to export sugar, its main commodity, exclusively to the United States. Other sectors emerged to aid the devastated Cuban economy. For Spain, the Spanish-American War signified the end of a period as a world power. However, Spain continued to have a significant impact on Cuban life as the intellectual contributions of the Generation of 1898 philosophers, poets, and writers fueled a rebirth of Spanish culture on the island.

An ambitious plan of Cuban reconstruction was carried out by the United States military governors. Health campaigns included the fight against malaria and yellow fever. Research based on the work of Dr. Carlos Finlay, a renowned Cuban epidemiologist who had discovered yellow fever, was conducted by Dr. Walter Reed. Many schools were built, and the public works infrastructure was improved and redesigned. The most difficult challenge to reconstruction was rebuilding agriculture since a vast majority of the sugar refineries had been destroyed. Adding to the problem was the devastating loss of livestock, manual labor, and the railroad system as a result of war.

Limited voting rights to participate in local elections were granted to Cubans as early as 1900. A constitution was created to protect universal voting rights and to promote the election of a president and a congress. The Platt Amendment, which ironically afforded the United States the rights of future interventions to protect Cuba's sovereignty, was ratified in 1901. It was finally repealed in 1934 after many decades of opposing arguments, but Guantánamo Bay Navy Base remained under the jurisdiction of the United States, a right granted in perpetuity.

ANDREA BERMÚDEZ

While significant historical events were developing in the country, so was the history of each individual family. One of the young diplomats stationed in Havana during the military occupation was dashing New Yorker Neil Brown. A graduate of West Point Military Academy, he went into diplomatic service and was sent to Cuba early in 1899 to work with the military attaché. When he first saw Roberto's grandmother, Lila, he was taken by her beauty. They had met at El Templete, a famous restaurant located in a neoclassic building whose entrance is graced by a stately ceiba tree. It was November 16, 1899, when the restaurant traditionally celebrated Havana's first town council, which had taken place three centuries before. The attraction between the young couple was mutual, and from the animated conversation they sustained that night, a love interest was born.

A short courtship was followed by a lavish wedding where both families met for the first time. The Browns spoke little Spanish, except for Neil, but Lila's family spoke some English. Needless to say, the encounter lacked the warmth most of these events bring about as the worlds they represented were so far apart. The young couple made their residence in Havana until 1902 when they moved to New York. Roberto's mother was born about that time, so adaptation to a new life with an infant was difficult for Lila. After five years of marriage, the Browns divorced, a scandal in those ultraconservative times. Neil was a distant father and an even more distant ex-husband, causing the familial connection to be dissolved. By the time Roberto was born, Neil had passed away.

Elena's grandfather on her mother's side, Máximo González, was first generation Cuban, so it was hard for him to declare his political loyalty. His father had fought on the Spanish side in one of the wars for Cuban independence. His duty as the oldest son called him to be supportive of Spain, but his heart was telling him differently. Dealing with this type of conflict had not been easy, but life had its way of resolving the contradiction. He met his bride, also named Elena, as a debutante, and soon after, they were married. Elenita, as the family affectionately called her, did not share Máximo's half-hearted allegiance to the mother country, so as the children arrived, a pro-*criollo* leaning became the family's political inclination.

Dr. Eloy Vidal, Elena's grandfather on her father's side, sympathized with the Cuban army. He had lent his support to the José Martí forces as a medical officer in Dos Ríos and was present when Martí lost his life. Soon after the war, Eloy married Ana, the youngest daughter of an affluent family. After retiring from the military, he went to work in the sugar industry. Their eldest son, Bernardo, was born during the United States military occupation.

Despite the fact that there were early assurances that the presence of the American forces in Cuba would be temporary, its effects were not. In 1901, the United States agreed to military withdrawal from the island through the Platt Amendment, which was responsible for changing the Cuban political and economic landscape. The document was also accountable for defining the future relationship between the two countries.

Cuban representation in government during this time was limited as only rich white males over twenty-one could vote. The economy was soon largely controlled by United States interests. Approximately 66 percent of businesses were American-owned, and a large majority of its economic trade, particularly sugar and tobacco exports, was exclusively with the United States.

Not everyone was thrilled with the change of guard in Cuba. While the paternal side, the Vidals, celebrated the events, Elena González, the maternal grandmother, was apprehensive of the power gained by the United States over Cuba. She kept telling her husband, Máximo, "Es el mismo perro con diferente collar" (It's the same old dog with a different collar). Grandma Elena's side of the family believed that the ideals of the Cuban revolutionaries had not been fulfilled and that the sacrifices of the past had been made in vain.

The first presidential election took place on December 31, 1901, but the newly elected president, Tomás Estrada Palma, did not take office until May of 1902. His motto "More teachers, less soldiers" made his presence in government popular among Cubans. The Republic of Cuba was being officially recognized after a history of political enslavement.

During the first three decades of the Cuban Republic, governmental policies were intensely influenced by the United States as prescribed by the Platt Amendment. Migration policies were revised and opened to include workers in good health who could be readily employed. Restrictions that before had included country of origin and religion were lifted, with the exception of Chinese laborers who would not be permitted to emigrate until after the First World War. The island's less-restrictive immigration policy lasted until 1933 and was seen as the Cuban version of the American dream, with promises of economic and social advancement. In the first years of the republic, over three hundred thousand immigrants came to Cuba, mostly from Spain, but also from the United States and Western Europe. A few Middle Easterners, mostly Turkish and Lebanese, migrated to Cuba, attracted by a buoyant commerce. After 1913, immigrants from Jamaica and Haiti arrived in droves to provide manual labor for the booming sugar industry.

During the First World War, Cuba became the number one exporter of sugar to the Allied nations. La Danza de los Millones (the Dance of the Millions) referred to this period of unprecedented economic growth, which lasted until 1920. The next decade would be known as a period of harsh economic conditions due to a dramatic drop in the price of sugar in international markets. This situation created an economic crisis in Cuba, which was accompanied by labor unrest, strikes, and unemployment. Quotas were established to curb immigration and protect Cuban workers.

The decades between the 1920s and 1950s were characterized by images of Cuba created by the tourism industry. A promised land for pleasure seekers, the island became a world-class tourist attraction. Luxury hotels and other venues were built to draw people from all over the world. The industry thrived at a very opportune time.

CHAPTER 5

Democracy Revisited

Those who make peaceful revolution impossible will make violent revolution inevitable.

—*John F. Kennedy*

U NFORTUNATELY, CUBA DID not enjoy a stable democratic tradition throughout its turbulent history. Oppressed by four hundred years of colonialism, numerous revolutions, foreign intervention, dictatorships, and war, Fidel Castro's reputed idealism was first seen as reprieve. However, the dream of a democratic Cuba was to be disrupted by new nightmares of tyranny.

Tomás Estrada Palma assumed the first presidency of the republic in 1902. He had fought in the Ten Years' War against Spain and had then become president of a short-lived provisional revolutionary government. He was captured at the time by Spanish forces and sent into exile in the United States. From this experience, he emerged a powerful political figure working alongside José Martí and other distinguished revolutionaries. When José Martí died in battle, Estrada Palma assumed leadership of the Revolutionary Party as a delegate-at-large.

He was a natural favorite of the United States government to become president of the new democracy. This first election was suspect as Estrada Palma had been the only candidate for whom Cubans could vote. His only opponent withdrew, complaining that there was too much favoritism for Estrada Palma on the part of the United States where he had remained during his presumed campaign for office.

Throughout his four years in office, Estrada Palma encouraged international trade and foreign investments in Cuba. Economic recovery seemed plausible as sugar and tobacco production rose. His pro-United States stance was evidenced in his preferential treatment of the country regarding trade and in his support of granting the United States rights in perpetuity to the Guantánamo Naval Base. Although respected for his honesty, his domestic policies did not win him the backing of his people. Without the tradition of, or knowledge about democracy, the Cuban political landscape became a tug of war among the various parties. The quest for political power and personal gain, *caudillismo*, rather than long-range plans to systematize the government, became an insidious threat to Cuban democracy.

Estrada Palma ran for office again in 1906, but strong opposition was present this time around. His attempt to stay in power set off a rebellion that prompted a second American intervention, which lasted three more years. Charles Magoon, a former governor of the Panama Canal Zone and minister of Panama, was named governor of Cuba. As governor, he concentrated on reorganizing the army and building the island's infrastructure. Valued by the United States government, Magoon was not a popular figure with Cubans who regarded him with distrust and even loathing. His detractors believed that Magoon's government had returned Cuba to the corruption of colonial times.

New elections in 1908 brought liberal leader José Miguel Gómez to power. As a major general of the army, he was a veteran of previous attempts for Cuban independence from Spain. Among his political credentials was his participation in the constitutional convention from which the first Cuban constitution emerged. Economic recovery had continued during the Magoon governorship, so the new president had a promising start.

Nicknamed the Shark, Gómez's presidency was marked by corruption from the beginning. Out-of-favor practices from colonial times, such as cockfighting and the lottery, made their return to Cuba. His rapid personal enrichment was questioned by many who felt his financial dealings were underhanded. National newspapers, funded by the government, were encouraged to publish exclusively progovernment views, a fact that helped spread some popularity among the people. However, scandal and restlessness seemed to prevail. In 1911, the National Council of Veterans complained that many of the Gómez associates had been Spain loyalists and, as a result, should have no place in government.

The United States, concerned about the situation with the veterans, warned President Gómez of the possibility of another intervention. In the meantime, the Independent Party of Color waged a war against racial oppression, which ended disastrously with the death of many Afro-Cubans. With the consent of Congress, martial law was declared in 1912. The times were less than ideal for a democracy to thrive, and when his term was up in 1913, Gómez did not seek reelection.

Mario García Menocal became Cuba's third president and governed for two consecutive terms. His support of big business brought economic growth to the island during some of those years, but Menocal did not escape unscathed, as his government was also suspected of corruption. Menocal authorized Cuba's entry into the First World War, just a day shy of the United States. Although Cuban contributions to the war were humble, its participation presented an opportunity for sugar production to be sold to the Allies, helping to create an economic boom for the island.

Menocal's first term brought financial reform, including a monetary system, and improvements in the areas of health, education, and agriculture. With time, his government began to lose focus. Opposition became fierce, giving Menocal's government a pretext to use repressive measures to contain the violence erupting around the country. His political rivals cried foul when he was elected president for a second term. Given the serious economic crisis created by a sudden fall in the price of sugar, Menocal's second term diminished his political legacy.

Elena's father, Dr. Vidal, often mentioned the friendship of his father, Eloy, to Menocal. He liked the president for his conservative views as well as for his love of Cuba but never shared his opinions about Menocal's political legacy. He did mention, however, Menocal's aristocratic upbringing as the son of a sugar magnate and his educational experience in the United States. A Cornell graduate in engineering, Menocal maintained close ties with his American fraternity brothers. Once back in Cuba, he was a participant in the 1895 attempt for independence. During the United States occupation, Menocal had been police chief of Havana for a short period.

The 1921 elections were challenged by the liberal camp complaining that voting had been rigged. Yet again, the United States intervened by sending General Enoch Crowder as an envoy to determine the extent of the fraud, to set a date for the new elections, and above all, to prevent civil war. Alfredo Zayas ran unopposed and became a one-term president amid thunderous protests. An intellectual rather than a politician, Zayas was the first nonmilitary president who had not participated in Cuba's efforts for independence. President Zayas inherited a country in financial ruin. Pressure for reform was strong from both Crowder and the Cuban people concerned about the conditions on the island. Despite the economic challenges his presidency faced, Zayas succeeded in accomplishing a series of reforms, including supporting women's suffrage, establishing freedom of expression for the press, returning of Isle of Pines to Cuba, supporting improvements in education, and launching the first radio station. He lost his party's confidence for reelection, so he threw his support behind Dr. Gerardo Machado who was elected in 1925.

At first, Machado enjoyed great popularity by capitalizing on the nationalistic spirit of the times, but soon after he became overconfident and autocratic. When the student leaders from the Directorio Estudiantil Revolucionario (Student Revolutionary Directory) opposed his tyrannical measures, Machado ordered disciplinary tribunals to expel them from the university. Through an amendment to the Constitution that he initiated, his presidential term was extended to six years.

A full-fledged economic crisis threatened the stability of the Machado presidency bringing about general transportation strikes and growing public dissatisfaction. Opposition voices became stronger and constitutional protections were suspended. Repression became the government's way to control hostility, but as time passed, it became clear that Machado was unable to succeed. Revolution was in the air, so it came as no surprise that the United States would again intervene, arranging Machado's resignation. The end of the *Machadato* (Machado regime) would make Dr. Vidal a direct participant in his country's history.

Dr. Bernardo Vidal's first military duty was in the eastern city of Holguín, circa 1931.

Medical Captain Bernardo Vidal

Public unrest and minor military skirmishes were common. While at home one day, Dr. Vidal noticed a large number of soldiers assembled on their porch. Armed with his German pistol, he opened the door to see what was going on. Dr. Vidal would later tell the story that the only vestige left of the soldiers were their shoes because they ran away so fast, propelled by the fearful sight of his Luger.

The 1930s marked the beginning of Army Sergeant Fulgencio Batista's ascent to power after the sitting president, Machado, was forced to retire. Captain Vidal was on active duty along with approximately three hundred men fighting the revolutionary forces led by Batista at Havana's Hotel Nacional. The artillery attack had been brutal and forced the officers to capitulate. Despite having admitted defeat, shots were fired at the officers, particularly the medical units, which included Bernardo Vidal. Eleven officers were killed and more than twenty injured.

Hotel Nacional

Dr. Vidal and his fellow officers were incarcerated for twenty days at the historic La Cabaña fortress, at the time used as a military prison.

The Vidal family had found Bernardo's name on a list of fatalities published by the new government. Grief-stricken, Sara Vidal was making funeral preparations for her husband. Looking at her five-year-old son, she wondered what other surprises the future would hold for them. Little did she know that her husband would be found alive among the imprisoned ex-*oficiales* (deposed officers). Joy and relief helped assuage the uncertainties the family was facing at the moment. Fortunately, the United States ambassador persuaded Batista to release the ex-*oficiales* unharmed. Dr Vidal regained his freedom and returned to his private life as a physician.

These were hard times for the country as economic dissatisfaction led to public turmoil. This situation gave Sergeant Batista the opportunity to seize control and become the real force behind a series of short-lived presidencies. Carlos Manuel de Céspedes, first in the series, was appointed provisional president after Machado's resignation. He was soon ousted by the military in collaboration with student rebels.

Dr. Ramón Grau San Martín, being a faculty member and dean in the School of Medicine at the University of Havana, was a favorite of the powerful student radicals. He became the seventh president in 1933. In a short year, a revolution led by Batista removed Dr. Grau from power as well. Carlos Mendicta assumed the presidency under very precarious conditions. Unlike his predecessor, Dr. Grau, the United States recognized Mendieta's government. A group of radicals opposing the new government organized bombings and demonstrations. Finally, a general strike followed in 1935 and forced the president's resignation.

Unsuccessful revolutions and a parade of unpopular and unimpressive presidents followed Mendieta: Carlos Hevia, Carlos Márquez-Sterling, José A. Barnet, Miguel Mariano Gómez, and Federico Laredo-Bru. The unstable situation offered Batista, now army chief of staff, the opportunity to become a political powerhouse. Of the five presidents, only Laredo-Bru served long enough to earn a presidential legacy. During his term, the army was revamped, and plans for reforms in education, agriculture, and welfare were put in place. The Cuban economy improved as well, and a new progressive constitution was ratified, paving the way for a much needed democratic process. However, an international incident exposed a more sinister side of Laredo-Bru, as he denied entrance to Jewish refugees fleeing Nazi Germany.

In the 1940 elections, Batista defeated Dr. Grau to become president. With a coalition supporting him, which included the Communist Party, Batista ruled under the new constitution. During his presidential term, he was able to undertake important progressive social reforms. Early in Batista's presidency, Cuba entered the Second World War, opening the door for trade agreements and other economic support from the United States. Term limits did not allow him to seek reelection.

Following Batista's four-year term in 1944, Dr. Grau was elected. Allegations of corruption and nepotism marred his second presidency. Despite economic support from the United States, Batista had left the country in financial chaos, so it was difficult for the new president to implement his plans for social and economic reforms. However, his efforts in those areas have been praised by historians. His protégé, Carlos Prío Socarrás, became the next president in 1948.

Prío had taken part in revolutionary activities opposing Machado in the previous decade and had also been a popular minister of labor during the second Grau presidency. Allegations of financial wrongdoing and his inability to curb violence made his presidency ineffectual. The shadow of corruption that had followed the previous administration remained a threat to Prío's legacy.

Cuba's democratic respite lasted until 1952 when another military coup brought Batista back to power. Three months before the elections, Batista, who was running a distant third, took control of military installations and the national media. Prío, unable to fight back the Batista forces, left for exile allowing Batista to assume the presidency.

Around this time, the Vidals lived in *Ampliación de Almendares*, an area near the *Cuartel de Columbia* (Columbia Barracks), command center for the military. Elena, then eleven, recalled the frantic activity preceding the news that a successful coup had replaced the elected president. She also remembered the sound of sirens, the sight of armed soldiers and tanks guarding the streets. Elena thought about how she and her friends watched in horror as a military plane crashed, killing the pilot whom they had known. She was too young at the time to overcome the tragic memory or to be able to understand the political implications of what had happened that day.

During Batista's years in office, Cuba had become a center of international attraction, making tourism an expanding industry. Cuba's popularity as a tourist destination brought years of prosperity, but it also brought mafia presence. Hotels and casinos, such as the Riviera, were being built or refurbished under the tutelage of controversial figures such as Santos Trafficante and Meyer Lansky. The multimillion-dollar enterprise included high government officials, and some close relatives of the president, who exerted control over gambling, particularly slot machines.

Life under Batista's regime was falling apart. Constitutional guarantees had been suspended once again, and the economy was taking a dramatic downturn. Dissatisfaction was beginning to mount, and Fidel Castro, a young student revolutionary, was making good use of this opportunity. On July 26, 1953, his forces attacked, unsuccessfully, the Moncada Barracks in the easternmost province of Oriente. After serving two years in prison, the

ANDREA BERMÚDEZ

Castro brothers, Fidel and Raúl, were released following an amnesty signed by Batista. They fled to Mexico where plans for another insurrection were developed and executed.

The promised elections of 1954 were a sham. Batista ran unopposed as the various candidates either withdrew or decided not to participate. The objectionable circumstances threw the country into deeper political crisis. Student demonstrations in the midfifties resulted in brutal clashes with the police, which forced the students to go underground and organize. In the meantime, Castro and a small group of followers, aboard the yacht *Granma*, arrived on the eastern shores of Cuba. These incidents marked the beginning of the end.

A successful *guerra de guerrillas* (guerrilla warfare) was waged with newcomers joining in, including Ernesto (Che) Guevara. As Batista's popularity declined, Castro's rose. The number of revolutionary victories in the eastern province continued to increase and, in direct relationship, the number of recruits multiplied. The political situation was critical. Batista's demoralized military, coupled with a disgruntled citizenry, were not the only indications that his rule was coming to an end. In 1958, the United States withdrew military aid to the dictator. That was the last straw. As Batista left for exile in Portugal and Spain, his twenty-five years of being an influential political force in Cuba ended, and hopes for a new beginning were being forged. Batista was never to return. He died in Guadalmina, Spain, in 1973.

PART II

Support Systems

CHAPTER 6

The Family as the Center of the Universe

Call it a clan, call it a network, call it a tribe, call it a family: Whatever you call it, whoever you are, you need one.

—Jane Howard

O THER THAN RELIGION or spirituality, there is nothing more influential in shaping the Cuban character than the family unit, which sometimes includes members who are not necessarily blood-related. The extended family may include friends or distant relatives who remain in close contact with the individual. In her younger years, Elena often wondered why she had so many aunts, uncles, cousins, when they certainly outnumbered her parents' siblings and kids. When she was five or six, she remembered her "sister" Meg, although she had no female siblings. They often dressed alike, so Elena thought maybe her sibling was a twin, although taller, fairer, and with her own set of very nice parents.

Elena and her friend Meg at Río Cristal, Havana, circa 1945

Meg's dad was the chief of police when the girls were young, so they were taken to school in a police car. Elena felt important although a bit scared of the machine gun lying by their feet. She found out much later that Meg's father had been on a hit list, so going to school was a far more adventurous circumstance than she realized at the time. Meg's family revered Dr. Vidal and treated Elena as if she were one of theirs. Elena and Meg's tight friendship lasted throughout their elementary school years. Attending separate high schools drove their destinies in different directions.

Elena was very fond of her father. Bernardo's life had a sense of balance with distinct priorities, which included healthy eating, exercising, and having hobbies to keep the child within thriving. There was always a room in the house dedicated to his train collection. He had recreated a childhood scene, complete with a sugar mill, small towns, and beautiful rural scenery. His father, Eloy, worked on the family plantation, although he was also a trained medical doctor. Eloy, a tall and lanky twenty-seven-year-old bachelor, had married Ana, the beautiful only daughter of a very distinguished family from Matanzas. Ana was a child bride at fifteen years old. Barely five feet, blond, and blue eyed, Ana and Eloy were undeniably a contrasting yet attractive pair. Their offspring included Bernardo, their first born, another son and two daughters.

Elena's Family Tree

Fabián Vidal
(1847-1905)

Eloy Vidal
(1870-1925)

Bernardo Vidal
(1900-2001)

Dulce Amaro
(1848-1917)

Carlos Piñar
(1845-1913)

Ana Borges
(1853-1925)

Ana Piñar
(1884-1973)

Jorge
González
(1844-1911)

Máximo
González
(1872-1923)

Sara
González
(1902-1976)

Elena
1941-

Sara Ortega
(1848-1927)

Arturo Lavín
(1845-1917)

Sara Carballo
(1850-1930)

Elena Lavín
(1876-1940)

Elena Vidal y González Family Tree

The family lived comfortably in Unión de Reyes, rural Matanzas, an area well-known for its numerous mills that processed the region's abundant harvests of sugarcane. Since schooling was not readily available in their immediate vicinity, Eloy and Ana employed a governess to homeschool their children. Bernardo remembered that class always started with his mother writing a maxim on the blackboard, her idea of teaching her children to value strength of character, solid morals, and respect for duty. "A smooth sea never made a wise mariner" was one he recalled as consoling when life would show an ugly side. Wise mariners they all became when in the late 1920s a crisis in the sugar market forced the Vidals out of business. Sugar had been first introduced early in the sixteenth century by colonial Spain, and by the nineteenth century, Cuba had become the foremost producer of sugar in the world. The island's economic fate had always been dictated by how sugar fared in the international markets and by how mercifully the hurricane season would treat the harvest.

Sara's background was quite different, although her family was also involved in the sugar industry for a time. Born to a family of seven siblings, Sara was the youngest and most indulged. Until Sara was in her teens, the family lived in Cárdenas, a large city 175 kilometers east of Havana. She attended school, had many friends, and relished the support of a very close-knit family. The family moved to Havana following the sugar market crash. The relocation to a city even larger than Cárdenas taught Sara the basic skills necessary to survive big-city living. From her parents, she also inherited a down-to-earth view of the world.

Despite the fact that Elena's grandfathers, Máximo and Eloy, had been brought up favoring different sides of Cuban history, the two men were to become good friends as their destinies intertwined through the sugar industry. It would be likely that their children, army medical captain Bernardo and beautiful Sara, would bring the families together with their marriage.

All of Elena's *abuelos* (grandparents) with the exception of Bernardo's mother, Mama Ana, had passed away before she was born. She heard of Abuela Elenita's sense of humor and of her *abuelos'* long-standing friendship. Elena's parents would take her to visit the Cementerio de Colón to pay their respects to the older generation now gone. Founded in 1876, the cemetery had been controlled by the Catholic Church until the Castro revolution. Those unfortunate enough to have died in sin, according to dogma, be it divorce or suicide, were not allowed to be buried there. The 140-acre cemetery was known for its elaborate memorials and became a national monument during the Castro years. The Vidal family pantheon was impressive with its massive marble statue of the Sacred Heart marking its site. During the early Castro days, respect for the departed had been violated as tombs were raided and remains stolen or lost.

Christopher Columbus Cemetery in Havana (*www.romanvirdi.com*)

Sara had inherited Abuela Elenita's witty and quick sense of humor, which occasionally tended to backfire on her. For one of her dates with Bernardo, Sara had decided to add a faux bun to her hairdo. They were attending a musical performance in a very crowded but elegant theater in Havana. Suddenly, she felt as if someone passing behind their seats had uprooted the hairpiece. When she looked, a big man wearing the typical white tropical suit just stood there looking sheepish with Sara's hairpiece caught on his zipper! Bernardo was red as a beet and unable to offer any help. After a short and awkward interval, Sara got her hairpiece back. With time, Bernardo learned to take similar incidents in stride.

Bernardo's mother and her unmarried daughter lived in stately quarters in one of Havana's older neighborhoods. Both women were musicians: Grandma, a concert pianist, and her daughter, an exquisite soprano. She would sing Gounod's "Ave Maria" at Elena and Roberto's wedding while Mama Ana accompanied her on the organ. When the aunt was a young woman, the Metropolitan Opera had been interested in her beautiful voice, but the elder Dr. Vidal would not even consider an audition for his daughter. It was not appropriate, in the mind of his generation, for a woman of means to have a job, much less in the world of entertainment. Both women were obsessed with age. Elena remembered her father's reaction when his mother was sharing with someone the year of her birth. He could not help but utter words that he should have kept to himself: "Now, Mother, you could not have been three when I was born!"

Sara had become a very enterprising woman who knew how to cut corners and make the best out of things. For a dinner party, she had borrowed a beautiful and delicate stuffed-dove centerpiece from her mother-in-law, a woman who loved to collect exquisite bric-a-brac. As preparations were made to decorate the table, Sara could not find the dove, which she had placed on a chair. She searched everywhere in the house with no luck. "Where on earth is Mama Ana's dove?" Sara kept asking everyone. Lady, the pet pointer, was the one to indirectly answer— a few feathers were found in Lady's bed as evidence of her guilt. Suffice it to say that replacing Mama Ana's dove was quite an expensive and embarrassing affair!

There are always characters in families, and Elena's seemed to have them all. On her mother's side, Tío Tato and Tía Niní were two of Elena's favorites. Tío Tato, poet and mathematician, was a renaissance man. Holding degrees in architecture and engineering, he had established a successful firm with his son, Rod. He enjoyed writing poetry and at times speaking in verse, always hilarious and entertaining. As were many of his brilliant counterparts, he was notorious for his absent-mindedness. Once, after buying a new car and forgetting that he had, Tío Tato arrived at home by bus, only to have to return to his office and retrieve his car. Another time, he was protecting himself from the rain by running from tree to tree, while his umbrella lay closed under his arm. The final straw came when he told his wife that he would purchase their goddaughter's birthday present so they could attend her party that afternoon. He bought a toy trumpet. Chachita, the goddaughter, was turning seventeen. As irritated as Tía Niní would get, the pair loved each other.

Elena thought of how generous Tía Niní had been to her and her family. Whenever Tía Niní returned from a trip to the United States, she would bring a trunk full of toys, clothes, shoes, and M&Ms. After Elena turned twelve, she began accompanying her tía on these trips and sometimes Tío Tato would join them as well. He would insist on being the interpreter, although his English was not quite up to par. In one restaurant, he asked for a blanket instead of a napkin. He could not figure out why the waiter gave him a funny look! Those experiences did not discourage him. On the contrary, he seemed to revel in the aftermath of what he had created.

Friday night wrestling at the tíos' home was a neighborhood event. In the early '50s, they were one of the first families to have television. It

ANDREA BERMÚDEZ

was a mammoth cabinet with a seventeen-inch round black-and-white screen. Creative vendors would sell you a tricolor plastic cover so you could colorize the images. The problem was that everything would be seen in red, blue, and yellow as the bands of color were parallel to one another. But it was fun to watch La Amenaza Roja (Red Menace), the most famous villain wrestler of the time. Every Friday night, rumors had it that his red mask was going to be pulled off and viewers would finally learn his identity. It never happened, but the neighborhood audience remained mesmerized.

There were quite a few other tías and tíos in Elena's extended family. There was not a moment when she was by herself. As she was always surrounded by people she cared about, she developed an identity that relied on outsiders for validation. "Does this dress make me look fat? Do I have enough makeup? Should I do this?" She would ask all kinds of questions, from trivial to significant, and they were always answered by someone outside of herself. This was not unique to Elena's predicament. It was the way of the culture. By never being alone, her thoughts were almost public. Her individuality became lost in her support system, and it was rare, and difficult, for her to make decisions on her own. She came to depend on her family, immediate and extended, to feel whole.

In times of need, her relatives were always there. They were also present when their help was not sought. Sometimes decisions were made to avoid hurting them, so the family's opinion would override individual judgment. Elena was a bit afraid that her attraction to Roberto had more to do with her parents' view of him rather than what her own heart felt. Be that as it may, she was planning a wedding and Roberto was to be the groom.

An important feature of Elena's family dynamics was the central role her mother played. In taking care of the children, she indirectly passed along her fears, her values, her preferences. The boys, particularly, developed a very close relationship with Mrs. Vidal. When looking for a spouse, they would be looking for qualities that would remind them of their mother. It was different for Elena, as in a way she and Mrs. Vidal were competing for her father's affection. If there were an argument, it would be Elena and her mother's. The boys would concede defeat early in the process. Dr. Vidal's assigned role as a father would be that of disciplinarian, except he did not have it in him to raise his voice or spank his children. When Bernie was young, he had the reputation of being a spoiled-rotten brat. After one of his many fits of temper, Mrs. Vidal warned him, "Espera que llegue tu papá" (Wait till your father comes home). Papa arrived and all he did was say,

"Niño, cuidado" (Be careful, kid). The reprimand did not seem like much, but the children still dreaded papa's arrival when they had misbehaved.

As generations passed, the role of the woman at home and in society changed in Cuba. In Elena's grandmother's generation, women were not educated since marrying well and having children fulfilled their important mission. They would have no say in what happened outside the home as voting rights were a male prerogative. Sara's generation progressed some. Women could vote, but it was still rare for them to attain higher education. None of Sara's sisters had gone beyond elementary school. They had developed beautiful penmanship, but whatever other education they attained was self-acquired. Sara broke the mold. She finished high school and went on to complete graduate studies at the University of Havana. This would serve as a powerful role model for Elena and her siblings who grew up viewing education as a basic need.

Sara also broke the mold when considering that "being the woman behind the man" was not really her forte. She loved her husband, but she would get her way as many times as he did. The marriage was pretty much quid pro quo. The strong ties of the pre-Castro Cuban culture to the Catholic Church had prevented women from attaining equal stature in society. The role of the church hierarchy was imprinted in social rules regarding gender. While an articulate man, for example, was considered smart, an eloquent woman was viewed as pedantic, as a know-it-all.

The dualistic nature of society regarding gender influenced how some families were structured. Roberto's family environment was quite different from Elena's. His parents were an example of how men always had the upper hand in family decision making. Patricio Medina was completely in charge, and the whole family lived by his rules with the sole objective of making him happy. Roberto's sister left for the Sacred Heart convent when she turned fifteen, so the male presence in the home was strong. Roberto was used to hearing his father pontificate about anything and everything. His mother acted as if she were not even there, as if her opinions were not valued enough to share with the family. At some point during Elena and Roberto's courtship, Mrs. Medina had told her that it was the responsibility of the woman to save her spouse spiritually. That comment should have been a clue to Elena about Roberto's upbringing, but she was blinded by her youth.

Extended families were also an integral part of the concept of family. Distant relationships were named, and good friends added to the "list." For instance, *primo tercero* (cousin thrice removed) became "*mi primo*" (my cousin) and *tía política* (aunt in-law), a certified relative. There were even *comadres* (godmother, referred to as comother) who, as stipulated in the Catholic baptism, accepted the responsibility for the child's spiritual development in the absence of the parents. In the same vein, there were *tatarabuelos* (great-great-grandparents) and *chornos* (great-great-great-grandparents) that, although time did not allow meeting them personally, their names were known and their stories told. Elena knew of General José Manuel Vidal, one of her thirty-two *chornos*, who was a friend of patriot Carlos Manuel de Céspedes and who had participated in the 1800's *Guerra de los Diez Años*. She even had a picture of this most distinguished and unsmiling general with his handlebar mustache and a remote resemblance to his great-great-grandson Dr. Bernardo Vidal.

One influential member of the extended family was Tata, on whom Elena most often relied for her wise interpretation of the world around her. She came to work for the Vidals right after Elena was born. Taking care of the demanding newborn kept her busy during the day and, sometimes, during the night as well. She did not mind. She was becoming quite fond of the tiny baby girl. Tata's name was María Rodríguez. Her real age was unknown, even to her. When asked about it, she would respond, "I was born the year of the flood." But which flood? 1875? 1893? 1903? With the active hurricane history that has always been part of island living, it was hard to pinpoint Tata's birth date. At any rate, Tata was strong and healthy with a no-nonsense approach to life.

She lived in the Vidal household and soon became an integral part of the family. Tata was treated with love and respect and her judgment sought in domestic matters. Her opinions reflected strong convictions and a solid value system. As Elena grew up, Tata's presence in her life became more dominant. If Elena took ill, Tata would not leave her side. If the young woman had a problem, Tata was always there.

Elena felt that of all that Castro took away, the loss of the family was by far the most difficult to endure. Many families had been torn apart by philosophical differences and a great number of others by distance. Time does not erase relationships, but separation loosens the ties that hold them together. Elena had to accept that her once tight-knit family was a thing of the past, a fleeting remembrance of what had been.

CHAPTER 7

At Home with the Vidals

Life is a rough biography.
Memories smooth out the edges.

—*Terri Guillemets*

SARA GONZÁLEZ AND Bernardo Vidal had met through their parents after their respective moves to Havana. Both sets of parents felt that their kids were perfect for each other, and fortunately, the young couple felt the same way. After a long courtship, they were married in 1926. The elder Vidals had been benefactors of the Catholic Church and had developed strong relationships with the hierarchy. As a favor to them, Sara and Bernardo were married on September 12 by the cardinal archbishop of Havana at the Parroquia del Sagrado Corazón de Jesús (Sacred Heart of Jesus Parish), an ornate nineteenth-century structure. In later years, Sara would refer to the event as being *de mucho ringo rango* (high society chic) because of all the influential attendees her in-laws knew in Havana.

Soon after, the young couple would make their home in the eastern city of Holguín, where they spent the first two years of marriage in Bernardo's military service before returning to Havana. After establishing his medical practice in the capital city, the Vidals moved to a quiet neighborhood in the Alturas de Miramar section. The street was lined by well-kept homes with expansive lawns and stately mahogany trees.

Elena was born when her mother was almost thirty-nine. She always suspected that she had been an "accident," although her mother reassured her that they wanted a girl to complete the family. Although her relationship to her mother was not distant, Elena would always turn to her nanny, Tata, for wisdom and solace. She was always there for Elena and had been since the baby was seven days old. Elena seemed to have it all: her mother's gregarious personality and her father's healthy attitude about life. She would have loved a little sister to play with, but she had her friend Meg and her younger brother who was close to her in age.

Davidsito was born twenty months after Elena. As a child, he had the reputation of being the genius of the family. Sara frequently told the story of a time when he was sitting on the floor with a goofy expression that alarmed her. "What are you thinking, Davidsito?" she asked, not sure she wanted to hear the answer. He replied, "That today is the yesterday of tomorrow." He was five. Early on, the two younger siblings would establish a special bond. They had been born late in their parents' lives, so Sara, in particular, had a harder time adapting to the larger family unit.

For the most part, childhood experiences were pleasant and orderly for the Vidal clan. Everyday school for the kids, domestic responsibilities for Sara, and a very demanding profession for Bernardo Sr. described the family activities. Christmas was the only other holiday the family celebrated besides Bernardo's saint's day. Going with Papi to buy their big tree was a special treat for Elena and Davidsito. Sometimes Alex would join them since Bernie was usually busy between his girlfriends and his medical studies. *Nueces, avellanas, turrón* (walnuts, hazelnut and nougat) were always available at Christmas time. Elena remembered the huge live turkey a patient sent once. She became enamored of the animal and even gave him a name. When it got to be time to make a meal out of him, nobody dared break Elena's heart, so Dr. Vidal, much like the presidents of the United States on Thanksgiving, had to "pardon" the animal so he could join fellow turkeys at his brother's ranch.

There were other priceless memories Elena held from her childhood. One day, when four-year-old Elena took part in an Easter procession as an angel, she became frightened by the trappings of Saint Michael the Archangel. Tata could not allow for the little girl to suffer, so she decided to walk along side of her, holding Elena's sweaty palms. It was quite a sight! Tata, whom Elena loved as a mother, had become an important presence in her life. Having known her all her life, Elena thought Tata could do no wrong. However, Elena was mistaken. There was one thing Tata could not do well, and that was making Cuban coffee. Bernie had nicknamed her Lucrecia, in remembrance of Lucrezia Borgia, daughter of Pope Alexander VI who was known for her poisonous concoctions. Tata would take Bernie's teasing in stride.

As a poor, uneducated black, Tata had experienced segregation to which she reacted without resentment. She felt strongly that only very ignorant people could feel superior to others. "Aren't we all going to die one day?" was her line when the subject of discrimination was broached. She saw segregation as a two-way street; she did not want to be with "them" anymore than they with her. She did make an exception for the Vidals. They were not "them"; the Vidals were family. Tata believed each individual was a child of God and, as a result, deserving of love and respect. Discrimination did not make Tata angry, it made her wise, and she made sure to pass this sentiment to Elena. Oftentimes, Tata would take Elena to her relatives' homes to play with her nephews and nieces. Her family would always welcome the little girl with open arms, almost as if her visits were a reason for joyous celebration.

Being around Tata made Elena feel understood and pampered. She treasured memories of taking the ferry across Havana Bay to visit the colonial town of Regla on the bay's southeastern shore. Once there, they would visit the hermitage of Our Lady of Regla, a seventeenth-century church popularly used in Santería celebrations. They would walk around the town, play in the park, and buy *dulce de maní* (candied peanuts) from a street vendor. After Elena's recovery from a particularly serious bout with strep throat, she and Tata offered a *milagro* (small silver amulet) to express gratitude to Our Lady for her miraculous intervention. For a small town, Regla's history was long and picturesque. As a strategic port, it was a smuggling center during the nineteenth century. It had also been said that famous Cuban patriot José Martí's first political speech was delivered from Regla's Lyceum.

Elena recalled her family neighborhood as a peaceful place, except for the rumors about a neighbor, Héctor Salazar, who lived alone in his 6,500 square feet white stucco home. A four-car garage sheltered his antique car collection, which had not been driven in years. He always took a taxi or the public transport that ran a few blocks away from the home. He never smiled or talked to anyone unless he was spoken to first. He was certainly an odd type. Rumor had it that years ago there was a Mrs. Salazar who had mysteriously disappeared. No one dared think he had anything to do with it, but everyone still gossiped about the possibility. After all, he was a peculiar neighbor. He had five people employed to care for the house, which seemed from the outer appearance to be in good shape.

When Alex was fifteen, he convinced Elena, who was nine at the time, to climb a gigantic ficus tree located between the two properties to see what was happening in Mr. Salazar's house. Maybe Mrs. Salazar had not really disappeared, maybe he had kids they could play with, just a bunch of maybes that sounded appealing to the two youngsters. Elena was the first to climb the tree. She just did not know she would be the only one. Elena was convinced that they would solve Mr. Salazar's mystery and put an end to the vicious rumors.

From her vantage point, she could see what looked like a kitchen. "Oh, there was a woman there looking very busy and moving rapidly from one end of the room to another," Elena observed. "Maybe it was Mrs. Salazar pacing the floor," she thought. Elena told Alex to join her so they could decipher what she was seeing. Alex did not answer. He was gone! She tried to get down from the tree but found out she couldn't. Where was Alex? "Well, maybe he went inside to get binoculars so they could do a more sophisticated kind of snooping." But no— he had run inside to call for Sara so she could find Elena "*con las manos en la masa*" (with her hands in the cookie jar). What could she say to explain herself to her mother? Elena had to take her punishment and learn from it. She would get even some day. Alex was that kind of guy, sneaky.

At least her older brother, Bernie, was direct. He was more of a "what you see is what you get" type who seemed to enjoy the attention lavished on being the first born. Following in his father's footsteps was expected of him as the eldest son. He took his responsibility well and seemed happy attending medical school. Elena did not always like or approve of what he did or said, but she felt he was forthright. He was also thirteen years older, so actually she did not know him that well.

Bernie was famous for his string of girlfriends who were constantly calling him on the phone. He would ask permission to invite them to dinner, and Sara would always seem to get attached. So when Bernie would break up with them, the girls would call Sara. From then on, there was a friendship established. When Sara's saint's day came along, two of them brought gifts, and wouldn't you know it? They were the same porcelain figurine of a Chinese girl looking dreamy. Sara loved everything Chinese but was pressed to exchange one of them for fear the girls would get suspicious if they ever saw the two identical figurines. They never found out the rest of the story. In time, however, Sara forbade Bernie from bringing any more girlfriends to the house unless he was pretty serious about them.

Being a middle child, Alex grew up with a sense that life was unfair to him. He was sandwiched between his good-looking and popular older brother and Elena, the only girl. Alex believed that Bernie got all the attention and that Elena could get away with anything. He felt he stood no chance, so he became secretive and angry at the world. Alex would look for any opportunity to lash out at Elena since he wouldn't dare cross his older brother. He did not have too many friends and turned to religion early on as an escape and a refuge. He was a time bomb, and it worried his parents who did not know what to do. Psychology, at the time, was seen with contempt, especially by Dr. Vidal who did not consider it a worthwhile science. He would say in private that dermatologists and psychiatrists made all the money because their patients were for life. This belief explained why Alex never received help with his glaring emotional issues.

Elena's daily routine consisted of going to a Catholic elementary girls' school and being at home. Her mother had gone to the same American Dominican Academy some forty years before, and she was partial to the experience.

Sara González circa 1916 in her
American Dominican Academy uniform

ANDREA BERMÚDEZ

Sara's daughter Elena thirty years later
following in her mother's footsteps

Elena was a bit of a handful during those early years. She could not sit quietly or pay attention for any extended period of time. She was mostly bored with the pace of instruction, so she found herself in trouble at times. It was pretty common that Elena would have to copy one hundred times "I will not talk in class" but, as most "repeaters" do, she failed to fulfill the promise.

She was a bit afraid of the nuns who spoke some Spanish but were not very deft in dealing with Cuban children. Her fourth-grade teacher, Sister Emma, confessed to the class that she thought Cubans lived in huts and wore *tapa-rabos* (thongs). Nothing could be farther from the truth. Cuba was, in fact, a highly developed and sophisticated country when it came to fashion and lifestyle. Those comments did not ingratiate Sister Emma with her students who from that moment on declared war. It was not long after Sister Emma had to be replaced by a less bigoted colleague. However, these fourth graders acquired the status of heroes or villains depending on whose perspective one would consider.

On a weekend, Elena and her friend Meg were planning to go to Meg's farm, and Elena was very excited. She could not settle down, thinking of riding horses and having fun with her friend. At the end of the school day, when she was in line ready to leave, she was pulled out by one of the nuns who thought Elena was being rambunctious and disorderly. The nun threatened to keep the girl over the weekend. She was petrified. She always thought the nuns were a bit creepy and probably lived among ghosts and apparitions. Elena could not stay there and die of fear, so when the nun was not looking, she got back in line and left school with Meg. The whole weekend had been ruined as Elena was convinced the nuns would be waiting to punish her upon her return. She worried unnecessarily since nothing ever happened as a result of that experience.

Elena did remember one fun experience at the school when she dubbed Al Jolson, America's famous 1930s singer, in his rendition of "California, Here I Come" for a talent show. She was so good! Applause from the audience called for an encore, which gained her the nuns' appreciation and her friends' jealousy. After that experience, everything seemed to click. Elena had found something she could do well, better than others, and that boosted her self-confidence. Gone was the boredom from which she had tried to unsuccessfully escape. There were no more lists to copy, no more complaining to her parents. A sudden change came upon her, and her life at the Dominican school improved dramatically. Years later, her high school experience at the academically demanding Ruston Academy was an entirely different story, and it turned Elena into a serious student. She frequently thought of this time as her happiest childhood experiences in Cuba.

For the boys' education, the Vidals felt Colegio de Belén, a Jesuit college preparatory, was the best choice. Bernardo Sr. had graduated from that school in 1918 and knew of its excellent academic reputation. Our Lady of Belen was founded in 1854 by a royal charter issued by Queen Isabella II of Spain. Nicknamed the Palace of Education, the school counted many illustrious Cubans among its graduates, including the eminent epidemiologist Dr. Carlos Finlay.

Most priests teaching at Our Lady of Belen were ultraconservative scholars from Spain, and they had tried earlier to discourage the family from sending Elena to an American school, labeling it as too lenient. Sara Vidal was determined to have her daughter attend her alma mater so the priests' warnings were not heeded. This type of independent thinking was not common in those days, particularly for a woman who thought of herself as religious. By instilling in their devotees a sense of guilt and punishment, most priests attained unquestionable control of their actions. However, this tactic did not work with Sara.

Despite the very strict environment of the school, the Vidal men had pleasant memories from the Belén days. Bernardo recalled a time when he and several of his friends decided to steal a bunch of bananas from a fruit vendor that parked in front of the school. After a short while, the guilt-ridden second graders decided to go to confession so they would "deserve" taking communion. After the fifth little boy admitted his role in the banana heist, the priest had had enough. He stood in front of the confessional and commanded "those who stole the bananas, go to communion." The boys recalled their own times of fun and mischief when childhood innocence was repressed by rules and authority. They received an excellent education as well, which later allowed them to pursue higher degrees.

Besides school responsibilities, an important routine at the Vidals' was dinnertime, a near-sacred event for the household. The family ate regularly at 8:00 p.m. when the clan was finally together from their various activities. It was not unusual to have a few guests join them, sometimes without any prior planning. Dinner started with a prayer of thanksgiving, which was followed by enough food to feed an army. Each person would choose what to eat and how much. Mrs. Vidal would do the honors and you had to stop her before you actually wanted to, as it was her habit to shell out two additional spoonfuls of whatever she was serving. The first course was chicken soup with a sliver of lime and sliced avocados. The rest of the courses were eaten together. Typically, they would be white rice and black beans, a choice from *ropa vieja* (shredded beef), *boliche* (rolled beef roast stuffed with ham), or *pargo* (red snapper) with a serving of green (*tostones*) or ripe (*maduros*) plantains and baguette-like bread. For desert, they had Dr. Vidal's favorite: a slice of guava paste and cream cheese on unsalted saltines (*galleticas de soda*). One of their engineer friends had once calculated how many kilometers of guava Dr. Vidal had ingested in his lifetime, and it was suspected that the number would encircle the 1,200 kilometer-long island at least a couple of times. Despite the large volume of food and the onslaught of "bad carbs," none of the Vidals were overweight.

Dr. Vidal was a man devoted to his profession. He loved his family and never missed a meal at home, even if it was interrupted by a visit to a patient. He indulged his children, most especially Elena as their only girl. When he mentioned her name, his eyes brightened up, and his smile gave away the depth of his feelings. So when she asked her parents if she could keep a pet monkey that her cousin had brought from a trip to Nicaragua, he couldn't say no. Ulises arrived on a Tuesday. He was so cute and cuddly. Elena had had a mental picture of dressing him up and having Ulises join them at the dinner table. However, Ulises was wild. He loved to climb the mango tree in front of the house and time Dr. Vidal's arrival with a quick sprint down the street. Dr. Vidal's lunchtime became a predictable experience: run after Ulises and bring him home. By Sunday, the experience was getting old, so suggestions were entertained to find a better environment where Ulises could thrive. Fortunately, a good friend of the family who owned a farm volunteered to adopt the pet monkey. Later on, the Vidals found out Ulises was actually a girl, had been renamed Cristina, and was living in grand style.

During Elena's teenage years, she was too busy with her friends to pay attention to her family life. Tata was the only exception as their bond strengthened with time. After meeting Roberto, Elena was dismayed to realize how quickly her childhood years had gone by and wished she had clung to them. "Unfortunately, one learns to appreciate the present when it is already gone," she told Tata as she was preparing to move on to another chapter in her life. When looking at her Tata, she was swept with wonderful memories of times they had shared. Again, she could not cling to the present to make it last.

ANDREA BERMÚDEZ

CHAPTER 8

The Circle of Friends

We are each of us angels with only one wing, and we can only fly by embracing one another.

—*Luciano de Crescenzo*

CLOSE FRIENDSHIPS WERE the core of Elena's extended family. They served as mirrors of her soul as they reflected aspects of her person not visible to the eye. It was through good friends that Elena developed her self-esteem. She discovered that she had a sense of humor when her friends laughed, that she had a good mind when she made them think. Life without friends, she thought, was a world without music.

Elena remembered her high school years at Ruston Academy, a college preparatory school in the Vedado section of Havana not too far from the waterfront. It was mostly attended by American children whose parents worked in Cuba, so the school offered Elena an opportunity to learn English and become acquainted with some aspects of life in the United States. In her senior English class, they had discussed chapters on the rat race and the survival of the fittest. She had no comprehension about what either concept meant since competitiveness was not a customary experience for Cubans. The Catholic Church had instilled in the Cuban culture a belief in predestination, which made fierce competition among people a moot point. Elena's day-to-day experiences did not familiarize her with the notion of any kind of race to survive. She was fortunate that at least Ruston prepared her intellectually to meet face-to-face these two important survival tips for navigating life in the United States.

Challenged in her studies for the first time, she still managed to make good friends that she would consider to be part of her extended family.

There were four friends, in particular, who were inseparable. Ofelia, Pilar, Teresita, and Xenia, who together with Elena, called themselves the Punjab after the Indian region "land of the five rivers." Although Teresita left high school to marry her football-star boyfriend, and contact with her had lessened, the sisterhood name stuck. The girls had even developed a language to communicate among themselves, a sort of pig latin that would allow them to create their own special world set apart from outsiders. Their sisterhood was exclusive, or so they believed, as sense of humor and smarts were the two most important requirements for acceptance, not that they would accept any more members. The Punjab girls were among the brightest and most popular in the school. Their popularity, however, had nothing to do with being easy with the boys, as this aspect of male-female relationships was not condoned by Cuban social mores. According to these tenets, girls had the responsibility of representing the family honor, and as a result, they had to behave respectably. On the other hand, boys, to grow up and become real men, had more latitude to experiment and not be judged. Two categories of girls emerged from this belief: the marriageable kind and the ones with whom to "have fun." The Punjab was definitely raised to marry "properly" when the time came.

The "Punjab" friends on graduation night in 1958. Left to right:
Xenia, Pilar, Elena and Ofelia

ANDREA BERMÚDEZ

Ofelia always wanted to be a writer, so from her you would expect words such as *plethora* or *onomatopoeia*. Smart as a whip, she was sort of the leader of the pack, in charge of keeping the group focused on their planned activities. She was always writing books that, although unpublished, showed promise of a talented writer. Xenia was reserved and moody but had a heart of gold and a good sense of humor. She was the philosopher in the group who tended toward an agnostic view of the world. Xenia was the only one of them whose middle name was not María, as her family shared her non-Catholic views. Xenia's dad was conspicuously absent, and she never mentioned him. The girls had figured that the parents had divorced at some point, and there was no contact with him. Pilar was the athlete. She competed in all sports, but tennis was her forte. In the early years, she would frequently travel to compete in national championships. Elena was the dancer of the group. Along with Ramiro, a senior in school, they could really show off their talent. With their energy and youth, they never took a break at the school dances. The writer, the philosopher, the athlete, the dancer, together they had it all. Those were happy days, innocent days. Reality was happening in a parallel universe.

Ruston Academy was pretty much the hub of the Punjab sisterhood activities. The Vedado District where the academy was located also included spacious old homes where many professionals lived in pre-Castro days. Its proximity to the Malecón, the popular boardwalk, made El Vedado an ideal place to watch for pirate ships threatening the harbor during colonial times. Ruston Academy was in three large buildings, suggesting remnants of old aristocracy.

Old Ruston Bachillerato building in the Vedado District

In one of those structures, a central courtyard was reminiscent of traditional Spanish architecture. A large banyan tree provided shade and ensured a comfortable temperature all year long. Mrs. Baker, the principal's wife, conducted choir lessons using a piano that sat under a roofed portion of the courtyard. Elena would have given anything to be in the choir, but Mrs. Baker had already told her that she could not sing. "*Más se perdió en la guerra*" (more was lost in the war), Elena thought to herself and proceeded to put the incident behind her.

She loved the old buildings. They had spirit and a history much longer and more interesting than hers. Unfortunately, in 1955 the school moved to new quarters. The buildings were modern and had all the amenities necessary: well-equipped classrooms and labs, great basketball and volleyball courts, plenty of space for track and field, large faculty offices, and a spartan principal's office. It only lacked character. It also lacked history, for now.

New Ruston in Alturas de Miramar, inaugurated in 1955

ANDREA BERMÚDEZ

Pilar was one of the cinco Marías who had been neighbors across the street since Elena was five years old. Sara Vidal and Pilar's mother, Marta Pons, were good friends, so the families spent a lot of time together. For a short time, Bernie had dated one of the older Marías. Dating, of course, meant taking along a chaperone, so Marta would likely be the responsible party. Mr. Pons was involved in politics. He had served as a senator from Camagüey, so he was Bernardo's conduit to the good gossip. It was a frequent experience for the two families to gather in the Vidals porch and exchange several generations of family stories. Oral history was a part of the learning experience of Cubans. They not only became acquainted with their past, but they would also acquire attitudes, biases, and values from the older generation. Through these social exchanges, Elena had learned a great deal about her wise grandmother Elenita for whom she had been named. Although Elena never met her, these conversations made her feel she had. As friends go, you could not have found a more amicable crowd.

Sometimes, the younger group would join other neighbors of the same age and gather in the garden to tell scary stories while some of them would play pranks, pretending to be a ghost or a stranger. They would sometimes dance to the latest fad, rock 'n' roll. Elena and Davidsito were a hit as they moved to the beat of "Rock Around the Clock." There was no alcohol served, no cigarettes smoked, only a record player and the fresh energy of youth.

Part of her extended family was the Robledo family. Their daughter Matilde had married Elena's cousin Rod. When their twins were born in 1953, Elena spent two weeks at the hospital keeping company to their mother, who almost died during childbirth. The babies were Elena's pride and joy, and she cherished the times she spent with them and with Matilde's family. The twins' grandfather, Raúl Robledo, was a real estate lawyer and had amassed a pretty hefty fortune. A charming and generous man, he was hardly impressed by his own success. Some weekends, he would invite Elena to join his grandson Ralph, then seven, to go horseback riding in the woods near their family estate. When the twins came home, the Robledo household became one of Elena's favorite places to visit.

When Matilde recovered from her childbirth experience, she and husband Rod invited Elena to go boating with them to celebrate their good fortune aboard their craft *The Miracle*. Elena had to beg her parents for permission as they were apprehensive about boating in September, the height of hurricane season. As fate would have it, once away from the coast, a storm formed out of nowhere, and for hours Rod fought the rough seas. Elena and Matilde were petrified, but rather than being quiet and forlorn, they could not stop laughing. The more nervous they got, the more they laughed. Poor Rod did not say a word, just barked orders when there was something productive the women could do. Fortunately, just as abruptly as the storm arrived, it left. *The Miracle* had earned its name. It had survived, and they were safe. When they returned home, they found a parade of Vidals and Robledos supporting each other at this time of panic. The women had rosaries draped around their fingers, a sign of the drama that had been played out during the young people's absence.

Then there was her good friend Antonia, the daughter of a TV producer, who was responsible for Elena developing a taste for the limelight. During this stage, Elena appeared in a couple of children's programs and was offered a bit part in a movie about the Cuban patriot José Martí. Her stardom died before it began as Dr. Vidal would not allow his only daughter to go into an acting career. History had repeated itself as years before Elena's grandfather had forbidden his daughter from pursuing an operatic career. The situation was a little different this time since Elena had only been offered a one-liner: "José, here is a glass of water," hardly a harbinger of fame.

Elena had quite a few male friends as well. As a matter of fact, at one point she knew three Miguels who created a lot of confusion when they would call and leave a message for Elena. Her visits with any boy were made under the direct supervision of Tata who at all times made herself pretty visible. Elena was fine with this even when she would catch Tata snooping through a cracked door. This zealousness was called for since Elena's behavior reflected directly on the family's honor. The boys could do as they wished, but Elena was another story!

Two canine friends, Rex and Lady, and Elena's horse, Onyx, completed her circle. Rex was a boxer whose looks betrayed his sweet nature. He was given to Dr. Vidal by one of his patients who could not do enough for the Vidals. Rex took to Bernie as both shared a mischievous side. Lady D'Irack was canine royalty, being the pick of the litter of a famous champion couple. The last name came with her, and her demeanor showed she was proud of it. Lady went on to become a champion herself. Her dietary requirements reflected her pampered circumstances and competed with Elena who lived on a permanent diet. The loyalty these animals had for the family would surpass that of any friend. When Rex died of kidney failure at age ten, the family went into mourning. There was incomparable grief for Elena who had experienced very few losses before. She swore she would never have another pet, but fortunately, she changed her mind. She got Onyx, her sixteen-hand-high Tennessee walker who became her escape during hard times. So Lady and Onyx were the children of the heart.

When Elena moved to the United States, she lost contact with her Cuban support system, but she added a few friends in the process. One of them was Dr. Jamie Baxter. Elena met her in Houston while Jamie was doing her residency in internal medicine at the University of Texas. She had been born in Key West where her father was the city aquarium manager. Jamie and her older sister lived with their parents in an apartment at the aquarium, which allowed them to grow up loving and respecting nature. As a child, Jamie remembers running with her sister to meet the Havana Ferry at Mallory Dock so they could wave at the arriving tourists. Elena and Jamie wondered how many times they might have waved at each other since Elena and her family would often travel to Key West by ferry to shop in Miami. Their friendship had been instantaneous and lasting. If Elena had a problem, Jamie would come to her rescue. She felt so lucky to have such a loyal supporter, particularly during heartbreaking times.

Another addition to the friendship circle was Marta, a colleague at the University of Saint Thomas in Houston. Marta, born in Argentina, was married and had three children. Their lives paralleled each other, so it was not a surprise that they would become good friends. They had even married on the same day, one in Havana and the other in Buenos Aires. Marta loved life and helped Elena enjoy the years they worked together. They shared some humorous experiences such as the time Elena and Roberto had invited Marta and her husband, Héctor, along with José de Rojas and his wife, to an evening pool party. Out of the blue, Elena received a phone call during the day from a friend, Alina, who was a student of Roberto's. The friend asked Elena to stop by her home to listen to her aunt playing Cuban songs on the piano. Elena had everything ready for the evening dinner, so she felt it would not hurt to visit her friend. She went ahead with the visit and, as a "by the way," invited her friend to stop by that evening for dessert and coffee since José was also her professor.

The evening guests had arrived and were enjoying themselves swimming and having a good time. All of a sudden, the doorbell rang, and to Elena's surprise, it was Alina with her mother and a cousin who had arrived before dinner was served. Confusion best describes the rest of the evening. As soon as they arrived, Elena noticed the mood of the party changing. José jumped out of the pool as if he had been hoisted by an invisible cord. Berta de Rojas, who seemed suddenly out of sorts, also left the pool and was talking to Marta's husband in hushed voices. Elena and Marta were unsuccessfully trying to make everything right and figure out where and why the party had suddenly gone wrong. Roberto was busily working on the barbecue dinner while entertaining the older ladies, but where was José? Where was Alina? They had disappeared.

Elena was totally frustrated. She had planned this party so well, and it was fast deteriorating. At one point, she told Marta, "If I were not the hostess, I would leave the party now." Marta looked horrified. "Don't you leave me with this mess!" she warned Elena who had no intention of doing so. Mercifully, the party ended and the guests left. Only then did Elena find out that José and Alina were having an affair, and Roberto did not feel right betraying the confidence. His trying to do the right thing had backfired. Berta de Rojas took a long time to realize Elena was a victim of naïveté and not a villain shoring up the illicit romance. Elena and Marta spent hours on the phone trying to interpret human nature. They decided that the aging professor had thrown his life away hoping that a young lover would make him young again. Unfortunately, it did not work this way.

From this point on, Elena became very selective about whom she would allow in her circle. She was known as a person with many friends. However, Elena would make a distinction between those that would be on your side, and by your side, no matter what and those whose support would falter during hard times. Her colleague, Father John Hanes, unfortunately, had disappointed her. Elena had been made chair of the Spanish Department where Father Hanes also taught. She was unaware of how resentful he had become having to defer to a female boss. As a priest, he was used to calling the shots, and it was nearly impossible for him to make the transition. Father Hanes had proven to be a good actor, able to conceal his true feelings about their professional relationship. What Elena did not know was that he was working behind the scenes to get her post. After this disappointing experience, she would say, "You will only know a friendship is true when it passes with flying colors the tests of life. Some people are born to love, others to be loved. Friendships are fed by givers, not takers."

It was her friends who were there when she needed direction. Elena was thankful that her journey had crossed their paths as each delivered a message that allowed her to believe in herself or a lesson that made her wiser. As has been said, friends open doors that had been closed or nonexistent before they came into our lives. Many times those doors are aspects of the self that had not been revealed before. Elena credits her circle of friends for giving her the love and support she needed to complete her lifelong search for her own identity.

ANDREA BERMÚDEZ

PART III
Understanding the Cuban Spirit

CHAPTER 9

Toward a Definition of *"Lo Cubano"*

Ordinary riches can be stolen, real riches cannot. In your soul are infinitely precious things that cannot be taken from you.

—*Oscar Wilde*

WHERE PEOPLE LIVE, their ancestry and how they interact among themselves determine racial makeup, language, and religion. These factors work together to shape the culture's worldviews and value systems. For these reasons, the essence of the Cuban people (*Lo Cubano*) cannot be appreciated if features such as race, language, and religion are not viewed as constantly changing factors that respond to external forces in the environment. The first challenge in defining Cuban culture is the fact that there is more than one, as influential forces have been varied and complex. Pre- and post-Castro Cuban cultures are poles apart, a vivid example of how the historical milieu has shaped those differences.

Before the Castro revolution, most influences came from the Western world, particularly, from the United States. This influence weakened and was replaced after 1959, when a relationship developed with the Eastern Bloc, for the most part with the USSR. Elena's memories of Cuba came to a halt as she departed in 1960, when for her Cuba froze in time. It is not surprising that her views on the defining factors of the Cuban spirit reflect that perspective.

The essence of Cuba is the Cubans, a product of a privileged geography and an intricate historical context. Part of their essence is the individual's identity, or claim, when choosing affiliation with a group. It can best be described as a person's sense of belonging and is reinforced by compatibility between the individual and others within the group. Of the various factors that intervene in developing group affiliation, a critical one is race. A person's color goes beyond a set of physical characteristics and becomes more of a subculture with its own set of values and mores. The majority of Cubans still living on the island are black while the reverse is true among exiled Cubans. Africa had long played a part in the history of Spain with the Moorish conquest that lasted eight centuries. A more recent occurrence has been African presence in Cuba. There, for almost five hundred years, Cubans of African ancestry have played a determining role in the development of Cuban culture. The segregation of races did little to impede Afro-Cuban influence in music, language, and religion from becoming a significant part of the culture.

Although chronicles regarding race and ethnicity in Cuba mostly emphasized the black-white story, there were other races participating in shaping its history. Anyone who fights a war to defend the interests of a nation becomes an integral part of its narrative. Nineteenth- and twentieth-century wars were fought in Cuba by a multiethnic military, which included Cubans of African and Chinese ancestry. However, the Chinese have been a silent minority, infrequently participating in Cuban national politics. After Castro, the Chinese became even more invisible. There were three known waves of Chinese immigration. In the mid 1800s, they came to the island as indentured servants to work in the sugar fields. Later, a group of successful California Chinese arrived in Havana fleeing from anti-Chinese prejudice. They laid the foundations for what later became the Barrio Chino (Chinatown), the largest Chinese community in Latin America. One last group arrived as political exiles from the 1912 revolution in China. Cuban antiforeigner measures of the mid 1900s forced the Chinese into small entrepreneurial activities. The Chinese-Cuban population remained small and self-supporting, and their strong identity ties have kept most of them in the *barrio*. Separate schools, a Chinese cemetery, a medical clinic, newspapers, radio stations, and social clubs kept them socially insulated from the rest of the Cuban population.

Elena recalled visiting the Barrio Chino with her mother and Tía Niní to go shopping at the *almacén*, a mixture of grocery and department store where good-quality foods were sold. Eusebio, the Chinese owner, loved Elena and always sat her on the counter to enjoy a small gift. He always said that her dark almond-shaped eyes and straight black hair reminded him of a dainty Chinese princess. Since Elena's mother had great affection for the

Chinese culture, she proudly wore her white silk blouse with hand-painted Chinese characters. She thought she would impress Eusebio who instead looked a bit surprised. Sara was the one surprised when Eusebio told her, "If I were you, I would not wear that blouse. What the characters say is a bit vulgar." Sara wanted to die!

To Elena, it was incomprehensible that the value of a human would be measured by social standards that favored one race over another, particularly when the architects of those standards stood to gain. She felt that cultural perceptions of race, much like those of language, were a political construct to keep some people under the thumb of the majority culture. Whatever race meant to others, to Elena it signified a critical factor in defining Cuba's multiracial character, which has greatly influenced the development of its language, religion, and music. Elena saw those three cultural features as vehicles to communicate: with each other, with the *más allá* (the beyond), and with one's soul, respectively.

In an attempt to understand *Lo Cubano*, language is among the most fundamental cultural attributes as it allows for communicating feelings and thoughts to others. The transference of culture from one generation to the next would be impossible if a commonly understood language did not exist. The beauty and complexity of Cuban Spanish, Elena believed, were shaped by unique geographical and historical circumstances and by their interaction with the individuals and the group. In Elena's travels to Spain and other Spanish-speaking places, her language was always the object of attention.

She tired of people declaring that Cubans mistreated Spanish and wanted so much to say in return, "We inherited Spanish from Spain for which we are grateful. But like children do, when they grow up, they become their own person, not a clone." Fast spoken Caribbean Spanish distinguishes itself from other dialects in the rendering of certain sounds, such as the aspiration of the *s* (*ehte* for *este*) and the weakening of the *r* in a final position (*po* for *por*). Elena recalled a time when Bernie and a Mexican doctor friend were chatting as they drove away from their hospital duties. Referring to the car coming behind them, Bernie said, "Ete que etá aca trá." Not understanding, his friend asked, "What is taca taca traca?" When Bernie repeated what he had just said, but this time in a more standard fashion, "Este que está aquí detrás" (This one that is behind us), they both doubled up with laughter.

Elena was proud of the language she spoke and made no excuse for her rapid and animated speech. Cuban vocabulary had multicultural influences as it included words inherited from aborigines (*bohío, hamaca, tabaco*) as well as from immigrants from every continent. For instance, people from Canary Islands, Spain, arrived in Cuba during the eighteenth, nineteenth and twentieth centuries and left a linguistic legacy (*guagua* [bus], *fajarse* [to fight]), which have given Cuban Spanish a unique flavor. Many European languages other than Spain's have also infiltrated the Cuban *Criollo* (Creole). Words inherited from French include *quinqué* (lamp), *matiné* (matinee), *catre* (cot); from Italian, *fotuto* (car horn); and from Portuguese, *chubasco* (shower). From West Africa and its variety of dialects came words such as *quimbombó* (okra), *fufú* (mashed plantain dish), *malanga* and *ñame* (root vegetables), and *marimba*. The various Chinese dialects have given *Criollo* numerous words and expressions as well including *champán* (champagne), *tibor* (urinal), and *chaucha* (food). Cuban Spanish has been enriched by this beautiful amalgam of inherited voices. When traveling, every time Elena used any of these words, people would immediately know that she was from Cuba.

With few navigable rivers and one central highway, communication between and among Cuban provinces was difficult, but it also created an opportunity in the prerevolutionary years for the development of a diverse culture, particularly as it affected language. Dialectal differences within the various parts of Cuba are evident in the choice of words as well as the cadence of speech. In eastern Cuba, words such as *macho* (pig), *balde* (bucket), and *guineo* (banana), for example, have become *lechón, cubo,* and *plátano*, respectively, in the west. Sometimes, words acquire different connotations, and an innocent choice could turn into a "four letter" word in one world or the other. There are theories that claim Taíno language has had a great influence in vocabulary and intonation patterns appearing in eastern speech. Cubans from Havana swear to the fact that speakers from Oriente have a *cantico* (sing song) while those from this easternmost province claim that *Habaneros* are the ones who have it.

Language, being in constant flux, has acquired new features within Cuba after three generations of the Castro regime, and also in Miami where a great number of Cuban exiles live. Added to the many Anglicisms already in the *criollo* vocabulary —such as *jonrón* (homerun), *picher* (pitcher), *lonche* (lunch), *mitin* (meeting), *parquear* (to park), *melón* (melon)— Miami Spanish exhibits, as expected, new terms applied to old habits, for instance, *choqueado* (shocked), *envuelto* (involved), *printeado* (printed), *sumarizado* (summarized). A great majority of Miami Cubans speak Spanish as well as English, a fact that has created discord between them and resentful monolingual English speakers.

Unlike Chinese, which is orally incomprehensible across dialects, Spanish is well understood among Spanish speakers worldwide despite its dissimilarities. Encountering these differences, however, can result in truly comical situations. Cubans tend to use the verb *coger* (to get, to grasp, to take, to hold) with high frequency. Unfortunately, the verb has a negative connotation for some Spanish speakers. When Elena met an Argentinean friend's sophisticated mother in Houston, she was warned not to use that word. The first part of the visit went extremely well because Elena was on guard. As she felt more comfortable in the conversation, her Cuban Spanish kicked in and she said to the lady the equivalent of "I am so glad you are here. Your daughter dreamed last night that you were *cogiendole* [holding] her hand." Marta cringed at the unintended vulgarity while her mother roared with laughter.

Cuban Spanish is also known for its very colorful colloquialisms. *Dicharachos* (sayings) are ever present in Cuban speech and provide the spice and earthiness for which Cuban Spanish is known. Examples of these idiomatic expressions abound. For instance, when someone is going through hard times, they are referred to as "Está pasando el Niágara en bicicleta," which literally means crossing the Niagara on a bicycle. Similarly, slang regarding baseball, a favorite Cuban sport, is also filled with earthy descriptions. "El bateador se ponchó" (the batter struck out) is literally translated as "the batter had a flat tire." One day, the Vidals were at the Havana baseball stadium sitting next to two men who were having an argument. One turned to Sara and said, "Señora, si se acaba la mierda en la Habana, este hombre se muere de hambre." (If Havana runs out of shit, this man will starve.) Sara, a very prim and proper lady, had no other recourse but to smile.

Language was not the only defining characteristic of *Lo Cubano* of the pre-Castro days. In the sixteenth century, the Diocese of Cuba was established by Pope Leo X who mandated the building of a church in Santiago de Cuba. Catholicism, the largest organized religion in Cuba, became a powerful influence in culture and politics throughout most of its history. During early colonial times, the mission of the church was evangelical, to convert the natives to Catholicism. Charles V, king of Spain, in charge of the church in the New World, condemned the *encomiendas*, a slavery system that positioned the conquistadores as guardians of the natives. Friar Bartolomé de las Casas, who portrayed the Indians as "docile" and "peaceful" tribes, added his voice against the cruelty and greed of some of the colonists who considered the Indians as soulless.

The growth of the church in Cuba was a slow but steady process.

Iglesia del Santo Ángel, Havana

By the sixteenth century, the Catholic Church, for the first time since the island was "discovered" and in the process of colonization, became a well-organized and powerful entity in Cuba. Sunday masses were the center of civil life where citizens would socialize and learn the rules that would control their lives. Strong actions were taken by the church to maintain its

ANDREA BERMÚDEZ

power, including an edict that would forbid businesses to be open before mass and on holidays. Various religious orders arrived toward the end of the sixteenth century, including Franciscans and Dominicans. Clarisan nuns started to arrive in 1644 establishing a convent that produced the first Cuban nun, Sister Ana de Todos los Santos.

Until the arrival of Fidel Castro, the church controlled most aspects of Cuban life. As a result, Cuban culture and social mores developed in concert with Catholic dogma, which defined duties and responsibilities of men and women, marriage, family, life, and death. It brought about a strict value system to determine acceptable behavior, gender hierarchy, and engendered guilt if its dogma was not followed. After the firmly secular Castro government came into power in 1959, the influence of the Catholic Church diminished. At first the Catholic clergy was supportive of Castro, but as his Marxist-Leninist philosophy became publicly acknowledged, Castro began restricting religious practices. Drastic measures against the church were taken, closing Catholic schools, nationalizing church property, detaining and expelling the hierarchy, including numerous priests and nuns. The church went silent. After the fall of communism in Eastern Europe, the church's influence on the island was resurrected making some inroads into the lives of the Cubans who live there. Approximately four-hundred priests and nuns are openly practicing today. The number of faithful has diminished as many have embraced the agnostic beliefs of the communist government.

Catholicism was not the only religion that was practiced by Cubans. There were few Protestant congregations as well as a small, but successful, number of Cuban Jews who had lived on the island for centuries. It is unclear when Jews first arrived in Cuba after being expelled from Spain in 1492. The Catholic sovereigns, Ferdinand and Isabella, had forced them to convert (*conversos*) to Catholicism, be punished by the Inquisition, or be expelled from Spain. To escape this fate, many immigrated to various parts of the world, including the Caribbean. Before Castro, it was estimated that close to 15,000 lived in Havana alone. With the nationalization of businesses after 1959, a majority fled. Cuban Jews, who playfully call themselves Jewban, had played an important part in developing the Cuban economy by participating productively in the sugar, tobacco, and garment industries.

Both Vidals had roots in the Iberian Peninsula, as their ancestors had emigrated from Spain in search of a new life. Although raised Catholic, neither one could deny the possibility of a Sephardic lineage. Their surnames indicated a probable connection. Elena's instinct further strengthened after discovering that contemporary DNA researchers had suggested that as much as a fifth of the Spaniards are descendants of the Sephardic Jews. Elena had long admired her Jewish friends Leah and Deborah, so having a possible connection to those cultures excited her. Her friends showed the determination Jewish immigrants have historically exhibited in adapting to alien circumstances. Little did Elena know that a similar history would be hers one day.

West African slaves in Cuba, mostly the Yoruba people, combined their religious beliefs with Catholicism, giving rise to Santería (worship of the Saints). The blending of the two religions was an attempt to disguise their beliefs in order to preserve them. Many Black Cubans, and a number of whites, believe that the deities (*orishas*) participate directly in human life to console and assist their faithful. The priests (fathers of *orisha* or *santeros*) and priestesses (mothers of orisha or *santeras*) serve frequently as diviners. Together, they reflect a male dominated hierarchy as the *santeras* have a secondary religious role assigned.

Santería rituals include the worship of selected Catholic saints that represent the various *orishas*, sacred *batá* drumming and limited animal sacrifice. Personal interactions with the deities are mostly in the form of offerings of food and money used to "pacify" or "persuade" them to act in a favorable way.

Batá drums

ANDREA BERMÚDEZ

The double-headed *batá* drums were also introduced in Cuba by the Yoruba slaves and are commonly utilized during religious ceremonies known as *bembé*. The leather used in making the drums comes from male goats or deer as the female hides are not considered acceptable. The various rhythms have special religious significance since they call upon the deities to participate in the rituals. Animal sacrifices, usually chickens, are performed only on rare occasions.

The '60s and earlier generations of exiled Cubans in the United States maintained, to a certain extent, the behavioral constraints posed by the church, including attitudes toward divorce, abortion, gender identity, and the role of the woman in a society ruled by men. Elena's older brothers were victims of *religión mal entendida* (misunderstood religion) and mistook cultural survival for sin. They never understood the need to change and adapt and spent their lifetimes living a life parallel to the mainstream. Fear of becoming anglicized kept the brothers marginalized. The threat of being consumed by a Protestant culture, or its puritan ethics, consumed them both. They would not accept Elena or her circumstances and were relentlessly critical of her decisions. Elena was forced to struggle to accept herself and to ignore their disapproval. There was little she could do to change their minds; after all, she was only a woman! Ultimately, Elena would find the delete button her best friend as she was able to make Bernie's ultraconservative e-mails disappear. It was fortunate that his children belonged to a generation that was not so indoctrinated. They had acculturated to an environment more influenced by religious freedom and had grown more accepting of differences in beliefs and opinions. It was inevitable that the generational divide disrupted the traditional passing of value systems to those born and raised in the United States.

Another important defining element of the Cuban character is music. Elena firmly believed that music was a medicine for the soul. She could not conceive of a world without song. Musical influences mirror the history of Cuba. Chronicles of Cuban music, as extensive as the history of the island itself, show that from its earliest beginnings, natives celebrated life with singing and dancing. Known as *areítos*, extravagant celebrations with hundreds of guests were considered by the aborigines to be central to their social life. Their song and dance, accompanied by *maracas* (pebble-filled wooden instruments), have been reported by early chroniclers. Since their culture was transmitted by oral history, little else is known about other musical contributions.

Later with influences from Spain and West Africa, Cuban music developed a distinctive sound. From the Spanish, Cuban *guajiro* (country) music adopted instruments such as the guitar and the tiple introduced by Spaniards from the Canary Islands. During colonization, many Spanish rhythms became popular, such as the *flamenco*, using castanets as a percussion instrument. Religious and military music were also Spanish exports. Once West Africans entered the scene, blended genres evolved. The *danzón*, derived from Spanish ballroom dances, and the *son*, a combination of Spanish guitar with African percussion, are two of the many examples of this amalgamation. Generally, the melodic elements have roots in Spain while the rhythms exhibit the African influence.

Popular music is mostly defined by Afro-Cuban contributions, and it has also had a great influence in defining *Lo Cubano*. Enjoyed around the world, Cuban rhythms are contagious and upbeat. They compel those who can't dance to want to dance while their lyrics expose the humor characteristic of the Cuban spirit. Both elements have propelled Afro-Cuban music to the level of an international trend. On a visit to the United States in the early 1950s to see her brother Alex, a junior college student in Virginia, Elena had stunned her mother with her dancing abilities. Mrs. Vidal had brought Alex a 45 rpm recording of Perez Prado's "Mambo Number 5," an Afro-Cuban rhythm that had become a craze in Cuba. As they were readying the record player, she told Alex that she wished he could see the mambo performed. To this Elena replied, "I can do that," and proceeded to show them her rhythmic moves. Sara Vidal's mouth dropped. She could remember how her daughter had loathed her ballet classes. "Elena wasn't even that good," she thought. Her legs had been bruised with reminders from her Russian teacher that the conventional positions or graceful movements were not quite right or missing. So where did she learn to dance so well at twelve years old? Elena was forced to confess that she had learned to dance with the kitchen help with whom she spent time visiting. Sebastián, the cook, was a musician on the side and used to sing and dance while he cooked. The lessons would be treasured by Elena who could not imagine living without dance, even at that early age. As a side comment, the word *mambo* is derived from a West African dialect and could be loosely translated as "conversation with the Gods."

Album cover of Pérez Prado's mambos (circa 1950)

Cubans have always cherished their music. Dr. Vidal frequently said that he was the only one born without rhythm. Fortunately, his kids did inherit the Cuban dancing gene. Before 1959, in various parts of the country, the famous *comparsa* (collective street dances) thought to have been introduced by African slaves in the 1500s took place in Spring before the annual carnival. Groups of Afro-Cuban musicians and dancers, each representing a theme, took to the streets. Dressed in flamboyant costumes with matching vibrant colors, the *comparsa* reflected the best of Afro-Cuban choreography. The *farolas* (long decorated poles) were twirled to the rhythm of percussion instruments and a variety of horns, including the popular Chinese trumpet. The public, lining the sidewalks, joined in the merriment by dancing and singing to the contagious rhythms. Several times throughout its history, governments prohibited the *comparsa*, but the tradition was usually reinstated during political campaigns. For two decades after the Castro takeover, the *comparsas* went silent. Attempts to revive the splendor of the past have failed.

It is impossible to grasp the essence of *Lo Cubano* without accepting its diversity in spirit and appearance. A simple definition would dissolve individual differences, creating a meaningless characterization. To truly understand the significance of *Lo Cubano*, we must look at the term from the multifaceted vantage point of race and its corollaries of language, religion, and music. When the point of intersection among these three forces is found, one has reached the core of *Lo Cubano*.

ANDREA BERMÚDEZ

CHAPTER 10

A Tour of Elena's Cuba

Beauty in song and in soul,
This is my Cuba

—*Andrea Bermúdez*

CUBA'S NATURAL BEAUTY, combined with the advanced infrastructure that existed during the pre-Castro era, had attracted thousands of tourists annually from all over the world. Its sugar and tobacco had no equal and became the core of its principally agrarian economy. Heavily dependent on the whims of Mother Nature, the Cuban financial system had been unpredictable throughout its history. Some coffee but mostly sugar trade brought about Cuba's prosperity in the nineteenth century. The arrival of the railroad at that time gave those industries a major boost. By the next century, tourism had become another major source of income.

The *Carretera Central* (Central Highway), connecting the island east to west, was built in the late 1920s during the Machado presidency. The two-lane road gave Cuba an economic advantage as it provided for more effective transportation of sugar and tobacco from one end of the island to the other. Driving the narrow *Carretera* was a dangerous undertaking, particularly its infamous *Curva de Cantarrana* (Singing Frog Curve), which was the site of numerous fatal accidents. The *Carretera* was celebrated not only for its commuting value, but also for its picturesque beauty, which attracted many tourists from around the world.

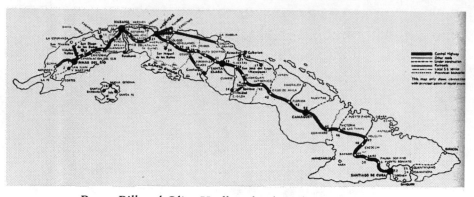

Route Bill and Olive Kroll took when they crisscrossed
the island with their travel trailer in 1956

By royal decree in 1878, Cuba had been divided into six provinces from west to east: Pinar del Río, La Habana, Matanzas, Las Villas, Camagüey, and Oriente. During the 1970s, Castro overrode the existing designation and further subdivided the island into fourteen provinces. Elena's tour of Cuba takes her through the original six, starting in the westernmost province, Pinar del Río, and ending in Oriente to the east.

Pinar del Río: Land of Pine Groves and Tobacco

Best known for its scenic beauty and variety, Pinar del Río is home to one of the three major mountain ranges found in Cuba, the Cordillera de Guaniguanico, oriented southwest to northeast. This mountainous area includes the Sierra de los Órganos to the west and the Sierra del Rosario to the east. The highest point to the north of the Sierra del Rosario is the Pan de Guajaibón, which stands over two thousand feet above sea level.

Elena had never been to Pinar del Río, so when her college friend Margarita invited her to spend a long weekend in November 1959, she accepted with pleasure. They took the Carretera Central and drove the 177 kilometers that separate Havana from Pinar del Río, winding through picturesque small towns and vast countryside lined by bohíos and palm trees. En route to her friend's home in the provincial capital of Pinar del Río, Elena and Margarita passed the Sierra del Rosario with its lush steep hills and stopped at the Soroa Botanical Gardens where over seven hundred types of orchids were grown. During the rainy season, a forty-nine-foot-high waterfall could be seen from *el mirador* (the lookout), a few minutes' walk from the gardens.

Soroa Waterfall

After feasting their eyes, Elena and Margarita stopped at the Castillo de las Nubes (Castle of the Clouds) to enjoy a late lunch. The castillo, located in the highest point in Soroa, was built in the 1800s as a home for a wealthy Spanish family. After the Castro revolution, the Castillo was appropriated and became a tourist attraction. After lunch and some bird watching, the girls continued their journey passing through the town of San Cristóbal with its quaint red tile roofs and colorful houses. Had they taken a detour northwest, they would have seen the natural springs of San Diego de los Baños in the foothills of Sierra de los Órganos. The small village is surrounded by forests and small lakes and is home to a great variety of birds and the indigenous Cuban deer. Before getting to their destination, they passed a typical colonial town, Consolación del Sur, anchored by a Catholic church and a small plaza.

Margarita and her family lived in a large home in the city not too far from several places of historical interest. With its narrow streets and neoclassic architecture, Pinar del Río had a very different flavor from other places Elena had seen around the island. The next morning, they visited a cigar factory and became fascinated with the rolling station. They watched the reader keep the rollers entertained by delivering news and reading short stories while over twelve thousand cigars were being rolled every day. The factory housed several rooms where various brands of cigars were selected, boxed, and labeled. Pinar del Río produced some of the best cigars in the world. Elena and Margarita hoped to have time on another day to continue westward on the Carretera to San Juan y Martínez in the area of Vuelta Abajo, where the finest tobacco on the island was grown.

Vuelta Abajo tobacco fields

Unfortunately, they had to choose which coast to visit, so they chose to go north. A southern route would have taken them to less populated and more-difficult-to-reach areas. So on Saturday morning, Margarita

ANDREA BERMÚDEZ

and Elena headed for Viñales Valley, located in the Sierra de los Órganos, between the city of Pinar del Río and its northern coast.

Viñales Valley with mogotes in the background

The valley gave Elena the impression of a lush garden submerged between the tall sierras to the east and west. The most unique aspect of its topography was the *mogotes*, limestone hills that can reach up to eighty feet tall and six-hundred feet wide, although these were not the most common. They would look like gigantic sponges if they were not covered in the tropical vegetation that gave them a domelike shape. Underground rivers and limestone caves were found in the area of the *mogotes*, and among them fertile valleys were used for planting excellent tobacco. Extensive pine groves, *pinares*, which gave name to the province, bordered the mountain range in the terraced hills of *Alturas de Pizarras del Sur*. Elena found the countryside north of Viñales the most stunning. If followed to the north, the road would have taken them to various caves, including Cueva del Indio (Cave of the Indian), used by the aborigines as shelter and cemetery.

The friends ran out of time and returned without reaching the northern coast with its mangrove-lined rocky beaches. In a next visit to Pinar del Río, Margarita promised to take Elena further west to either *Cayo Levisa* (Levisa Key), a small coral island with the best white beaches in the province or to its westernmost beach María La Gorda.

Sunset at María La Gorda Beach

Both were described by Margarita as snorkeling paradises that showcased the beauty of the area's abundant marine life. *Cayo Levisa*, as part of Los Colorados Archipelago, is surrounded by thousands of small cays and inlets that could only be reached by ferry.

This trip would have to wait indefinitely.

La Habana: Seat of Government

Havana is located between the provinces of Pinar del Rio to the west and Matanzas to the east, with coasts to the north and south. East of the provincial capital is the small fishing village of Cojímar, the place that served as backdrop for Hemingway's famous novel *Old Man and the Sea*. The bicoastal province is dotted with beautiful sandy beaches. To the north there is the small, but infamous, port of Mariel, a place well-known historically for the 1980 boatlift during which thousands of Cubans fled the country. Not too far from the port is the sugar district of the province which included Central Mercedita, one of the many sugar mills dismantled by the Castro government.

Central Mercedita circa 1900

To the south of the original site of the city of Havana is the Surgidero de Batabanó, departure point for the Isle of Pines, the largest island near Cuba. Located one-hundred kilometers off the southern coast, Isle of Pines had been part of the municipality of Havana for two centuries. In 1978, Castro renamed it Isle of Youth and declared it a "special municipality," independent of any province and directly under the jurisdiction of his government. While Elena was growing up, part of the island served as a prison. Elena never got to visit Isle of Pines, so she never had the opportunity to enjoy its striking black sand beaches, a result of volcanic activity in the area.

As an industrialized province, agriculture did not play as important a part in La Habana's economy as it had done in the rest of the country. The balanced combination of natural beaches and burgeoning city life made this province a special destination of the tourist industry. Being so close to the United States, it was not unusual to have weekend visitors to attractions such as Tropicana nightclub, a spectacular "paradise under the stars" as it was commonly dubbed.

Born and raised in the Cuban capital of La Habana, Elena knew her way around the city pretty well, and memories of its historical traditions and beauty became a part of Elena's being. One of her most vivid recollections included long strolls along the Paseo del Malecón (Seawall Boulevard), which connected Old Havana with its newer sections.

View of the Malecón (Seawall Boulevard) with the
Morro Castle at a distance

Elena and her friends would stop to enjoy a glass of *guarapo* (pure sugar juice) while listening to concerts and watching the occasional parades. Magnificent sunsets accentuated by the soft salty breeze became symbols of her lost youth. This was a time in her life when, despite its reality, everything seemed so uncomplicated.

ANDREA BERMÚDEZ

Among the sights Elena remembered during these strolls down the Malecón was the Castillo del Morro (Morro Castle), the picturesque sixteenth-century structure at the entrance of the bay, which could be observed for miles. A smaller fortress also built around the same time, the Castillo de la Punta, stands on the western side of the harbor and was meant to provide the possibility of crossfire in case Havana were attacked by pirates.

La Punta Fortress

Continuing west of La Punta is the area of La Habana Vieja (Old Havana) where the Cathedral and the oldest square in the city, the Plaza de Armas, were situated.

Cathedral of Havana

Old Havana was the site for many world-renowned restaurants. One of Elena's favorites, historic El Templete, was built on the original site where the city was founded in 1519.

El Templete Restaurant

ANDREA BERMÚDEZ

There were also a number of churches in the area including San Francisco de Asis, *Espíritu Santo* Parish, *Santo Cristo del Buen Viaje* (Holy Christ of the Safe Journey), and *Nuestra Señora de la Merced* (Our Lady of Mercy). The latter, dating back to the seventeenth century, took over a hundred years to be built, and stands out as an extravagant architectural creation. Continuing south three notable landmarks could be found: José Martí's modest place of birth, the illustrious Payret theatre and the Central Railway Station with its Moorish inspired design.

South of the Malecón and as an extension of Old Havana, in the Centro, two distinctive government buildings worth noting were the Capitolio (State Capitol), the seat of legislature until 1959, and the neoclassic Palacio Presidencial (Presidential Palace)

National Capitol, no longer the seat of Congress

Presidential Palace, now Museum of the Revolution

After Castro, the Ministry of Science, Technology, and the Environment moved into the Capitol building while the Presidential Palace, which had been occupied by all presidents from 1920 to 1959, became the Museum of the Revolution. Directly beneath the dome of the Capitolio, there was a diamond replica marking kilometer zero. The real diamond had disappeared, and rumor had it that it had later reappeared among the first lady's valuables during the second Grau administration. As an aside, it may not have been coincidence that she also won the lottery. True or not, popular mythology becomes history when shared by the people who lived it.

Away from Old Havana and rising over the Malecón, Elena remembered the Maine Monument erected to commemorate the sinking of the SS *Maine* and the start of the Spanish-American War of 1898. The American eagle on top of the monument was removed in the early days of the Castro revolution, and now the tall columns lie bare and forgotten, except for a plaque that blames the *Imperialistas Yanquis*, Castro's favorite moniker for the United States, for the *Maine* tragedy.

Elena had attended the University of Havana, one of the first institutions of higher education founded in Latin America. Starting as a Catholic institution in 1728, it became secular a hundred years later. The building sat majestically on a hill overlooking the Vedado district. A large number of

ANDREA BERMÚDEZ

steps, which led to a bronze statue of the alma mater, marked its imposing entrance. Because of its autonomous status, the university became a focal point of student revolutionary activities. Elena well remembered being caught in a shoot-out between opposing factions during which her life and those of other innocent bystanders were placed in danger. Batista chose to close the university in 1956 to stave off the threat of insurrection. It reopened in 1959.

University of Havana

There were so many other sites in the Havana of Elena's memories that would never be forgotten, but there were also experiences that made her smile whenever she thought about them. A favorite one was the spring carnival whose route followed the seawall. Decorated floats, trucks, or convertibles, colorful costumes, music, and dance added to the gaiety of the event. Elena and her friends would enjoy selecting themes to decorate a borrowed truck, including their last parade in 1958 before their high school graduation, when they all dressed up as carousing pirates. Several decades earlier Sara had also celebrated this tradition, and in keeping with the times, with a less rambunctious all-girls crowd in an elegantly festooned vehicle.

Sara González, top right, and her friends at a carnival circa 1919

How could Elena forget the *piruleros* (hard candy vendors) and their sugary concoctions or *guarapo* sold along the Malecón? She hung on to memories of seemingly insignificant experiences that served to validate her recollections. When there is continuity in people's lives, memories become reinforced by friends or by the environment in which they live. For the exile population, the continuity they expected to have at home in Cuba was abruptly disrupted. Consequently, for them, memories become the validation that those experiences and the people who participated in them actually existed.

Matanzas: The Athens of Cuba

Having been the birthplace of famous Cuban poets, Matanzas was known as the Athens of Cuba. Both Vidals, as well as their Cuban ancestors, were from the province of Matanzas, so Elena felt great affinity with its environs. Considered coastal plain because of its largely flat topography, sugar and tobacco crops became the core of its economy until the sugar industry moved east to Oriente. Even now, numerous sugar mills are located in the province.

The northern coast is partly rocky and lined with mangroves. However, situated along the Hicacos Peninsula, to the northeast is one of the finest beaches in the world, Varadero, known for its crystalline turquoise waters

ANDREA BERMÚDEZ

and powder-fine sand. The stunning Varadero that Elena remembers lost some of its natural beauty when part of the open spaces was replaced by a resort atmosphere catering to international tourists. The International Hotel in Varadero, built in 1950 and now a four-star resort, was one of the few luxury hotels that existed when Elena and Roberto spent their three-day honeymoon prior to leaving Cuba. The mansions she recalled, including one belonging to the DuPont family, were confiscated by the government after 1959 and turned into restaurants or hostels to serve the tourist population.

Varadero Beach

From Varadero, Elena had been able to visit the Bellamar Caves several times, as they were only forty kilometers southwest of the resort. The extensive underground cave system took her breath away on every visit. A world of its own, the gigantic stalactites and stalagmites created an eerie environment made more dramatic by the tranquil sound of underground rivers and streams. Formations, such as the Fountain of Youth or Coco Rallado (Grated Coconut), were striking natural displays that seemed different to her every time. The experience always left her with a desire to return. She said to herself many times, "The caves have been there for thousands of years. They will still be there when I return."

Bellamar Caves

Two kilometers north of the caves is the provincial capital, also named Matanzas, where Elena's Grandmother Ana was born and raised. Folklore had it that the name *Matanzas*, literally translated as "slaughter," referred to the mass killing of Spanish soldiers attempting to attack natives in the area. To cross the river, the soldiers asked local fishermen to assist by providing them with boats. Once in midriver, the fishermen turned over the boats, drowning the soldiers.

ANDREA BERMÚDEZ

Among several industrial centers in Cuba, the city of Matanzas grew to be one of the most important. Situated on the northern coast of the province, it is bordered on three sides by the picturesque Bay of Matanzas. The Parque de la Libertad, with its imposing century-old bronze monument to José Martí, was the focal point of the city. Over half a century ago, the square was the site that marked the entrance of Castro and his forces to Matanzas. The park area was surrounded by history: the Palace of the Governors; the nineteenth-century Hotel Louvre; the Biblioteca Gener y Del Monte, one of the oldest libraries in Cuba; and the Pharmaceutical Museum with its vast array of turn-of-the-century porcelain medicine flasks, books, and other pharmaceutical supplies.

Pharnaceutical Museum

Nearby, the neoclassic San Carlos de Borromeo Cathedral offered its first mass in 1693.

Encircled by hills, also in the northern part of the province, the Yumurí Valley is one of the most scenic on the island. Royal palms thrive in the area giving character to the valley, a rich habitat for numerous bird species. Traversed by two rivers, its fertile soil supports a variety of crops, especially sugarcane.

Yumurí Valley

Surrounding the valley, Monserrat Hill is home to the Ermita de Montserrat (Hermitage of Montserrat), established in 1875. During Catholic holidays, the church would organize community events attended by families from neighboring towns. Elena could see in her mind's eye her Matanzas-born grandparents enjoying these festivities as children. She wished she knew what they had been like then, but she had no one to ask anymore.

Cárdenas, east of the city of Matanzas, was Sara Vidal's birthplace and childhood home. Her father Máximo held business interests in *Central Dos Rosas,* sold later to an American chocolate manufacturing company. Cárdenas, founded in 1828, developed rapidly due to the completion of the railroad a few years later.

Parrochial Church of Cárdenas where Sara was baptized in 1902

The city had the historical distinction of being the place where the Cuban flag was first raised in 1850. Cárdenas was also the site where several battles were fought during the Spanish-American War of 1898.

South of the city of Matanzas, in the center of the province, is Unión de Reyes where Bernardo Vidal and his father, Eloy, were born. In 1844, the town started as a railroad station near an already existing tavern, and by 1879 grew to become a successful center of commerce for the area. For Bernardo life centered on the sugar mill *Conchita* and the railroad; a simple life that shaped his stable personality.

The southern half of the province is largely occupied by wetlands and mangroves and was habitat to dozens of bird species, many endemic.

Wetlands in southern Matanzas

Known as the Ciénaga de Zapata (Zapata Swamp) and located north of the Bay of Pigs, the region had the largest marshland in the Caribbean. The area also had historical significance, made notorious by the failed Bay of Pigs invasion of 1961. One of two beaches found in this area, Playa Girón, was the site of the disastrous landing. Notwithstanding its sad history, Girón's translucent waters —which allowed swimmers to enjoy its underwater corals, flooded caves, and sponges— made this beach a favorite of the southern coast.

East of the Zapata Peninsula in central Matanzas is Jagüey Grande, known for its massive citrus harvests, one of the largest operations in the world. Central Australia, a now defunct sugar mill in the area, was the site from which Castro led the counterattack against the Bay of Pigs insurgents.

Las Villas: Home of Colonial Trinidad

Located in Central Cuba, Las Villas exhibits a variety of landscapes. To the north, rural life is embodied by a number of small fishing villages, cays, sandy beaches, and coral reefs, while central Las Villas boasts sugar plantations and colonial towns.

ANDREA BERMÚDEZ

La Boca Village, Las Villas

The Escambray Mountains with abrupt peaks, deep valleys, and lush vegetation line the province to the south.

Escambray Mountains in the background

In the 1970s, Castro subdivided Las Villas province into three: Villaclara, Cienfuegos, and Sancti Spíritus, which Elena continued to regard as cities.

Santa Clara, in the center of the province served as the capital of Las Villas and remains the capital of the newer province of Villaclara. The city had played an important part in the Castro revolution, having been the site of the last successful battle against Batista, led by Che Guevara. After Che's 1967 death in Bolivia while exporting his socialist brand of revolution, his remains were returned to Cuba and interred in a Santa Clara mausoleum. At the center of the city and occupying an entire block was the Parque Vidal, which acted as the city's social hub. An older custom, no longer practiced, was for young women and men to walk around in a circle with women taking the interior path and men the exterior. Many romantic relationships had this type of beginning. Elena's mother recalled a similar custom as typical of her generation in her native Cárdenas.

Moving north from Santa Clara, Santo Domingo offered an opportunity to appreciate the flora and fauna of the area. Distant relatives of Elena lived in the village, so to Elena, Santo Domingo was also the place where the city girl first experienced life in the wilderness. Her visit to her relatives' outhouse would make for an amusing scene in a reality show. It was a "she came, she saw, she panicked" experience, which forced her to understand that basic needs do not wait for fancy bathrooms!

A noteworthy landmark for Elena was Tata's birthplace, the city of Sagua la Grande, on the north coast of the province. Sagua had planted its historical roots in one of the wars for independence. Elena loved to hear Tata's stories about her birthplace including how the city and its port, Isabela de Sagua, had been important trade centers during her childhood. She used to talk about being sent fishing in the Sagua la Grande River, the largest river in Cuba to drain into the Atlantic Ocean, and coming home empty-handed. Tata had a soft spot for defenseless creatures, so her mama never asked her again, suspecting that her daughter had done her best not to catch any fish. Elena never had the opportunity to visit Sagua, but she promised herself that it would be one of the first places she would like to visit when and if she ever returns to Cuba.

In the southern part of the region, the Escambray Mountains, Elena was fortunate to see the Salto del Hanabanilla (Hanabanilla River Waterfall) before it was destroyed by the Castro government to build a hydroelectric plant that is no longer in use. Elena vividly remembers the multiple cascades, the highest on the island, surrounded by a number of coffee plantations, lush natural vegetation, and abundant fauna. When

ANDREA BERMÚDEZ

Elena found out that the *salto* was now a lake, she felt a deep sense of loss for the irreversible damage to the island's ecosystem. Her incredulity made her wonder if there would be anything left the way she remembered. "Very unlikely," she sadly admitted.

Also near the Escambray, colonial Trinidad is a city small in size but grand in appeal with its five-hundred-year history. Its colorful architecture, red terracotta roofs, and cobblestone streets are a magnet for tourists visiting Cuba. The Plaza Mayor, in the center of town, is surrounded by several eighteenth- and nineteenth-century structures.

Trinidad Plaza

Some historians refer to Trinidad as the "museum city of Cuba" because of its genuinely colonial flavor. Besides tourism, tobacco formed the basis of its economy. North of Trinidad, the city of Sancti Spíritus lies along the banks of the Yayabo River. The city, now elevated to province, was founded in the sixteenth century. It had held an important place in the Spanish colonization of the Americas as it was from there that the Spanish departed to conquer Yucatan, Mexico.

In the southern part of the province on the shores of Bahía de Jagua, Cienfuegos has been nicknamed Perla del Sur (Pearl of the South) for the striking beauty of its bay.

Cienfuegos Bay

In the eighteenth century, the Spanish built the Castillo de Jagua, a military fortress at the entrance of the bay for protection from the attacks of pirates. At the center of the city, one could find the José Martí Park enhanced by a large sculpture of the Cuban hero. Dominating the large plaza is the commanding Arch of Triumph, which reminds visitors of May 20, 1902, when Cuba finally became a free republic. Via Cienfuegos Boulevard, the park connects to the Paseo del Prado, the city's main artery, and from there to the picturesque Malecón.

With so much natural beauty, the province of Las Villas has become a destination for the tourist industry. The economic shifts from cattle to sugar in the eighteenth century, and presently, from sugar to tourism, have come at an opportune time in the province's economic development. Sugar production lost its prominence after the Soviet Union, a major sugar market, collapsed.

Camagüey: Where the Cattle Roam

Largely flatland, the province of Camagüey is well-suited for the cattle industry. It is bordered by coral reefs on both coasts, to the north by Jardines del Rey and to the south by Jardines de la Reina. Both archipelagos boast hundreds of islands, sandy beaches, and cays with plentiful flora and fauna and are considered paradises of biodiversity.

Cayo Guillermo in Jardines del Rey Archipelago

Cayo Sabinal Lighthouse

Elena affectionately referred to Camagüey as the Texas of Cuba. It is the largest province and is commonly associated with a *vaquero* (cowboy) culture for its cattle-dependent economy and rodeo festivities.

Cultural sophistication and tradition were also two well-known traits of this quaint province. Elena's friend Pilar, one of the cinco Marías, was born in Camagüey where her father was a well-known political figure and her mother considered "old aristocracy" because of her kinship to a war-of-independence hero. Elena remembered many stories about Camagüey's historical traditions from her conversations with Pilar. One that made an impression was the story of Ana Betancourt, one of the first Cuban feminists who, in the 1860s, fought for Cuban independence and women's rights. Ana was captured during the Ten Years' War and sent to exile in Spain where she died in 1901. Elena and Pilar had had long and serious conversations about their mothers not having a place at the table in political decisions made at the time of their youth. Neither one could conceive such inequality and developed an appreciation for those women who fought their battle and made it easier for the younger ones' voices to be heard.

Cayo Coco (Coconut Key) is the second largest island of the Archipelago of Camagüey. Situated off the north coast, Cayo Coco has about seventeen kilometers of white sand beaches and crystal blue waters. Santa Lucía Beach, with its remarkable coral gardens and extensive marine life, is a fine example. A frequent visitor to the area was Ernest Hemingway in his favorite boat Pilar.

Cayo Coco is connected to Cayo Guillermo
by a natural causeway

ANDREA BERMÚDEZ

Santa Lucía Beach

Also on the northern coast, Nuevitas, on the bay of its same name, was the trade center for rural Camagüey. With its proximity to Playa Santa Lucía and Cayo Sabinal, tourism has contributed a great deal to its elevated status. It is believed that Christopher Columbus visited the Port of Nuevitas during his first voyage.

The provincial capital, also named Camagüey, was originally located on the northern coast. The city was moved to the central part of the province during the sixteenth century to avoid the constant threat of piracy. One can hardly picture the city of Camagüey without the typical *tinajón* (large clay pots) whose original intent was to collect rainwater for a city with very seasonal rains and a lack of adequate water supply. In modern days, the *tinajón* has remained a symbol of Camagüey, and the subject of local lore.

Mansion with typical "tinajones"

At the center of the city is the eighteenth-century mansion and birthplace of Ignacio Agramonte, general of Camagüey's armed forces during the Ten Years' War of independence against Spain. Streets, alleys, and park plazas were intentionally built in a labyrinthine design to confuse potential invaders during colonial times.

Another city of interest to Elena was Ciego de Ávila, in the southwest section of the province. Founded in 1840 when the first few hundred settlers arrived, it grew into a vibrant city with a diversified economy based on cattle, agriculture and industry by the early 1900s. Farther east from Ciego de Ávila, on the Caribbean Coast, the city of Santa Cruz del Sur was hit in 1932 by a category four hurricane that killed over three thousand people in Cuba, and devastated the city. This late-season hurricane was one of the deadliest hurricanes to hit the country. Pilar's grandparents lost their home, and almost their lives, forcing the family to move inland.

Bordering the Oriente province, the city of Guaimaro is a place of historical significance. Liberated during the first war of independence, it is

ANDREA BERMÚDEZ

Santiago de Cuba Cathedral

the center of the city is the colonial Céspedes Park with its
statue honoring Carlos Manuel de Céspedes, responsible for
Ten Years' War. An elaborate and colossal cathedral, built in
wers above the park. One of the best known streets is *Padre*
limbs to the top of the city and provides a panoramic view
Another *Morro* fortress was built in the 1630s at the entrance
guard Santiago against enemy attacks. From its overlook, a
see the city and the imposing Sierra Maestra with its largest
is *Pico Turquino* over six-thousand feet above sea level. One
tural contribution of this city is the famous carnival. With a
ating back to the seventeenth century, the Santiago Carnival,
a's in extravagance and gaiety. The dance troupes rehearsed
oaration for the highly anticipated festival.
y city of Bayamo, now the provincial capital of Granma,
: largest cities in Oriente and the second founded by Diego
1513. Situated on the Bayamo River, the city had been an
d commercial center of note during colonial times. It had
al part in the Ten Years' War with a strong *criollo* presence,
the birthplace of Carlos Manuel de Céspedes. Colonial
identified with its strong patriotic roots, was also the place

where the Constitutional Assembly of the Republic in Arms met in 1869.
The all-male revolutionaries were against slavery but, ironically, opposed
women's right to vote.

Oriente: Revolutionary Trailblazer

The easternmost province of Oriente became five when Castro
reworked Cuba's geography in 1976 (Tuna, Granma, Holguín, Santiago de
Cuba, and Guantánamo). The province is bordered by Camagüey to the
west, the Atlantic Ocean to the north, the Paso de los Vientos to the east,
and the Caribbean Sea to the south. On the north coast visitors could find
beautiful beaches, while the swampy southern part of the province was best
for cultivating sugarcane.

Guardalavaca Beach in the north coast

The province also has a long historical legacy. It is believed that
Christopher Columbus landed on the north coast of Oriente in 1492.

Monument to Christopher Columbus, Guardalavaca

His passionate remarks about the island's natural splendor have been extensively chronicled. Oriente was also the site where the independence movements against Spain originated, and where the Communist revolution was nurtured and fought.

Guantánamo, in southeast Oriente, includes the Punta de Maisi, the southernmost point on the island.

Humboldt Park, (

Since 1903, the United States has h
the Guantánamo Naval Base is locate
shows a marked influence of the Fren
Haiti, were given lands in the area to b
    Until 1589, Santiago de Cuba had b
its role at that time to become the pro
the years, Santiago has played a ma
important battlefield during the wars o
revolution saw its start in Santiago d
forces unsuccessfully attacked the Mo
in Santiago where six years later Castro
and took command of the island.

Marking
large bronze
initiating the
the 1500s, t
Pico, which
of Santiago.
of the bay to
visitor could
peak known
important cu
long history
rivaled Hava
all year in pro
    The win
was one of th
Velázquez in
agricultural a
played a cent
having been
Bayamo, a cit

Humboldt Park, Guantánamo

Since 1903, the United States has had jurisdiction over the area where the Guantánamo Naval Base is located. The city's distinct architecture shows a marked influence of the French who, after being forced out of Haiti, were given lands in the area to become cacao and coffee planters.

Until 1589, Santiago de Cuba had been the island capital, relinquishing its role at that time to become the provincial capital of Oriente. Through the years, Santiago has played a major historical role having been an important battlefield during the wars of independence. In 1953, the Castro revolution saw its start in Santiago de Cuba when Castro and his rebel forces unsuccessfully attacked the Moncada military barracks. It was also in Santiago where six years later Castro claimed victory over Batista forces and took command of the island.

Santiago de Cuba Cathedral

Marking the center of the city is the colonial Céspedes Park with its large bronze statue honoring Carlos Manuel de Céspedes, responsible for initiating the Ten Years' War. An elaborate and colossal cathedral, built in the 1500s, towers above the park. One of the best known streets is *Padre Pico*, which climbs to the top of the city and provides a panoramic view of Santiago. Another *Morro* fortress was built in the1630s at the entrance of the bay to guard Santiago against enemy attacks. From its overlook, a visitor could see the city and the imposing Sierra Maestra with its largest peak known as *Pico Turquino* over six-thousand feet above sea level. One important cultural contribution of this city is the famous carnival. With a long history dating back to the seventeenth century, the Santiago Carnival, rivaled Havana's in extravagance and gaiety. The dance troupes rehearsed all year in preparation for the highly anticipated festival.

The windy city of Bayamo, now the provincial capital of Granma, was one of the largest cities in Oriente and the second founded by Diego Velázquez in 1513. Situated on the Bayamo River, the city had been an agricultural and commercial center of note during colonial times. It had played a central part in the Ten Years' War with a strong *criollo* presence, having been the birthplace of Carlos Manuel de Céspedes. Colonial Bayamo, a city identified with its strong patriotic roots, was also the place

ANDREA BERMÚDEZ

Monument to Christopher Columbus, Guardalavaca

His passionate remarks about the island's natural splendor have been extensively chronicled. Oriente was also the site where the independence movements against Spain originated, and where the Communist revolution was nurtured and fought.

Guantánamo, in southeast Oriente, includes the Punta de Maisi, the southernmost point on the island.

ANDREA BERMÚDEZ

where the Constitutional Assembly of the Republic in Arms met in 1869. The all-male revolutionaries were against slavery but, ironically, opposed women's right to vote.

Oriente: Revolutionary Trailblazer

The easternmost province of Oriente became five when Castro reworked Cuba's geography in 1976 (Tuna, Granma, Holguín, Santiago de Cuba, and Guantánamo). The province is bordered by Camagüey to the west, the Atlantic Ocean to the north, the Paso de los Vientos to the east, and the Caribbean Sea to the south. On the north coast visitors could find beautiful beaches, while the swampy southern part of the province was best for cultivating sugarcane.

Guardalavaca Beach in the north coast

The province also has a long historical legacy. It is believed that Christopher Columbus landed on the north coast of Oriente in 1492.

where the Cuban National Anthem was written. Its narrow, winding streets could be visited in horse-drawn carriages, a favorite transport in the city. The historical center included the Cathedral of Bayamo and the city square. Coffee, grown in its mountain region, was the basis of its economy. Southwest of Bayamo, on the Caribbean Sea, is Cape Cruz which is part of the Granma Landing National Park.

Cape Cruz lighthouse

The infamous boat Granma was used by the Castros and Che Guevara in an unsuccessful attempt to overthrow Batista.

In the northwest area of the province, the city of Holguín was home to the Vidals during the early days of their marriage. It was in this city where Bernardo served as a medical lieutenant, later promoted to captain, during the Machado government. The city had several small parks including the *Parque Calixto García*, built in honor of the Holguín-born hero of the Ten Years' War. Coincidentally, Dr. Vidal would later in his career become director of the Calixto García Hospital in Havana.

Tunas, a province after 1976, had been known to Elena as a small town named Las Tunas in the central eastern section of Oriente. The city bordered by the *Carretera Central* had been the site of a victory for Spain in 1869 being renamed Victoria de las Tunas at that time. In 1895, Cubans reclaimed the city and removed *Victoria* from its name in an effort to erase the vestiges of Spanish colonialism. The center of the city is graced by the typical colonial plaza that, along with the baseball stadium, acted as focal points of social life.

Although the similarities among Cuban provinces are strong in language, religion, and culture, there are a few dissimilarities that contribute to the unique character of each province. For instance, there are some differences in vocabulary and intonation patterns despite the fact that Spanish is the official language. The same can be said about food. Although both eastern as well as western Cuban cuisine were distinctively *criolla* (mixture of Spanish and Cuban), a tendency toward its European roots appeared more in cities like Havana where continental cuisine with its elaborate desserts was common. Eastern provinces, being more rural and in closer proximity to Santo Domingo and Puerto Rico, exhibited more Caribbean and African influences with dishes such as *congri* (mixture of white rice and red beans) and *fufú* (mashed plantains with pork, shrimp, or beef).

Ideological and historical differences notwithstanding, Cubans share extraordinary courage and optimism, distinctive characteristics that, hopefully, someday will make them one people again. Cubans at home or in exile have been blessed to experience the island's beauty; to those in exile, a past kept present in their hearts and minds. This is the Cuba Elena will always remember and love. The island was etched in her heart forever, brought to life through memories of its vitality and beauty. Truly a paradise lost.

CHAPTER 11

Flora and Fauna of Cuba

Look deep into nature, and then you will understand everything better.

—*Albert Einstein*

CUBA, WITH ITS beautiful palm-fringed shores, has long been considered a tropical paradise by botanists, tourists, and most importantly, Cubans themselves. Situated strategically at the entrance of the Gulf of Mexico to its west, it is bordered by the Atlantic and the Florida Straits to the north and the Caribbean Sea to the south. Cuba known as the "pearl of the Antilles" is the largest and westernmost island in the West Indies. From Punta de Maisi in the east to Cabo San Antonio in the west, the fertility of her soil and her diverse tropical environment, from flat to hilly to mountainous, produced extraordinary fruits and vegetables, particularly coconut, mangoes, bananas, plantain, sugarcane, oranges, pineapples, and a host of others. With Havana only ninety miles from Key West, the straits can tell the story of the many who have tried to escape Castro's regime. Only these waters know how many did not succeed, a tragedy that has been unfolding for many years.

To Elena, it was impossible to understand the essence of a people without knowing about the natural environment that nurtured them. She was always conscious of the value of the plants and animals that thrived in her world. Elena appreciated trees and palms of all kinds, particularly the royal palms, which to her were a symbol of a free Cuba.

Royal Palms

During her *hachillerato* (secondary) studies, she fell in love with Leví Marrero's *Geografía de Cuba*. The book gave her a knowledge and respect for other forms of life also living on her island. She kept her yellowed class notes that allowed her to relive that experience. For an enrichment course she took while on sabbatical leave, she wrote a paper on "The Flora and Fauna of Cuba," which her professor highly praised. One of her sources was her notes from Dr. Marrero's 1951 edition. Excerpts from Elena's paper follow.

"Agricultural productivity, the basis of Cuban economy, is determined to a great extent by its soil and climate. The long and narrow shape of the island allows sea to land breezes to moderate the climate year round. The average temperatures, 75° F in summer and 70° F in winter, coupled with relatively copious rainfall, increase the potential for agricultural production. With two-thirds of the island being a slightly undulating savanna with rich clay soil, planting is suitable for a variety of crops, particularly sugar and tobacco. When the Spanish colonizers arrived in the 1500s, a great majority of the island was covered by forests, some of which have since been sacrificed for sugarcane cultivation.

Sugarcane

Adding to the savanna and forests, there is a small desert area in the easternmost province of Oriente where cacti and woody shrubs thrive. On the whole, Cuban soil is about 80 percent productive for one crop or another. In its mountainous tropical forest regions, coffee, cocoa, and *henequén* (sisal) are grown.

Paradise found is only interrupted by tropical cyclones that may occur during the May-to-November hurricane season when nature has her way of balancing its affairs. Ecologically, Cuba is a hurricane-adapted system, which includes its people who learned to live with their threat. Tropical cyclones generally form off Cape Verde and move in a westerly direction, but they can also form in the Gulf of Mexico, the Atlantic, or the Caribbean. It seems that Cuba's strategic location makes it a likely target of the hurricanes' path. Several merciless storms have hit the island through the years leaving behind a trail of horror and destruction. In 1963 Hurricane Flora, one of the five deadliest in Atlantic history, slammed into Haiti and eastern Cuba, further stalling over Cuba and leaving over seven thousand people dead in its course.

With thousands of plant species found on the island, Cuba shows a greater variety than the rest of the Antilles, making up about 2 percent of the world's flora. More than half of those are endemic plants, and the rest have been introduced by a variety of possible sources, including currents and the fact that the island is on the flyway of birds depositing seeds as they migrate between North and South America. Considered a natural botanical garden by some biologists and a miniature continent by others, Cuba's flora is most similar to South America's northern coast. Native plants dispersed as well to other parts of the world, including Florida, where one can find flowers and trees native to Cuba. Flowering species alone are estimated at about eight thousand with hundreds of species of colorful orchids and wildflowers. Among the flowering species, the exquisite *mariposa* (butterfly jasmine), Cuba's national flower, reigns supreme.

Mariposa (Butterfly Jasmine), the Cuban national flower

ANDREA BERMÚDEZ

Many of the extensive coastal areas are bordered by magnificent coral reefs as well as various types of *manglares* (mangroves), island builders that create habitat for many species of plants and animals. *Los Jardines de la Reina* (Queens Gardens), off the southern coast of Central Cuba, include many small islands reaching into the Caribbean, showcasing the most beautiful red mangroves and pristine coral reefs. In a sense, mangroves, which occupy approximately one-fourth of the coast, regulate the environment as their seedlings slow down currents and allow sediments and nutrients to settle. Mangroves also promote natural cooling and protect the coast from erosion caused by the sea currents. As the island grows, it attracts various species of animals. In addition to its natural functions, the wood of the mangrove is used in construction, furniture, and in the production of charcoal. Environmental pollution threatens the future of this critical ecosystem.

Red mangroves

Among the many palms found in Cuba, the royal palm is the national tree, which lends character to the vast savannas.

Rural landscape in Las Villas

Standing fifty to seventy-five feet tall, this elegant palm has a canopy than can spread twenty-five feet wide. Beyond its beauty, the palm offers tremendous utility to farmers as its fronds are used to build *bohíos* (rural dwellings) while its oblong purple seeds (*palmiche*) constitute an important food source for swine. Both Santería and Christianity have attached religious significance to the royal palm, thus making its powers transcend the natural world.

Another survivor from the forest clearing to grow sugarcane is the ceiba (silk cotton tree). Also found in the savannas, the tree can grow over two-hundred feet and live several hundred years. The ceiba has a utilitarian value in that it produces the raw materials for stuffing pillows and mattresses. This tree also enjoys a spiritual symbolism having been identified with a sacred African counterpart that is said to have safeguarding powers over the fury of the gods.

In terms of domesticated crops, sugarcane, a class of several interbreeding species of tall grasses, has been said to be a landscape modifier as it has taken over a large portion of the Cuban terrain. Introduced to Spain by the Moors during their eight-hundred-year rule, sugarcane was brought to Cuba during Spanish colonization. As the major agricultural product, the Cuban economy rises and falls with the price of sugar. The island has lost its place in world production since other countries such

ANDREA BERMÚDEZ

as Brazil, India, and China have become more prominent. Byproducts, which include ethanol and bagasse (*bagazo*), have critical importance for energy conservation. Ethanol can be blended with gasoline as an alternative fuel, and bagasse, the remains of crushed cane, can be burned to produce electricity or be used as raw materials for other products such as paper.

Tobacco and coffee follow sugar in the farming hierarchy, and the three taken together represent the majority of the agricultural production. When tobacco was first introduced in Cuba is still in dispute, but it is known that early on the natives used it for medicinal purposes. With the arrival of the Spanish colonists, tobacco became known to the world. The nineteenth century marked the end of Spanish monopoly on exports and fostered the rapid growth of the industry at that time.

Much like sugar and other products, tobacco has been at the mercy of the markets, which to an extent are determined by political events. The 1960s United States embargo against the Castro's regime disallowed exporting manufactured goods to the United States, a fact that has penalized agricultural productivity. The best tobacco comes from the western part of Cuba, particularly the Vuelta Abajo zone in the province of Pinar del Rio where sandy soil mixed with clay provides the ideal environment for this crop.

Tobacco field

Coffee was introduced to Cuba by French immigrants from Haiti about the time that Spain lifted its monopoly on exports. Mountain ranges in the east seemed to offer the appropriate soil requirements for coffee to thrive; therefore, most of the coffee production came from these areas. By the 1800s, it had become one of the top crops in Cuba. The high demand of internal consumption, which nearly exceeded the supply, all but guaranteed the success of the coffee industry. By the time of the Castro revolution, coffee had established itself as a major export. The United States embargo against Cuba also affected its export levels, which, coupled with bad crops, have reduced its production.

In the category of "minor crops," fruits were meant for both internal consumption and export. About one-third of Cuban *fincas* (farms) had fruits as one of their products, with few having them as a sole product. Pineapple, banana, and orange were the principal crops, but the fruit variety was endless: *mamey, anón, mango, guava, chirimoya, guanábana, zapote, caimito, tamarindo*, and *mamoncillo*. Rich in flavor and nutrients, these fruits were among Cuban's favorite foods and constituted a primarily domestic market. After the government started requiring supply booklets, internal consumption of fruits declined.

Since flora and fauna are interrelated aspects of the natural environment, a corresponding diversity and abundance of wildlife are also observed in Cuba. However, deforestation has caused many species to become extinct, and many more endangered. In general, the number of mammals found on the island is sparse, with the exception of large colonies of bats. About a third of the species of bats present during colonial times have become extinct. Their excretions, known as guano, have great economic value as a fertilizer.

Declining at an alarming rate is the *solenodon* or *almiquí*, a very large insectivore. At one-and-a-half foot long, the ratlike mammal is an odd nocturnal creature that is most commonly found in the eastern and central regions of Cuba. Regarded as a living fossil, the *almiquí* was thought to be extinct several decades ago. However, rare sightings have occurred since. Another mammal, the enormous manatee, was once a common presence in Cuban waters but today has almost disappeared. Through the years the manatees have fallen victim to hunters who sought them for their food value.

Of the rodents, the various species of *jutía* are, perhaps, the most typical. The largest land mammal measuring ten to eighteen inches in length, the *jutías* are considered gentle and shy tree rats that have also fallen victim to deforestation, as well as to the introduction of invasive exotic species of European rats. Considered a delicacy by some, the *jutía* can be found almost anywhere in the Cuban archipelago.

Among the hundreds of species of birds in Cuba, the most notable is the *Trogón* or *Tocoloro*, with its distinctive dark blue-violet crown. Chosen as the national bird, it measures about ten inches long and is still found abundantly in the forested areas of the island and on the Isle of Pines. A rare species, the *zunzuncito* (bee hummingbird) is the smallest bird in the world, measuring two and a half inches long. Characterized by its vibrant red, green, and blue colors, the tiny bird, most commonly found in the woodlands, is frequently mistaken for a bee. A slightly larger relative, the Emerald or *Colibrí* hummingbird prefers the coastal areas and forests of Cuba. It was thought to be sacred by the Taínos.

Emerald Hummingbird

It would be an impossible task to exhaustively describe the hundreds of noteworthy species of Cuba's avifauna, which in many cases have shown their ability to adapt to and survive in the changing natural landscape. Some *cotorras* (parrots) and *periquitos* (parakeets) are protected species since the colorful *guacamayo* (Cuban Macaw) became extinct during the nineteen century. It has been said that the last specimen may have been shot in the Zapata swamp in 1864. A fruit eater, *guacamayos* were known for foraging on guava, banana, and other fruit crops.

Bird species that thrive in aquatic habitat have been less threatened. Amid this group is the multicolor Cuban tody (Cartacuba), which can be found along the borders of rivers and streams, as well as the long-legged *flamenco* (flamingo), which favors coastal lagoons, brackish lakes, and ponds.

Flamingos

Nature has assigned birds important ecological tasks. Crops threatened by destructive pests are protected by insectivores such as the *bijirita* (prairie warbler), or by predators, including the *lechuza* (barn owl), which attack rodents that feed on grains. Other species, for instance the *aura tiñosa* (turkey vulture), are recyclers, helping to clean up the environment by disposing of carcasses. Countless other birds spread seeds for our flowers and trees. All indulge humans with their beauty and grace. The *sinsonte* (mockingbird) has a beautiful melodious song and frequently mimics other birds. It emits a special harsh sound to alert its kin of potential danger. The *ruiseñor* (Cuban solitaire) has been considered one of the most extraordinary vocalists of the Caribbean for its distinctive flutelike song. Its habitat is in the eastern and western mountainous areas of the island.

The hundreds of reptiles in Cuba, a majority endemic, are not considered poisonous to man. Of all the species, the crocodile is the most

ANDREA BERMÚDEZ

primitive, and its two species are largely found in the Zapata swamp, and in the Lanier swamp in the Isle of Pines. Adults measure on average ten feet long. Decline in population is mostly due to illegal hunting.

The highly endangered Cuban crocodile (*Caimán*)

Half of the species of reptiles are in the lizard group, including the *salamanquita* (gecko) which at one inch long is one of the smallest in the world. Because they are insectivores, the numerous and varied *lagartijas* (lizards) inhabiting the island help control insect populations.

On the other end of the spectrum, the endemic rock iguana is one of the largest in the West Indies, with males measuring up to five feet. The species was once the basis of the natives' diet. Currently considered an endangered species, the rock iguana favors the coastal areas of southern Cuba.

Of the approximately twenty-six varieties of snakes, the *majá* (thick-bodied snake), approximately ten to fourteen feet in length, and its considerably smaller version the *jubo*, measuring about three feet, are the most common. The *majá*, also known as the Cuban boa, will not attack humans unless cornered and prefers to feast on birds, rodents, and poultry. The *jubo* is a very swift-moving reptile that is also harmless to humans. Freshwater turtles include the *jicotea*, endemic of Cuba. They are commonly found in rivers and swamps and are considered vulnerable to extinction. Several fisheries in southern Cuba had been harvesting the *caguama* (sea turtle) whose feeding and nesting habitats were threatened by man-made events such as pollution and egg collection. Because the *caguama* became endangered, the Castro government was forced to take steps to ban its harvest.

Numbering more than sixty native varieties of amphibians, the group includes the biggest specimen, the tree frog, as well as the Habana robber frog, the fourth smallest in the Western hemisphere, measuring about half an inch. The tree frog, an invasive species, is known for its ability to travel and adapt to different environments, at times changing color to fit its surroundings. The Habana robber frog can be found in low, moderate, and higher elevations across the island and is considered to be vulnerable to extinction. There has been a worldwide decline in the number of amphibians, most likely due to loss of habitat, pollution, and disease.

Mollusks have one of the most varied environments in the Cuban fauna. They may appear anywhere from the deep sea to the mountains or the prairies. There are thousands of different species with a high degree of endemism. Marine mollusks, include the *cobo* (queen conch), one of the largest edible marine snails in the Caribbean, which was used by natives to make utensils. Although not considered endangered, it is threatened by overfishing. The land snails are by far more numerous and generally better known as the painted snails for their colorful beauty. *Liguus fasciatus*, a tree snail, is similarly beautiful and exhibits a great variety of colors. They are recyclers as they feed by scraping off a thin outer layer of bark, where nutrients are found, and fertilize their host trees by dropping fecal pellets to the ground.

There could not be beauty without a counterpart. Insects and arachnids are also abundant in Cuba with thousands of species of insects and several hundred arachnids identified. Insects have proven to be destructive to crops and a nuisance to humans. Insect-eating birds and lizards, among other fauna, help minimize this threat. Of the arachnids, the nocturnal *alacrán* (scorpion) as well as the *araña peluda* (tarantula) are the most common examples found on the island. The over forty species of scorpions are among the less venomous in the world and can be found in different types of forests, savannas, and semideserts. The poisonous tarantula, also nocturnal, prefers dark places and can grow to be about the size of a baseball.

Of the many types of fish that inhabit Cuban rivers, lakes, streams, and coastal waters, almost half are endemic. One of the rarest species is the freshwater gar or *manjuarí*, which inhabits western Cuba, most prominently in the *Laguna del Tesoro* and the Isle of Pines.

ANDREA BERMÚDEZ

Laguna del Tesoro in the Zapata Peninsula, Matanzas

Considered by many as one of the most primitive, this living fossil is the rarest among gars. Many of the freshwater varieties are threatened by extinction, such as the endemic biajaca, a Cuban cichlid, which is being displaced by the invasive exotic tilapia.

Fishing is a critical industry in Cuba supported by a large number of species of food fish. As a result, a number of sharks inhabiting the oceans surrounding Cuba are attracted by the abundant fish and mollusk communities. The most dangerous is the great white shark that may measure up to twenty-one feet long. A specimen was caught off the town of Cojímar in 1945. It has been said that in a single bite, this type of shark can consume thirty pounds of flesh.

It would be impossible to fully describe the richness and diversity of the Cuban flora and fauna. It should suffice to say that an island blessed with beauty and abundant natural resources is threatened by human carelessness. The danger posed by pollution, habitat loss, and human greed, among others, have placed the island at risk of becoming a paradise in ruins. The future of Cuban natural gifts is uncertain unless strong policies are enforced to protect its natural bounty."

At the end of her term paper, Elena's professor wrote, "I can tell how much of your heart is in this paper. I wish you luck returning to your paradise." The only correction in red pen was the name "Isle of Pines," which the professor changed to "Isle of Youth." Elena had known that Castro had renamed it, but she refused to acknowledge the fact. Castro had altered the course of history. She would not recognize his attempt to change geography as well. The professor followed his comments with a big red A+.

Elena's return to Cuba had not yet happened in 2009, when as she was perusing a Cuban bookstore in Miami, she found Dr. Marrero's last edition of *Geografía de Cuba*. To Elena, it was like a welcome reunion of memories she kept alive in her heart. She remembered the many nights the Punjab sisterhood skipped sleep studying these pages. The memory brought smiles and sadness all in one.

CHAPTER 12

A Cuban Recipe

Some people dream of success . . . while others wake up and work hard at it.

—Unknown

ELENA THOUGHT IF she had to describe a Cuban as an imaginary "recipe," how would that go?

2 cups of humor
3 cups of fortitude
1 cup each of determination, hard work, and optimism
Add sea salt and sugar to taste
Mix gently
Makes a one-of-a-kind Cuban.

History has shown that in the face of hardships, Cubans, on the island and in exile, have proven to be survivors. Be it their determination, resiliency, or their sense of humor, they have been able to "roll with the punches." Dr. Vidal believed for all time that "if at first you don't succeed, try and try again." Cubans have shown their ability to do just that. Dr. Vidal knew it firsthand. When he came to the United States at sixty-two years of age, he had to take the foreign board eligibility exam to be able to practice general medicine. Since he was staying with his brother's family in Coral Gables, he had no transportation to his review classes in South Miami. That would not stop him. He walked for miles to the bus stop and most of the time skipped lunch so he could attend the intensive sessions. He passed the test with flying colors, a fortunate event since he already had a job waiting pending the results.

Dr. Vidal's career was long and productive. He retired at ninety-five after having had two previous retirement attempts, recognition from the U.S. Congress, congratulatory letters from three American presidents (Reagan, Bush, and Clinton), and a myriad of grateful patients. When Dorchester County, Maryland, published a book of patriots and community leaders that had made important contributions, Dr. Vidal was cited among them. Every year, Dr. Vidal would be Hurlock's Grand Marshal in their Fourth of July parade. To honor the dedicated physician, on his death at 101 years old, a passenger train was named after him. Elena would never forget his funeral procession. The people from Hurlock had insisted that the cortege drive the doctor's remains around the town. They congregated in the streets to pay tribute to a man who had spent his lifetime making the world a little better.

An important factor fueling the Cubans' courage to survive has been their sense of humor. Turning life's happenings into humorous events has been elevated to a fine art by Cuban lore. During Ramon Grau's presidency, 1944 to 1948, it was thought that his sister-in-law, Paulina, was the real power behind the man. Since Grau was unmarried, she served as his first lady. In the mid 1940s, the president built an enormous illuminated fountain, close to the airport, that served as a roundabout for the heavy traffic of the vicinity. Some evenings, Dr. Vidal would take the family for a ride to the area and watch for the changing multicolored lights. Despite its beauty, the fountain was commonly known as *el videl de Paulina* (Paulina's bidet).

Cuban success stories of real people —be they professionals, entrepreneurs, white-collar workers, or students— reveal their belief that luck over skill is a myth. These individuals have worked on the premise that success is a byproduct of determination, hard work, and risk-taking. They have challenged their fate to follow their dreams. In the words of a woman entrepreneur: "When dreams become plans, you get there, despite the bumps along the way. Being successful is no longer exclusively a male privilege, since success is truly a function of how much risk you want to take, and how much sleep you are willing to miss."

A proof of resilience and determination is the story of the Cuban *balseros* (rafters) who have looked death in the eye and confronted it. These men, women, and children risk their lives crossing shark-infested waters with nine- to thirteen-foot waves towering over precarious man-made rafts. The professions represented by the *balseros* run the gamut from physicians to blue-collar workers searching for a new life that can realize their hopes of a better future. Many are elderly; such is the case of a blind ninety-year-old woman who left Cuba in a raft with her son's family. Another *balsera*, a sixty-four-year-old teacher-single mother survived the treacherous journey accompanied by her son. Shortly after her arrival, she found work as a hairdresser relying on previous experience she had had as a young woman. Many who undertake the journey are still unborn. Some are rescued in the high seas after days or weeks adrift. Of those who survive the voyage, many arrive dehydrated and near death.

Abandoned *balsa* found and photographed by
Dr. Deb Shaw in Islamorada, FL circa 1994

Elena usually refers to this chapter in her exile history as "one of the greatest tragedies. How desperate these brothers and sisters have to be to put themselves through such agony at sea." A great number of *balseros* do not survive the crossing, and many others are sent back to Cuba. It pains Elena to think what will happen to those who are repatriated since many of them were harassed and fired from their jobs just because they had chosen to leave Cuba. Before 1994, the *balseros* were considered political refugees;

after that date, most were classified as illegal aliens. The "wet foot, dry foot" policy determines that the refugee must have at least one foot on U.S. soil to have the opportunity to stay. Those who lost their lives in the crossing at least died with their hearts full of anticipation for a better life.

Founded in Miami, Florida in the early 1990s, "Hermanos al Rescate" (Brothers to the Rescue) was the organization behind the search and rescue missions that helped *balseros* reach United States shores. In 1996, two of their six Cessnas were shot down by the Cuban Air Force, and four of the members killed. The incident was denounced worldwide as an act of violence. A park complex has been built in southwest Miami to commemorate the death of these four brave men.

One of the most famous *balseros* is Elián González who, at age six, accompanied his mother and a number of others attempting to make the crossing in a small aluminum boat. The boat capsized, drowning Elián's mother and ten other refugees. The little boy and three other survivors drifted in an inner tube until rescued. He became the object of a tug-of-war between his father in Cuba and his exiled relatives in Miami. The U.S. attorney general at the time determined that Elián should be returned to his father in Cuba since his mother had taken him out of the country without the father's authorization. The case of Elián González divided public opinion. Elena herself was not sure what to think. On the one hand, his mother had sacrificed her life to provide a different future for the little boy; on the other, she thought his biological father had a right to decide. Anywhere Elena went, she was accosted by the same question: "What do you think should happen to Elián?" She found herself giving contradicting answers as she hesitated about what would be in the best interest of the child. Years later, pictures of Elián, as a young adult in his military fatigues, reminded Elena of how close he had been to freedom. Elián has since been used as a prop by the Castro government, and neither he nor his father is allowed to talk to outsiders, particularly the press. Elena wondered for what kind of life was his freedom relinquished.

There have been other amazing efforts to escape life in Cuba such as turning surfboards, mattresses, and even refrigerators into dangerously vulnerable crafts to attempt the passage. It has been said that "necessity is the mother of invention," and *balseros* have proven the truth of the saying many times over. In 2003, an old Chevy truck serving as a vessel for a dozen *balseros* was captured by the coast guard south of Key West, and the men returned to Cuba. The vessel, a model of inventiveness, moved about five miles per hour powered by a small propeller connected to the motor of the flatbed. The Chevy stayed afloat by a series of empty oil barrels connected to it. Seven months later, eleven *balseros* tried the journey again, this time in a vintage Buick sedan. Caught by the U.S. Coast Guard, the crew was sent back to Cuba and the Buick destroyed, as had been its Chevy predecessor.

Determination and resilience are also manifest in the experiences of others, perhaps more fortunate, who have been able to redirect their destinies in successful endeavors without the challenge of such brutal beginnings. There is the Cuban college president who has transformed his institution from a little-known community college to a premier institution of higher education. Elena met the veteran trailblazer personally and had the opportunity to work at his institution. She was in awe of this man's abilities and intelligence. At about five feet five in stature, he would dominate a roomful of people. "A short man with a giant soul," Elena thought. Creative in his thinking, indefatigable in his work, and with a clear vision as to where his ideas should lead, this man has translated his dream into the largest community college in the United States and possibly in the world. Elena was impressed that despite his Ivy League degrees and accomplishments, he still took the time to express an interest in those who had not achieved as much as he had. Graduates from his institution have continued to develop their intellect and training and now hold important leadership roles in building their communities. The list of prominent alumni is endless: physicians, judges, musicians, bank presidents, politicians, teachers, nurses.

There are many other success stories that prove how Cubans have been able to reinvent themselves to deal with the realities at hand. There have been many instances of teachers who have been able to influence the dreams of the next generation through their dedication. One such person is the retired Cuban professor of Spanish linguistics and literature, almost blinded by advanced juvenile diabetes, who continues to research and make important contributions to her field. She has received numerous honors and accolades during her long career, including membership in the Spanish Royal Academy, a remarkable distinction for someone not born in Spain. There have been numerous stories about entrepreneurs that show how dedication and fearless risk-taking have fueled their accomplishments. A case in point is a Cuban-American businessman well-known for his anti-Castro activism who became the CEO of the largest Hispanic-owned business in the country, a multinational corporation first to be a part of the New York Stock Exchange.

Not all Cubans have enjoyed such public recognition, a fact that does not minimize the importance of their contributions to their families and their community. There are many unsung heroes, such as Rogelio, who arrived in a raft with his wife, their little boy, and two other male adults. They landed in Islamorada in the Florida Keys and were fortunate that the "dry foot, wet foot" policy allowed them to stay. At the time of their arrival, no one spoke English and their work experience in Cuba was not much help in getting jobs. Rogelio joined a cousin who had a pool-cleaning business, and his wife found a job as housekeeper. He would bring his little boy, who was soon helping his dad by performing simple chores. Before long, Rogelio's impeccable work ethic and positive attitude gained him a vast clientele. Soon the son was translating for his father while learning the value of honorable work. In just a few years, Rogelio was running his own business, allowing his wife the time and financing to attend nursing school, her dream. Rogelio's family never missed a meal. His little boy was going to school and learning English. Their lives seemed to justify the risk they had taken in leaving Cuba.

A number of Cubans, having experienced a history of failed politics, have chosen a political career as a means to bring about beneficial changes to the lives of their respective constituencies. They represent the gamut of the political spectrum from elected school and university board members to United States senators. For example, the state of Florida, where most Cuban exiles live, has elected the Díaz Balart brothers, Marco Rubio, and Ileana Ros-Lehtinen to represent the Republican constituency of the state. Mel Martínez, former senator from Florida, was the first Cuban-American to serve in the U.S. Senate. He had previously served as chairman of the Republican National Committee and as secretary of Housing and Urban Development. After his resignation from the senate, Martínez became a lobbyist and a partner in an international law firm. Florida is not the only state to recognize Cuban leadership in politics. In 2006, New Jersey elected a Cuban-American, Democratic senator Bob Menéndez. His long record of public service as a school board member, city mayor, state legislator, and member of the U.S. House of Representatives gained him the distinction. As a son of immigrants, Menéndez grew up in a Union City tenement and turned his life experience into a motive to attain higher education and worked to improve the lives of his family and his community.

Cuban voices from the world of entertainment have had the opportunity to publicly showcase their stories of resolve and grit. A beloved Cuban icon, Celia Cruz is a powerful example. She was born in Cuba circa 1924 from humble parentage and passed away in 2003, a famous international star living in exile. Her talent was evident at an early age when she would sing lullabies for her three siblings. Around age twelve, Celia started singing in public in exchange for tourist tips. Despite the fact that her singing helped provide for the family, her father did not approve of her musical inclinations. He would have preferred that Celia become a teacher, one of the few options available for career-oriented women of the time. Trying to satisfy her father, she started studying to be a teacher but soon dropped her plans in favor of attending the National Conservatory of Music.

Celia soon joined the *Mulatas de Fuego*, an international troupe, followed by the famous *Sonora Matancera* orchestra where she met and married Pedro Knight. After 1965, both left the *Sonora* and Celia went solo, represented by her musician husband. In the United States, she joined several famous band leaders and sang with a number of musical legends. Known as the queen of Afro-Cuban music, Celia stole the hearts of her audience in Cuba and around the world. When she left Cuba in the mid 1960s, she became very outspoken about her opposition to the communist regime, especially after she was not allowed to enter the country to attend her mother's funeral.

Celia's musical career was stellar and varied, from singing in famous venues to appearing in movies, and winning the coveted Grammy award several times. Through song, Celia Cruz expressed her longing for Cuba and her desire to see the island again someday. Her wishes would not come to pass. At her death in 2003, Celia had become an icon of Cuban music, famous and beloved around the world but still living in exile. Her distinctive shout of *"azúcar"* (sugar), often interjected in her songs, will live forever in the hearts of her vast international audience.

Representing a younger generation of crossover musicians, Gloria and Emilio Estefan also deserve enormous recognition for bringing Cuban rhythms to mainstream America. Gloria Fajardo Estefan fled the country as a little girl when her father, a soldier and Batista bodyguard, had to leave for exile. While in the United States, he participated in the failed Bay of Pigs invasion and, years later, in the Vietnam conflict. A victim of Agent Orange, he was diagnosed with multiple sclerosis soon after his return. Gloria, being the oldest child, inherited the responsibility of caring for her sick father and for her younger sibling while her mother, a teacher, worked to support the family during the day and attended school at night. Music was all Gloria had to help her cope with her difficult circumstance. In 1975, she met Emilio, and soon the talented musician was a lead singer in Emilio's band.

Three years later, the couple married, and the band, renamed *Miami Sound Machine*, became an instant hit in the 1980s. Almost immediately, their Spanish albums were a success in Latin America and in the United States. Having sold over ninety million albums worldwide, Gloria has collected a succession of music awards, including several Grammys. Her album, *90 Millas*, is a tribute to her native Cuba. The title is indicative of the distance between Cuba and the United States and the music an amalgam of Cuban rhythms and American pop. Successful music is not the only flourishing endeavor of the Estefans as they own a variety of businesses worldwide, including several Cuban-themed restaurants.

There are numerous other private and public success stories of Cubans whose life experiences chronicle their endurance and self-confidence in the face of insurmountable challenges. "What drives your people?" her friend Marta had asked Elena. Her response has always been: "It is not wealth alone that motivates my people to be the best they can be. Their 'stick-to-itness' comes from the awareness that each individual has a unique mission in this life, and that realization becomes the driver of all action." That statement also described Elena. The "what's in it for me?" was not a motivator. She looked at the grand scheme and tried to figure out how her next step fit into the big picture. "I am climbing mountains one step at a time," she would often say. "How would you describe your fellow Cubans in one word?" someone asked Elena. To this, she answered, "One word? Are you kidding me? That's impossible, you need a whole dictionary! After seeing how they have coped with life, I would say Cubans are humorous, optimistic, courageous, determined, people-oriented, and industrious— all the right ingredients to make them survivors."

These life stories, as well as the myriad of untold ones, document that a great number of Cubans living in the United States have made the American dream a reality. It is evident from their narratives that attaining the elusive dream has not been an easy accomplishment for any of them. Elena compares the search for the American dream with the childhood game of *Chutes and Ladders*. Going up ladders wins the game, but it is not as easy as it seems with all the threatening chutes taking the player down along the way. The significant difference is that in the game, the only consequence of finding the chute, instead of the ladder, is that one has missed an opportunity to win, and perhaps has made an opponent happy in the process. In real life, the chutes are a more serious hazard, which only the very resolute and savvy can overcome. It helps that many have pursued education or training to improve their chances at winning the game.

The success many Cuban-Americans have experienced is a function of not having lost sight of their goals, and when encountering "chutes," they have not let disappointment distract them. Considering "chutes" as just a bump along the road, they have gotten back in the game and played it with determination. "Was theirs an 'American dream' or a well-conceived and executed plan?" Elena considered. "Dreams are passive and fleeting. In them, you wait for something to happen. In a plan, you must act decisively to make things come about. These individuals have definitely not waited for life to take place. They have worked hard to make it materialize."

PART IV
The Anatomy of a Revolution

CHAPTER 13

A Retrospective of the Castro Revolution

Si alguna vez la Revolución significó algo, hace mucho tiempo que se transformó en mentira. (If ever the Revolution meant anything, it's been a while since its transformed itself into a lie.)

—*Vicente Botín*

THE BENIGN CLIMATIC environment of Cuba was an "*arma de dos filos*" (double-edged sword) as it allowed the island to be a tropical paradise while providing shelter to the mobile war carried on by the anti-Batista revolutionaries in the Sierra Maestra. Known as guerrilla warfare, this type of combat is characterized by short unexpected attacks, raids, and sabotage, while constantly moving from target to target, and a "friendly" environment is a requisite to its success. Sierra Maestra, the largest mountain range on the island, had already proven its historical significance during colonial times when chieftain Hatuey resisted the arrival of the Spanish and, later, when the various wars of independence were fought against Spain.

Fidel Castro Ruz had made revolution his life mission. Born in 1926, he showed an early interest in politics and history. Fidel and his six siblings had been born out of wedlock in a prosperous environment. His father, Angel, born in Spain, had fought against Cuba in one of the wars for independence. He became a wealthy, self-made landowner and investor after moving to the island. Fidel's mother, Lina Ruz, had been Angel's common-law wife until their marriage when Fidel was in his midteens. According to one of the children, Juanita Castro, their childhood environment was happy and not at all unusual as their father had separated from his wife and lived with Lina and the children.

As a student of law at the University of Havana, Fidel Castro became involved in revolutionary politics. He was able to use to his advantage the university's autonomous status, which allowed him to store weapons and train future insurrectionists without governmental interference. After receiving his law degree, he ran for the House of Representatives, a move that was doomed by Batista's coup in 1952, which cancelled the elections.

Less than a year later on July 26, Castro organized an attack on the Moncada military barracks where two-thirds of the assailants were killed. After the failed offensive, Castro and a few of his allies fled to the Sierra Maestra. In the fall of 1953, Fidel and his brother Raúl were captured and imprisoned. His notoriety was beginning to gain him some necessary recognition for his future plans. A new movement had been born and was named the 26th of July, in honor of the failed attempt. While in the Isle of Pines prison, he never stopped organizing efforts to topple Batista's government.

When Fidel and Raúl Castro were released two years later as a result of an amnesty signed by Batista, they fled to Mexico to plan Fidel's next steps. In exile, they joined forces with guerrilla warfare expert Dr. Ernesto (Che) Guevara, a physician by training and a committed revolutionary. The Argentine-born Che had already shown Marxist leanings when he met the Castros in Mexico, and decided to join their revolutionary movement. As a young student, Che travelled throughout Latin America, concluding that the poverty he witnessed was the result of capitalism This experience triggered his direct involvement in the socialist government of Jacobo Arbenz in Guatemala during the early 1950s when Che fought against the U.S.-backed overthrow.

Cuban coin commemorating Che Guevara

ANDREA BERMÚDEZ

In the meantime, Cuba was imploding. There were student demonstrations and riots to which the police responded with brutality and repression. A failed Batista assassination attempt began eroding the loyal support of the military that had maintained Batista's stronghold on the island. His support had started to unravel with the mock election of 1954 in which his opponents withdrew with suspicions of fraud. The situation in Cuba was chaotic. To avoid civil war, efforts were made to find a compromise between Batista and the revolutionaries. Colonel Cosme de la Torriente, well-respected for his experience as a former secretary of state and veteran of the 1895 war of independence, was designated to lead the dialogue with the government. The Diálogos Cívicos (Civic Dialogues) took place between Batista and de la Torriente, but unfortunately, nothing positive was achieved, including Batista's refusal to hold elections in 1956.

What followed was a period of total instability as Batista slowly lost control of the country. Police force was unsuccessfully used to address the bedlam. Student leaders were killed, including the president of the university's Federation of Students, José Antonio Echeverria, who had led the Revolutionary Directorate, an underground student movement. Echeverría and his men, unaware that the attempt to assassinate Batista had failed, took over a radio station to announce Batista's death. Police intervened and Echeverría was shot to death while his student followers were wounded in the skirmish.

Castro's underground movement in the cities had been led by Frank País, a close collaborator, who after successfully organizing opposition cells in urban centers joined the 26th of July Movement. As the key person responsible for coordinating urban action and sabotage against the Batista government, he has been touted as the architect of the revolution. Castro communicated his plans to invade Cuba, and País appealed to the Cuban people for a mass demonstration against the government. The urban leader wanted to distract the police so Castro and his eighty men could land an invasion undetected. País was captured and later released, becoming the head of the movement's underground efforts in Oriente. After his brother's death, País went into hiding. In July 1957, as he attempted to escape, he was shot and killed by the police. Without the work of País and the urban underground, victory for the Rebel Army was made more difficult.

At the end of 1956, Castro landed a small boat, the *Granma*, on the southeastern coast of Cuba. Batista's forces were ready and captured or eliminated more than half of the invaders, as well as some members of the urban underground. Fidel, Raúl, Che, and a few other men escaped to the Sierra Maestra. Rising sharply from the sea, the Sierra created the perfect hiding place for the insurgents. Batista forces had not been trained to fight guerrilla style, so it was an added advantage that allowed the rebels to regroup, and wage the ultimately successful revolution against Batista.

During the next couple of years, the urban underground, largely composed of middle-class Cubans, went to work while the revolutionaries reorganized. Some historians have argued that it was not until 1958 that Castro and his Army took charge. The rebels in the Sierra were almost a forgotten story making hardly a clatter when, in 1957, Herbert Mathews, a foreign correspondent from the *New York Times*, published a series of articles about the insurrection. The contents of the series infused life into Castro's cause and awakened interest and support for the revolutionaries.

Other key figures and icons of the 26 of July Movement include his brother Raúl, Camilo Cienfuegos, Huber Matos, Celia Sánchez, and Vilma Espín. The first two were *Granma* survivors. Raúl Castro fought alongside his brother and has since lived in his shadow. Despite the fact that he did not win any important battles for the revolution, he earned a number of titles, including that of brigadier-general, in charge of the armed forces. As heir apparent to his brother, Raúl had been second-in-command for most of his life. On the other hand, Camilo Cienfuegos earned the rank of commandant in the Rebel Army. After winning the Battle of Yaguajay, his column along with Che's and others took the city of Santa Clara without much opposition from the Batista forces.

This was the last important battle of the Castro insurrection. The next day Batista fled Cuba. Cienfuegos went on to play an important role alongside Castro, including his participation in the Agrarian Reform passed between 1958 and 1963 for the purpose of breaking up large landholdings and redistributing them among peasants and farmers. Camilo died mysteriously in October 1959 when his Cessna vanished on a flight from Camagüey to Havana.

Huber Matos joined the urban underground after the arrival of the *Granma*, but was caught supporting the rebels after the transports he used identified his family business. Matos requested asylum at the Costa Rican Embassy and was soon able to rejoin his clandestine support for the rebels, only this time with weapons and munitions. Toward the end of 1958, Matos participated in the battle that took Santiago de Cuba, a critical victory for the rebels. Although he was high on the hierarchy as a commander of the Rebel Army, his public criticism of the Castro government's Marxist sympathies earned him twenty years of imprisonment only nine months after the victorious arrival in Havana. From his exile in Miami, he has denounced the atrocities of the Castro government, including human rights violations against political prisoners.

Celia Sánchez, whom most Cubans believed to have been Fidel's right-hand person, had been a member of the urban underground since 1952 and was partly responsible for the arrangements to land the *Granma* and provide the necessary reinforcements. Little is known of her childhood, except for the fact that her father was a dentist and she seemed to have had an affluent upbringing. In her early thirties, Sánchez joined the rebels in the Sierra Maestra and participated in combat side by side with her male comrades. Loyal to the revolution, she worked closely with Fidel Castro and earned the title of secretary to the Presidency of the Council of Ministers. Her life was very private, only portrayed by rumor or myth. She died of cancer in 1980. In death, she has been catapulted to the level of a revolutionary icon.

Another woman fighter, Vilma Espín, a chemical engineer from the Massachusetts Institute of Technology, was also an early member of the 26 of July Movement. She collaborated with Frank País and his urban underground activities where she acted as conduit between País and Fidel Castro. Espín would soon become the head organizer of clandestine undertakings in the Oriente Province. In 1958, she joined the Rebel Army in the Sierra Maestra. On January 26, 1959, she married Raúl Castro and had four children, including their son Alejandro thought to be a possible heir to the Castro legacy. As president of the Cuban Federation of Women, among other political responsibilities, Espín had the opportunity of working to advance women's issues. She was awarded the Lenin Peace Prize in 1979. Vilma Espin passed away in 2007 following a long illness. She was seventy-seven. Vilma Espín and Celia Sánchez, as role models and activists, eventually helped change the function of the woman in Cuban society, from domestic to militant. With the revolution, there was more encouragement for women to fully participate in war and politics and to pursue education and careers at par with men.

General strikes, bombings, riots, kidnappings, and sabotage in the cities described life during this difficult transition. The final straw came in March 1958 when the United States declared an embargo against Batista that stopped the supply of armaments. These actions alone would have sufficed to make his regime vulnerable, but there was more in store. Operación Verano (Operation Summer) in May 1958 was a last-ditch effort by the Batista forces to subdue the rebels and any other opposition forces, but it failed dismally. The rebel forces were continuing their victorious march, finding little or no opposition from Batista's army, which had become demoralized after losing confidence in their leader. Batista fled Cuba in the early-morning hours of January 1, 1959, leaving it in the hands of a powerless military junta whose duty was to select a provisional president. Castro refused to acknowledge the new president and seized control of the country without any resistance. The revolution had come to an end, and now a new government had been declared with assurances to the people that democracy would be restored. Fidel arrived in Havana on January 8, 1959 with promises of freeing the island from the yoke of a tyrant and, instead, became the longest living dictator in the modern world. He had a hero's welcome by those who believed in his ideals but were betrayed by his demagogy.

1999 stamp depicting Fidel Castro and Camilo Cienfuegos commemorating the 40th anniversary of the revolution

After the victorious arrival of the *barbudos* (bearded rebels) in Havana, Manuel Urrutia, who had been in exile, assumed the first presidency under Castro. Urrutia, a jurist by profession and a politician by vocation, had a long string of revolutionary credentials. He had been active in fighting the dictatorships of Machado and Batista and was seeing now an opportunity for a democratic resolution. His role in the success of the revolution was significant as he was the person who dealt with the United States and who successfully advocated for the arms embargo against the Batista military. However, as in the Matos case, Urrutia fell into disfavor early on by making decisions that Castro felt were too slow in coming and not radical enough. Even though Castro had not assumed any title other than armed forces commander, he would publicly announce changes without consulting with the president. It became obvious who was truly in charge. While Castro had not yet declared his allegiance to communism publicly, Urrutia's fierce anticommunist stance was seen as a possible stumbling block. After only six months in power, he resigned the presidency and left the country. Osvaldo Dorticós was appointed president, and Fidel Castro resumed his position as prime minister, a post he had held since the previous February.

Radical measures were taken early on. Property from American investors and Batista supporters was the first to be confiscated. Equality seemed to mean the rich would lose their wealth and the middle class its income while the poor remained so. The National Institute for Agrarian Reform, INRA, was created to bring about reform legislation, and Che Guevara was appointed to direct it. INRA broadened the scope of governmental seizures by adding foreign and domestic privately owned land. Another far-reaching measure was the government takeover of media outlets, which began the slow, albeit effective, mass indoctrination agenda.

It was not until December 2, 1961, that Castro finally acknowledged through a televised address that his social revolution was Marxist-Leninist inspired from the onset. As a communist state, Cuba soon became allied with the USSR. As time passed, it became clear who was to benefit from the Castro revolution. The "Cuba for Cubans" slogan seemed to have narrowed its scope, and the term *Cubans* redefined to mean only those with Marxist-Leninist leanings.

CHAPTER 14

The Early Years of Castro's Cuba

Any existence deprived of freedom is a kind of death.

—*General Michael Anoun*

ELENA REMEMBERED THE fateful New Year's Eve of 1958. The day had been weighed down with uncertainty, and as the evening progressed, there was a warning sense of gloom. The country felt something of substance had happened, but what it did not know was that the president had left for exile. Who was really in charge now was unclear even to those "in the know."

There were not the usual multiple parties to attend. Dictator Fulgencio Batista had resigned, and he and his closest associates had fled the country that very day. Elena thought about Jack Blanco, one of her classmates and a dear friend. His father was a general in Batista's army, so she feared for his fate. On a whim, Elena decided to call Jack and wish him something. But what? Happy New Year? What she really wanted to ask him was, "Are you and your family OK? What's going on?" She could not think of what to say; words would not come easily. They chatted briefly, and when they said their good-byes, Elena felt the uneasy sensation that she would never see Jack again. She wept the loss of her friend and the loss of the only life she knew. She wanted to hold on to the present memories and not let go, but there was no choice. The future was set in motion and there was no escape.

Castro's triumph over the powerful Batista regime was celebrated by an overwhelming number of Cubans, predominantly youth and the disenfranchised. Batista had been a dominant figure in politics since his first coup d'état in 1933. Elena experienced personally the exuberance of the masses on January 8, when a victorious Fidel and his army of rebels arrived in Havana. Elena did not know how to feel about the sudden change. On the one hand, her immediate family was threatened as a result of their distant connections with the previous government, but on the other, she was young and youth was idealistic about the future. She kept these conflicted feelings to herself.

The beginning of Castro's regime was filled with promises of justice and equality. However, persecution and fear precipitated by numerous harsh measures initiated by the government created an exodus that included close relatives and friends of Elena's. Almost immediate nationalization of businesses and industry forced the wealthy to extinction and the middle class to lose their modus vivendi. That about covered everyone Elena knew. Her American acquaintances from Ruston were some the first ones to flee Cuba as the mass propaganda "Cuba sí, yankees no" was beginning to take root.

One of the first experiences with the new government was the televised trial and execution of one of Batista's army generals. The event was meant as a lesson of what could happen if one dared become an enemy of the revolution. The military tribunals were led by Che Guevara at La Cabaña, the same fortress were Dr. Vidal had been imprisoned twenty-five years before. Those convicted of treason were either executed by a firing squad or received long prison sentences. Sending prisoners "to the big wall" (*el Paredón*), meant condemning them to the death squad without the benefit of a fair trial. There were countless Batista supporters whose televised trials brought protest. The public spectacle turned private, and the "cleansing" continued.

Elena would see the trial of her cousin Manny in her mind's eye for many years. He had been an officer of Batista's army, but with his desk job, he had never participated in battle. He was still given a long prison sentence. It was believed that judges had already prepared the sentencing in advance of the trial. Manny was condemned to a rat-infested dungeon flooded with sewage, which obviously showed the little consideration given to human rights. Manny's only entertainment was a lizard that visited him every day. To keep his sanity, he spent his time trying to train the curious visitor.

After the trial, Manny's family had to go into hiding. Elena would help them move from one location to another, sometimes late at night. She recalled an evening when she was helping to move Manny's mother who disguised herself by wearing dark glasses at night. Amateur counterrevolutionaries did not stand much of a chance. Fortunately, after a few months, Manny's family was able to return to their home.

The Vidals were targeted by the Castro regime from the very beginning of his administration. Dr. Vidal had retired from his army career as medical captain when Batista first took over the country in 1933. A private man devoted to his loyal patients, Dr. Vidal never engaged in any other political or military activity after that time. However, familial connections to his brother, Senator Vidal, placed him and his family in jeopardy with the Castro operatives.

Just like a fading memory, the Punjab sisterhood had gone their separate ways. It did not come as a surprise to Elena that Xenia had joined the government militia during Castro's first year in office. Her "absent" dad had reappeared from his underground pro-Castro activities and had become an influential figure in Xenia's life. Her green fatigues were a reminder of the disparate worlds separating the girls now. While Elena attended the University of Havana, Ofelia had already left the country to marry her U.S.-born fiancé. Although Pilar and her family were still in Cuba, they were discussing plans to move to Spain in the next two to three years.

After her high school graduation in 1958, Elena had been accepted to the School of Architecture at the Saint Thomas of Villanova University, a private Catholic institution founded in the 1940s and highly respected for its solid academic preparation. Elena had fallen in love with the idea of becoming an architect like Uncle Tato and cousin Rod. The father-son team had had a very productive career together. Uncle Tato was the man of numbers behind the team, and Rod a very talented designer. When Elena was age seven or eight, they would take her to the office and let her sit at a drawing table to create her own designs. Rod would always be gentle in pointing out things like "If you want to add rooms upstairs, you have to do something downstairs as well" or "Remember you need a door here or there to get from one room to another." More than just learning, Elena fell in love with the process of building. She dreamed of the day when she would be designing homes for real. It was natural then that architecture became her first career choice. However, attending Saint Thomas was a short-lived affair as Castro appropriated the university in 1959, and classes were suspended indefinitely. Later, in 1961, the founding Augustinian friars were expelled from Cuba.

ANDREA BERMÚDEZ

Meantime, Elena and Roberto were getting serious about their relationship, and marriage plans were germinating. Elena decided to shift careers and enroll in the Escuela de Idiomas (Language School) at the University of Havana like her mother, Sara, had done a few years back. Sara had always considered education as the key to freedom of the mind and spirit, a belief that she instilled in her four children. Close to age fifty when her brood was old enough for Sara to build a life for herself, she hired a physics tutor to prepare her to complete the only subject she was missing for a high school diploma. Sara Vidal's elder sisters had not even finished elementary school since women of their time were raised to marry well and have children. Sara, however, was a gutsy pioneer and, most definitely, an inspiring role model for her daughter when, years later, Sara had completed the equivalent of a master's degree. Not only had she challenged tradition by pursuing higher education, but she also found employment as principal of a language school.

Gone were the days when the family would sit on the porch with neighbors and friends and trade stories until late in the evening. A curfew mandated an early retirement. Lights out, no visitors allowed. In order to enforce the clampdown, Castro had created neighborhood committees to maintain surveillance on potential enemies of the revolution. Their scope was later expanded to include flushing out counterrevolutionaries and homosexuals. It was probably a member of this committee that informed on the family having Senator Vidal's car hidden in the garage. The militia showed up and towed the car away as if it were the lawful thing to do. Rumor had it that one of Castro's associates was seen driving it. The family was fortunate that the loss of a car had been the only consequence to what was interpreted as disloyalty to the revolution. Loyalty to the state was more important than loyalty to the family, so more than once individuals became *chivatos* (snitches) and gave away family members, even their next of kin.

Life was not easy on many other fronts. The simplest act was difficult. A phone call had to be preceded by a recording that stated, "Patria o muerte, venceremos" (Country or death, we shall conquer). Taking a bus was dangerous as more than once a shoot-out disrupted traffic. Elena and Roberto had gone to Tropicana nightclub on *el Día de los Enamorados* (Valentine's Day), only to be caught in a bombing that killed an innocent nineteen-year-old girl. This incident weighed heavily on Elena's mind. She did not know the girl, but she was well aware that the young woman's journey was incomplete. It could have been her. Not even church attendance was safe. Many a time churchgoers were threatened or ridiculed by the revolutionary militia standing outside. Elena thought of the many times shots were fired and she ended up running for cover at unforeseen places such as a church, a park, a school.

The Catholic Church, the most dominant influence in Cuban culture prior to the revolution, was losing its grip. Before Castro, the Church exerted control over every aspect of the lives of its followers.

San Francisco de Asís Basilica Old Havana

One day in 1957, the Catholic bishops required each parishioner to publicly condemn a Brigitte Bardot movie entitled *And God Created them Equal.* The offender was the actress's shapely rear end exposed in one of the scenes. When the priest requested at mass that those in attendance stand up and take a vow of condemnation, Elena stayed seated. To the dismay of her very conservative family, she simply explained that she thought it was hypocritical to condemn a movie she had stood in line to watch!

During the early part of Castro's regime, things had changed for the Catholic Church in Cuba. The government had nationalized church property such as Colegio de Belén and the University of Saint Thomas, while entire orders of priests and nuns had been expelled.

Family life had become constricted. Their connection to Senator Vidal attracted frequent visits from the militia with one excuse or another. Social exchanges became limited as well. Parties were not fun anymore with imposed curfews that restricted the hours friends and family could congregate. Elena, unable to see her Punjab friends, had very few outside contacts. Watching drive-in movies became the pastime for Elena and Roberto who were always accompanied by another adult. At the time, it was considered inappropriate for an unmarried woman to be seen in public in the company of a man without a chaperone. Tata loved to play that role. Despite the fact that she did not understand English and had trouble reading the subtitles, she could follow the plot. Tata would say, "Just tell me who the bad guys are, and I will go from there." Sometimes the story line Tata manufactured was even better than the movie itself!

Elena made the best out of attending school. Her friend Celia would take her and Pilar to the Instituto de Idiomas every day. Celia had taught at Ruston Academy, and now they were classmates. The three of them became close as they spent hours trying to escape their unpleasant reality through enjoyable times together. One afternoon, they were walking along an open area at the Instituto when a gigantic Cuban flag that hung from the third floor lost its hold, fell three floors, and totally swallowed them up. Elena and Celia were terrified. Pilar was giggling. Two armed militia came not to help untangle the flag, but to interrogate the women. They were allowed to go, but not without a stern warning. When Pilar confessed, the other two found out she had pulled the end of the flag, causing the hullabaloo that almost landed them in jail.

All good things come to an end. Pilar started dating Luis, a young dentist who had joined Castro in his fighting days at the Sierra Maestra. Long haired and bearded, Luis flaunted his green fatigues. Elena could not get over that her friend was dating a *barbudo*. "Love must really be blind," she thought. Fear was a state that does not breed trust, and Elena was living with apprehension about the world that surrounded her now. Could she still trust Pilar? What were Pilar's loyalties now? The answer was clear to Elena when Pilar and Luis became engaged, and plans for their entire family to leave the island were put on hold indefinitely.

Before Elena's wedding to Roberto, Celia suddenly left Cuba without a single word of explanation. A phone call to Celia was met with a recording indicating that service to that number had been disconnected. Elena later found out that Celia's husband, Alfredo, had been active in the underground movement against Castro and had to leave in the middle of the night to avoid capture. Elena prayed that her friends had succeeded.

One summer day in 1959, Bernie was arrested at the hospital where he worked. Militia forces did not need warrants to justify detention or imprisonment. They just appeared at a doorstep or place of work, and the victim was hauled off to prison, sometimes violently. The day after Bernie's arrest, a nervous coworker alerted the family who by now was sick with worry not knowing what had caused his absence. A few days later, Bernie was released with little or no explanation. The reason for detaining him was a note with a "suspicious" phone number found in his pocket. The note had been planted, and the alleged crime was nothing more than a signal that their lives were imperiled and that it was time to leave. Who had snitched on them this time? The family would never know.

A connection with the Catholic Church allowed Mrs. Vidal to get a visa for Bernie. Elena could remember going with her mother to the back of a church in Old Havana to retrieve the document. She never asked any questions as knowledge of the facts would have placed them in danger. That same summer, Bernie left for the United States "until matters settled." The die had been cast, and it was just a matter of time and opportunity before other members of the family would join him.

Elena's younger brother Davidsito had been an esquire with the Knights of Columbus, a secret religious society working side by side with the Catholic Church. The first Cuban chapter had been established early in the 1900s and by the time of the revolution, it had approximately thirty chapters throughout the country. Several of the knights were arrested when Castro took over, forcing the organization to disband in 1960 and secretly destroy all documents identifying its members. The Vidals still feared for Davidsito's safety, so anytime he was late for a meal, they thought the worst had happened.

By 1960, Castro had nationalized most privately owned businesses, including U.S. oil companies, banks, property, and any assets belonging to the Catholic Church. Despite the claims made by the United States against Cuba, sufficient compensation for the losses never took place. In retaliation, the United States canceled the remaining sugar quota. Castro turned to the USSR for help and obtained it. This decision prompted another wave of exiles. During the first two years of the revolution, a great number of well-educated Cubans left the country, including doctors and teachers. The exodus created a brain drain that forced Castro to prohibit certain age groups and professions from leaving Cuba. The close of the '60s witnessed the nationalization of all private enterprises, including street vendors.

It seemed that life was changing by the second, and not for the better. It scared Elena to think what would be next. She thought how terrible their lives had become, always looking over their shoulders, afraid that their private thoughts would be exposed. Roberto and Elena were leaving behind a life of fear, a life they once thought to be perfect.

ANDREA BERMÚDEZ

CHAPTER 15

En Route to Exile

All changes, even the most longed for, have their melancholy; for what we leave behind us is a part of ourselves; we must die to one life before we can enter another.

—Anatole France

I T DID NOT take long for August 20, 1960, to arrive. Everyone was pretending to be calm and upbeat. Attempts at humor were unsuccessful, as was making the effort to smile. Elena, Roberto, the Vidals, and Tata drove together to the airport, located nine miles southwest of Havana in Rancho Boyeros. The Medinas' big Chevy followed. It felt like an eternity of a car trip to all involved. Few attempts at conversation were made as each person was assessing the enormity of the moment.

The airport, authorized in the late 1920s, had frequent flights between Miami and Havana. The Tropicana Flights from Miami had been popular with U.S. tourists who enjoyed a weekend visit to the spectacular nightclub and casino, an open-air paradise surrounded by lush tropical gardens. A Compañía Cubana de Aviación turboprop aircraft would take Elena and Roberto to Fort Lauderdale. Previously, the airline had been privately owned by Cuban capital, but it had been taken over recently by the revolutionary government without compensation to its legitimate owners. That was the government's official definition of nationalization.

Rancho Boyeros Airport, renamed
José Martí International Airport, Havana, Cuba

Travel etiquette required dressing in one's Sunday best. Stewardesses, as they were called at the time, were thin, tall, young, also requirements. Smoking was permitted, and no seatbelts were available. These rules did not inspire confidence, but safety regulations were fewer and less stringent in those days. There had been three hijacking incidents in the recent past, one resulting in several fatalities and the loss of the aircraft. Despite the revolutionary leaders' apologies, those incidents added to everyone's apprehension.

At this time, governmental security required selecting two passengers by lottery to be fully searched. They were ordered to disrobe and suffered the humiliation of being inspected even in their most private areas. Luckily for Elena and Roberto, they were not the two chosen. Another anxious moment was going through customs where the officers made sure the travel requirements were in order (a total of sixty pounds of baggage weight, $5 USD, and an excused round-trip). Elena and Roberto were directed toward the aircraft, an indication that this part of the ordeal had concluded. Their sixty pounds of personal belongings had been further restricted by fifteen-pounder Duke, a beautiful Boston terrier belonging to Roberto's uncle who lived in Miami and sorely missed

ANDREA BERMÚDEZ

his dog. That was all Elena and Roberto had to start their new life: $5 USD, forty-five pounds of personal belongings, a fictitious honeymoon permit, and somebody else's dog! Quite an auspicious beginning for the young couple!

Looking out the small window of seat 9A, Elena could see the grim expressions of her loved ones. Tata could not even look at the plane. She was looking down and probably fighting the need to cry. That image would haunt Elena for the rest of her life. The Vidals were doing their best to remain calm, waving as if they could see their daughter waving back. It was good they could not see Elena's tears or her cheerless demeanor, hardly that of a honeymooner. Roberto was also consumed by the pain of the farewell but was trying to be a man and be his wife's strength. It was unfortunate that he could not admit his own feelings of loss at this moment. In Roberto's world, that would not have been acceptable. Men had to remain strong for the sake of their women. What a travesty to both of them!

Arrival at Fort Lauderdale International Airport was chaotic as family members and friends of the passengers noisily jostled one another to hug and welcome their kin to the new country. Tia Rosa, Dr. Vidal's younger sister, had volunteered to house the young couple until they found an apartment of their own. Duke would go home with his owner, Uncle Max, who was beaming with happiness at the sight of his dog. He had not seen Duke since he left Cuba on December 31, 1958. Uncle Max had worked for Batista as his chief of staff and had left Cuba with the Batistas on a military plane. Luckily, the Boston terrier did not need a passport as it would have connected him to the deposed regime!

Roberto had negotiated a job through a cousin who lived in Miami. It was to pay him $350 a month, and it was not clear to Elena what the job actually entailed. He also borrowed $600 from his generous uncle so they could get a car and rent a modest place to live. Working as a lawyer in the United States was not an option since Cuban civil law was based on the Napoleonic Code, as was common to parts of Europe and Latin America, while the United States' most powerful legal source was its constitution. This disparity resulted in a lack of reciprocity for Cuban attorneys to practice law in the United States.

The young Medinas stayed with Tia Rosa's family for two weeks before they found a livable efficiency apartment in southwest Miami. Just a month later in September 1960, they had the unexpected visit of Hurricane Donna. The door to their tiny apartment was ready to surrender to the swirling winds of the hurricane, a vicious living force bent on destruction.

Hurricane Donna, at times reaching category 5 strength, was one of the worst storms to hit South Florida. It left many deaths and billions of dollars in damages along its path, After the frightening experience, Elena and Roberto moved to a safer place within the same apartment complex. Memories of the 1944 hurricane in Cuba came to mind, and she wished her Papi were with her.

After the hurricane passed, the young Medinas were ready for their first investment, a two-tone 1950 Studebaker that they bought for $375. Their first adventure was driving to Key West in their nifty old car. What an incredible sight the Keys were! Elena remembered Islamorada with its beautiful purplish colors as she looked down while flying out of Cuba for the last time. She was in awe of the scenery as they travelled down the narrow road and crossed its forty-some bridges. With water on both sides of the Overseas Highway, she did not know where to look, the ocean side or the bay, afraid she would miss something worth seeing. The Keys had already played a part in her life. She had fond childhood memories of taking the Havana Ferry with Aunt Niní and her mom to go shopping in Miami. Those ninety miles separating Cuba and the United States seemed now interminably distant.

She felt cultural ties with Key West, a city that had played a part in Cuban history. Prior to becoming a Spanish settlement in the 1800s, the waters of Key West (*Cayo Hueso*) were often visited by Cuban fishermen. Key West had belonged to Spain until 1822, when a commodore of the U.S. Navy landed the USS *Shark* and planted an American flag claiming it as United States territory. By the end of the nineteenth century, a great number of residents were of Cuban lineage, and some had achieved political status. Several of Key West mayors were Cuban, including Carlos Manuel de Céspedes, son of the famous patriot of the same name. The elder Céspedes had been known as the father of the Cuban Republic, having led the first of its three wars of independence from Spain. José Martí was also among the several political figures that had made Key West home. He founded the Cuban Revolutionary Party in 1892 while in exile in that city. Elena was overjoyed to connect with Key West's shared roots and benefit from a visit to the legendary San Carlos Institute founded by Cuban political exiles in 1871 as an educational, civic, and political entity. It had been named La Casa Cuba by José Martí. This trip made her feel close to home, especially when she stood at Key West's southernmost point, indicating that Havana, 90 miles away, was closer to her now than Miami.

ANDREA BERMÚDEZ

The Southernmost Point, Key West

Roberto worked and travelled all the time. This gave Elena an opportunity to figure out the world surrounding her now. Although she had attended American schools all her life, her English was bookish, and the Miami culture felt alien. Her Aunt Rosa was her salvation. She lived in Coral Gables with her American husband and their two little girls. An accomplished musician and painter, she was the picture of stability. That was exactly what Elena was missing, a sense of balance and harmony in her life. One morning, after Roberto left for the day, Elena was stricken by a severe pain in her lower abdomen. While in Cuba, she had been a very healthy youngster who could always rely on immediate medical care from her dad. Unfortunately, he was not here now, and she knew she needed help. She tried to distract herself by walking to the post office, but as time passed, the pain was getting more acute. Since she did not have a phone, she knocked on the apartment manager's door to ask if she could use hers to call her aunt. Elena was doubled up in pain by now. To her astonishment, the manager told her that she could use the public phone in the lobby and closed the door in her face.

Elena was hurting too badly to recognize this experience as her first brush with racism. Having grown up white in Cuba, she had not experienced being the target of racial prejudice. Elena was taught by example that all humans had equal value as they were all children of God. She had loved her black Tata like a mother, so the idea of a superior race would not have crossed her mind. Elena realized at this instant that not everyone felt this way. The shoe was on the other foot, and by virtue of being in a different world, Elena had become a "lesser" human being. There was no room, however, for self-pity at the moment. She could be dying now and needed someone's help in a hurry.

It took Elena another hour to connect with her aunt who rushed her to Mercy Hospital in South Miami. By then, they had located Roberto who appeared by her side without delay. The hospital had provided a wheelchair but would not admit her unless they could advance two hundred dollars in cash. Roberto left at once to borrow the money and promptly returned with the required sum. At this time she could not think straight but later thought the name of the hospital, Mercy, was an ironic misnomer.

Elena had suffered a painful kidney stone, which surgery was unable to remove. She recalled waking up from the anesthesia and seeing a priest sprinkling holy water all over her, while a solemn looking nun held a lighted candle. As the priest said something like "may the Lord pardon thee for whatever faults thou has committed," Elena's eyes got big as saucers and she wondered if she had actually died. Later Elena was told that since she was a Catholic, the hospital chaplain had decided to administer the sacrament of Extreme unction, given usually to people in danger of dying.

When a very somber doctor appeared to tell her that one of her kidneys had stopped working and needed to be removed, Elena thought she had had enough. Her father had assured her on an earlier phone call that she was not suffering anything fatal, and that with time she would naturally pass the kidney stone. Without a word to the doctor, she stepped down from her bed, pulled out all the tubes, said thank you, and left the hospital against medical advice. Fortunately, she passed the stone the next day, and life was back to normal. At age nineteen, Elena was showing a glimmer of grit, an important trait she had inherited from both of her parents.

A month after the event, Elena and Roberto were getting ready for the Medinas' arrival in Miami. The young couple was busy with the preparations and had found a small furnished apartment for Roberto's parents close to shopping areas since neither one drove. During the end of 1960 and early 1961, those who wanted to leave Cuba could do so with nothing more than what they were wearing and a dime to make a phone call upon arriving in the United States. Elena and Roberto availed themselves of the benefits provided by the federal assistance refugee program and obtained basic food staples for the senior Medinas. This program was so successful that, a year later, it developed into the Cuban Refugee Center (*El Refugio*) established by the United States Department of Health, Education, and Welfare. The program helped thousands of Cuban exiles until its demise in 1994. Along with the federal assistance, there were many other nonprofit organizations, including churches of various denominations, ready to assist Cuban refugees, so Elena had made sure that her in-laws had what they needed for a fresh start in their new environment.

Roberto was glad to have his parents out of Cuba. His father had been a very successful trial attorney but had run into trouble because of his close ties to the Catholic Church. The Medinas had given shelter to a Jesuit priest accused of counterrevolutionary activities. The priest had been found hiding at the family home, which made the Medinas a target of constant militia harassment. They managed to leave Cuba without further trouble.

Elena's younger brother David was next in line to arrive. He had had difficulty getting the necessary permits but was finally able to leave. He was going to stay with Tía Rosa's family now that Elena and Roberto were on their own. Tía Rosa had told him that there was a community college nearby that he could eventually attend until he could figure out what to do with his life in exile. Elena had gone to get him at the airport, and both siblings were happy to see the other. They talked nonstop until their arrival at Tía Rosa's, and David seemed relieved to have made the trip without harassment from the Cuban airport officials. He told his sister that the Vidals were doing as well as possible back home and were planning with great anticipation their imminent trip to the United States.

In just a few days, David had found employment sacking groceries at a nearby shopping center. The Vidals were proud of hard work, and this job opportunity gave their youngest son a chance at saving some money for schooling. David started his English night classes next to improve what he had already learned at school in Cuba. He had proven himself to be quite helpful to Tía Rosa's family, doing odd jobs on the weekends, so she gave him an extra room they had over the garage and told him he could stay as long as he needed. With Tía Rosa's help and his own hard work, he was soon on his way to successfully adapting to life in exile.

David finally shared with Elena his frightening experience a month before he left. It happened that he was thrown in jail with a group of his friends without cause or explanation. They had been to a movie and had assembled in front of the theater. According to David, they were discussing the movie when the militia arrived and forced them into the back of a truck where two armed men held them at gunpoint. They stayed in prison for a week, not even allowed to contact their parents. The Vidals were in agony, once again not knowing what had happened to their son and fearing the worst. Fortunately for the boys, there had been a mistake on the part of the militia, and they were released to their parents. David said they all looked like goons when they returned home, with long unkempt hair and scruffy beards. Their clothes were wrinkled and seemed two sizes bigger than what was left of his already thin frame. He told Elena he had never been more scared in his life.

David's was not an uncommon happening as nonmilitary youth was seen by the government as a potential source of trouble. Bernie had had a similar experience except that he was let go after a couple of days. A week in hell was more than the family could take. The Vidals were now more than anxious to get Alex out of Cuba. Their plans to leave could not wait much longer.

Not too long after David had arrived in Miami, Elena received the devastating news that her Tata had passed away unexpectedly. She had been distraught with Elena's departure and had decided to join the young couple in Miami. Unfortunately, these plans were not to be realized. On an early morning of 1961, Mrs. Vidal found Tata slumped over her prayer book. A simple candle was lighted next to a small statue of La Virgen de la Caridad (Our Lady of Charity). As the candlelight became extinguished, so were the hopes for Elena and Tata to ever see each other again.

CHAPTER 16

The End of a Dream: The Bay of Pigs Invasion

One may know how to gain a victory, and know not how to use it.

—*Pedro Calderón de la Barca*

ROBERTO AND HIS cousin Amaro Rubio were leaving for the weekend "to take care of a job-related matter." Elena knew not to ask too many questions. She hated to feel not trusted, or even worse, she hated the possibility of Roberto lying to her. That weekend, however, was not to be. She received a late call that Roberto and Amaro had been involved in an accident, and that they were hospitalized for their injuries. Elena rushed to the hospital with Amaro's wife and was stunned to see Roberto in such bad shape. This event took place close to Christmastime 1960.

Elena was in a daze. She just stared at her husband and wondered if he was going to survive. She had no room to worry about herself. In his present condition, there was only room for him. Actually, this had been the case all along as he always came first.

Roberto opened his eyes and offered a tentative smile. She smiled back, not sure if she had looked reassuring or plainly terrified. Elena was a juvenile nineteen-year-old, ill-prepared to meet this kind of life head-on. She was beginning to relate to bad times as magnets that attract more bad times.

A doctor interrupted her despairing thoughts. "Are you Mrs. Vidal?" he asked, unconvinced that the young woman in front of him could be facing this level of responsibility. Elena nodded as the kind doctor proceeded to tell her that Roberto was going to be fine, and that the most serious injury was his three broken ribs. Roberto opened his eyes and greeted the doctor with a weak but steady voice. Aside from the pain he was enduring, he had been lucky. A few days stay for observation, and he would be good to go.

After the doctor left, Elena rushed to her husband's side. She had promised herself that there would be no tears, but they seemed to have a mind of their own. Between sobs, she was able to ask him how the accident had happened. Amaro had apparently dozed off and had lost control of the car. The next thing they both saw was a humongous tree and then darkness. Roberto, who had been in the passenger seat, was truly lucky to be telling the story. He could feel Elena's distress, so he decided to tell her the whole truth. Amaro was taking Roberto to visit a training camp in Homestead where their fellow counterrevolutionaries were training for a planned invasion of Cuba sometime during the next year. President Eisenhower had approved a program in early 1960 promising covert support through the State Department and the Central Intelligence Agency. The United States did not want to appear to be directly opposing the Castro government, so helping Cubans to defeat Castro was a more acceptable option.

By the end of 1959, Castro's regime had taken a dramatic turn to the left and was fast becoming a CIA concern. Two events added to the apprehension of the U.S. government: Castro's efforts to export the revolution to other Latin American countries and the escalating nationalization of banks and other privately owned businesses. Plans for a counterrevolution were already in place by exiles living in the United States and Mexico. Fire-starting bombs were being dropped in various places on the island during that time as a sign of a civil war about to begin. Castro accused the United States for these events and for the formal training of anti-Castro insurgents that had been taking place in the United States and in the Panama Canal since November 1960. The dictator was already making pronouncements in Cuba about the possibility of an invasion or war, which he promised would be fought "to the death."

Had it not been for the accident, Roberto would have joined the Homestead camp in two short weeks. In an unsuccessful attempt at light humor, Roberto indicated that the mishap could not have occurred at a more convenient time. Elena was unable to react. She was stunned. How come she had not known? Was he going to leave without word? Elena was too naive to take offense and too worried about their future to react appropriately.

Roberto felt the urge to come clean and explain to Elena the full extent of his political involvement. His actual job had been with the Cuban Revolutionary Democratic Front, which had relocated to Miami after being asked to leave Mexico. Known in Spanish as the Frente Revolucionario Democrático, they had been planning to participate in an invasion of Cuba through its military brigade. Roberto's "mysterious job" had to do with the extensive planning that had to precede the invasion. Now, Elena had been indirectly implicated with the counterrevolution, and she feared for her parents' safety in Cuba. It was too late, however, to worry about any possible damage having been done to them by her unknowing participation in Roberto's plans.

Throughout this time, Elena had maintained frequent phone communication with her parents. Her father was planning to leave by the end of 1961, soon to be followed by her mother and brother Alex. Elena and her parents had developed a sort of a code so they could talk with less fear of being monitored. They knew that phones were tapped, so they were still careful how they phrased their exchanges. The family chats had kept Elena informed of daily happenings in Cuba.

Meanwhile, Castro's appropriation of private enterprise —including manufacturers of textiles, sugar, perfume, and milk products— was progressing at a fast pace. Life in Cuba was all but calm. Fear and anxiety were taking over as bombs and other devices exploded in what used to be sacred grounds —the university, schools, parks, and churches— with civilians seriously hurt or killed as a result. Anti-Castro propaganda was being dropped in key areas of the country and transmitted from a powerful radio station on Swan Island in the western Caribbean. Castro, on the other hand, was warning the Cuban people that there were impending threats of an invasion. Life could not be taken for granted.

The relationship between the United States and Cuba had been progressively deteriorating in direct proportion to the extreme measures Castro's government was putting in place. In response to the constant threat to American interests in Cuba, the United States declared an economic embargo against Cuba in October 1960. Travel restrictions to the island followed. In January 1961, diplomatic relations were severed, and the U.S. Embassy in Cuba dismantled. Both Elena and Roberto worried about the impact of the antagonism between the countries on Elena's family.

While Roberto was recovering from the accident, the couple lived in a small one-bedroom apartment in an old section of southwest Miami.

They had found the place by looking in the classifieds and reading that it was located "in a quiet neighborhood." The apartment was clean, and yes, the neighborhood was quiet as one would expect from a well-kept large cemetery across the way. Elena was literally "learning on the job" as it related to her domestic responsibilities. She was not a very experienced cook, if she was even qualified to be called one. Elena had been doing her best not to let her husband starve, so she was slowly venturing into simple recipes that looked a bit more interesting. One Saturday, Elena felt like showing off and set a really nice table with fresh flowers and candlelight. She had followed religiously her Cuban cookbook to fix baked chicken. Roberto was pleasantly surprised and very complimentary of her efforts to create a beautiful table. He sat and took a first bite, which he thought was pretty tasty. "This is really good," he said with a smile and added, "Wow, and it is stuffed too." It was only then when Elena realized she had forgotten to remove the giblets. Somehow, the story made it to Cuba since her mother had mentioned the very infamous episode on their last communication.

By February of 1961, Roberto had fully recovered and was finally ready to leave again for his military duty. In his green fatigues and imposing black boots, he bade farewell to Elena and his parents. She would remember this day for the rest of her life. The invasion was their only hope of returning to the homeland. Brother Bernie had come back to Miami, having also volunteered to participate in the invasion as a physician. His orders to report to camp were a week away. Elena wanted to call her parents in Cuba so they could talk to Bernie as well. However, he could not bear to talk to his mother, knowing of the possibility that neither of them would return safely. Elena talked to her parents briefly but did not share with them what was really happening with their lives. The parents asked about Bernie, and Elena assured them that he was fine. When she hung up, she realized the immensity of their anguish. It broke Elena's heart to hear trepidation in her mother's voice.

After Roberto's departure, Elena's top priority was to get a driver's license. She was a pretty good driver, but she did not want to run the risk of being stopped without a permit. The next day, she would drive herself to the DMV in her old Studebaker and take her driving test. Regrettably, she flunked and was told she could not take the test again for several days. She still had to drive home, and if she got caught, she'd be in a heap of trouble. More trouble she did not need. After she convinced herself it was safe to drive the getaway car, she went home. For three days, she drove everywhere

ANDREA BERMÚDEZ

in her much-loved car, which for now was her best companion. Fortunately for Elena, she went back for her driving test as soon as it was allowed, and this time, she passed without a glitch.

The young woman had been taught to drive by her father. She had relished the lessons as it afforded her time to be with him and learn about his life. Elena admired her father's glass-half-full attitude about everything. Dr. Vidal had had his share of grief, but he would always tell Elena, "If you fall from a horse, get back on it and ride forward." It was a valuable message Elena would never forget.

The first week after Roberto left was tolerable although she worried constantly about her loved ones. She had managed to take care of her affairs without the help of anyone but was getting lonesome and a bit apprehensive. This was the first time in her life that Elena had been by herself. Her in-laws invited her to stay with them, and although she did not like them that much, she agreed.

The senior Medinas were very set in their ways. Elena's mother-in-law doted on her children, particularly her only daughter, a Sacred Heart nun, and Roberto, the youngest. Exceedingly religious, they saw the world exclusively through that lens. Elena dreaded conversations about sin and salvation at dinnertime and could not comprehend the narrowness of their thinking. Many times Elena wondered how they could be right in believing that the promised reward was for the "chosen few," undoubtedly those like themselves, while most others were cast at the doors of hell. The idea of a heaven full of people like the older Medinas was not very appealing to Elena. As expected, Mrs. Medina tried in vain to instill her ultraconservative views about marriage in her young daughter-in-law. One bit of advice, in particular, made Elena cringe: "Remember that husbands are always right." She would also refer to her in-laws' views as "*religión mal entendida.*"

Elena was coming from a lineage of very independent women who would not have adhered to such demeaning messages. Her Aunt Olga had married Tío Juan, a very straightlaced engineer who disapproved of her leaving the house while he was at work. She had been known to get lonesome and go visit her parents. In trying to keep her from doing that, Tío Juan put a lock on their armoire to prevent her from leaving. Tia Olga wasn't about to let him have his way, so she took an ax and demolished the piece of furniture. Surely he noticed but was smart enough to never mention the incident again. A part of him had to admire Tía Olga for her doggedness. The pair went on to celebrate their sixtieth wedding anniversary before he passed away at age ninety-one.

It helped that Elena was not paying attention to rumors about the impending invasion of Cuba. One of them described how El Encanto, one of Havana's favorite department stores, had burned to the ground in an intentional fire. Elena was anxious enough as it was and did not need the added concern. She was constantly thinking about Roberto and Bernie and wishing with all her heart that they would return unharmed. Elena also worried about some of her friends who had been part of the exile brigade: Amaro, Alberto, José Ignacio, and a host of others. "How sad," she thought, "that Cubans are killing one another for the fanatical dreams of one man."

On April 20, her father-in-law had asked her to drive him to the post office. There was so much apprehension in the air, but neither one was letting the other one know. Mr. Medina had been reading the papers and listening to the radio, so he knew the latest, and the news was not good. Elena preferred not to know, so they turned their nervousness into an innocuous conversation that did not hide their uneasiness. When they returned home, Elena could not believe her eyes. Both Bernie and Roberto were standing right in front of her in their green fatigues. After all the training and anxious wait, their operations had been cancelled, so they never left Miami. Bay of Pigs had failed. Elena wanted to know everything now. While she was happy Bernie and Roberto were safe, she was saddened by the knowledge that others had not been as fortunate.

Before hearing the details of the doomed invasion, they called the Vidals in Cuba. Elena's mother was so emotional she could barely talk. Two days before, a picture of a dead rebel had been published in the Cuban newspaper *Granma*, and she had thought he looked like Bernie. She did not say anything to her husband who had had the same reaction to the photograph. They had both mourned a death that, fortunately for them, never came to pass.

As Bernie and Roberto told the story, Elena was saying a silent prayer for her fellow countrymen. According to Roberto, the original invasion plan had included attacks from land and air to seize a beachhead and install a provisional government that would be recognized by the United States at a later time. The expectation was to have a general uprising following the landing. By the time the invasion was underway, the use of air cover and airstrikes had been stopped by President Kennedy, following the advice of some of his most trusted advisers. The exiles had been sent to their deaths.

Adding to the ill-fated decision, the Communist Intelligence Service had located the site for the invasion, *Bahia de Cochinos* (Bay of Pigs) in southern Cuba. Castro declared a state of alert for the country, and his forces were ready and waiting for the insurrectionists. Earlier, the government had imprisoned thousands of suspected counterrevolutionaries so that the internal support to the invasion would be cut off. Prisons, fortresses, and even a sports arena were bursting at the seams with hostages. On April 17, 1961, the invasion landed in Playa de Girón in the Bay of Pigs. In three days, the exile forces had been defeated by a better-equipped Castro army.

Playa Girón in the Bay of Pigs, its beauty
belies the tragic events of 1961

Over one thousand combatants were captured and close to a hundred lost their lives in battle. Some escaped into the mountains and the swamp along the coast. They had no place to go. Amaro had been captured near the Zapata swamp on the western side of the bay with several of his men and sent to prison. By September of that year, negotiations to free the Bay of Pigs prisoners commenced, and in December 1962, Castro and the United States reached an agreement. The prisoners were released to United States custody on December 23, 1962. In return, Cuba received millions of dollars in food and medicines.

Historical events have a human connection for those who lived through it. The story of Celia and Alfredo was for Elena the human face of the Bay of Pigs tragedy. Elena had reconnected with Celia, her college friend from Cuba, who had disappeared two years before in the middle of the night with her husband Alfredo. They had been part of clandestine movements that had fought against the governments of both dictators, Batista and Castro. Celia and Alfredo's ten years of marriage had been spent in hiding, most of the time in danger of being captured, or of losing their lives. Now one was gone. Elena knew that Celia had visited Cuba to learn as much as possible about her husband's death, but it took several years for Celia to be able to share the details of her incredible saga.

Alfredo and his comrades aboard the *Houston* never reached shore after having to abandon ship in the area of *Traviesa* Cay. Three men, Alfredo, a man who had been Elena's schoolmate, and one other stayed together for the first few hours planning to swim through the countless cays and inlets of the archipelago until reaching shore. Without water or supplies their fate was sealed. The first day Elena's schoolmate disappeared. Alfredo and the other man continued swimming, trying to make it to land. During the long struggle Alfredo succumbed to dehydration. The remains of the six-foot-four star athlete were found by a fisherman who brought his body to shore. In Miami, Celia had heard that Alfredo was alive in prison, so she immediately decided to return to Cuba so she could be with him. Without a word to anyone, she made quick preparations and left, only calling her parents from the airport to let them know what was happening. She had arranged to stay with a friend's aunt whom Celia did not know. She was hoping that the note she was carrying from her friend would secure a place to stay.

She arrived in Cuba and, fortunately, ran into an old friend of the family at the airport who felt compelled to help her. He first drove her to the place where Celia was supposed to stay. Before Celia could show the woman the note she was carrying, the door had been slammed in her face . . . . In Celia's style, the experience was not about to deter her. At this point the regrettable incident was unimportant. Celia's family friend offered to take her to his two widowed aunts who would be able to house her for a couple of days. The next day, Celia and the family friend marched to the prison with hopes of seeing Alfredo. The place was a mob of anxious relatives waiting for their loved ones. The officials started calling out last names but never got to Alfredo's.

By the end of the day, the news of his death had reached Celia. The fisherman who had found Alfredo's body had come forward and wanted to see her. The experience tore Celia's heart, but she felt it had been necessary.

ANDREA BERMÚDEZ

She was able to identify her husband and see to it that he receive a proper burial. The fisherman also gave Celia the ring and watch Alfredo had been wearing when his remains were found. The fact that she was able to accomplish this much without risking her own safety was remarkable. At the airport when she was returning to the U.S., the immigration official looked at her papers, and in a commanding tone said to her: "*Señora,* you go, but the watch and the ring stay." Celia, a very dignified lady in the fullest sense of the word, faced the man and with the sweetest whisper responded "You will have to kill me." She had given the man two options; either a scene that would make him look bad or to let her go without further harassment. He chose well. Celia had risked her life to make certain that Alfredo's remains would be treated with the dignity a hero deserved. Her courage and strength of character had not abandoned her at this difficult time. Celia had lost her soul mate, but not her soul.

The Bay of Pigs fiasco brought about the end of an era. Hopes for a return to Cuba had been shattered creating the need to turn exile into a way of life. Elena was feeling envious of the ability animals have to adapt to their environment with apparent ease. "Migrations in nature follow instinct," she thought, "and the survival of a species is disaffected by bureaucracy or war. Unfortunately, human migrations are strenuous, and problematic struggles that work against survival." Rather than an easily reached American dream, exile was to be a hard-fought battle to adapt and live on.

PART V

In Search of a Homeland

CHAPTER 17

Life after Bay of Pigs

Nobody can go back and start a new beginning, but anyone can start today and make a new ending.

—*Maria Robinson*

THE REALIZATION THAT there would be no return to the homeland was difficult to fathom. Elena and Roberto had emotionally kept their bags packed so that they could deal with the separation from family and friends as a temporary experience. The life they had expected to be a short-term episode had been extended indefinitely by the Bay of Pigs disaster.

Roberto found employment with Yellow Cab as a taxi driver while a friend of Elena's found her a job as girl Friday in the warehouse office of a boutique chain. She was so proud of herself making $33.70 a week. The job required her to answer the phone at times, which was the bigger challenge as her English skills were not quite as sophisticated as those of a native speaker. "Good morning, Morris Levy Stores" sounded like an easy task, but adding anxiety to the experience made it quite cumbersome for Elena. She recalled an incident when someone wanted to talk to Mr. Levy who had passed away several years before. Elena thought that saying, "He is dead," was not appropriate, so she was trying to locate a softer expression. She thought she had found it when she responded, "He passed out." The silence on the other end of the line puzzled Elena until a coworker slipped her a note saying, "Passed away."

Driving a taxi in Miami was no small feat for Roberto. The city had been built in a grid system, which felt more like a complicated maze to a newcomer. Life got easier when Roberto finally figured out that Flagler Street divided the North and South quadrants of the city while Miami Avenue, the east and west. The young Medinas were doing better financially, and with the help of frequent generous tips, he was soon able to support the family. By July 1961, Elena was expecting their first child. She had been taught that a marriage was not complete without children, and the delay in getting pregnant had been obsessing her. Elena and Roberto were thrilled when the pregnancy test resulted positive. She was planning to work until early February since the due date for the baby's arrival was early March.

Bernardo Vidal had been trying to leave Cuba for weeks, but physicians were prevented from receiving governmental authorization to do so. Once again, his wife Sara's ingenuity and gutsy spirit allowed her to secure a passport identifying Dr. Vidal as a businessman. There was a frightening instant at the airport when they saw that the immigration official checking passports was a former patient. Luckily, the uniformed officer inspected the passport and, without looking at Bernardo, signaled him to go on. When he arrived in Miami, Elena and her father had not seen each other for a year; their embrace spoke volumes.

Her father looked thinner, but as usual, he was in great spirits. Elena thought, "This man never lets anything get to him. I want to know his secret." Her apartment was too small, so Bernardo would be staying at his brother's home. He informed Elena that Alex had run into a bit of trouble with the militia when they came for the nth time to search the premises. Her brother had had a screaming fit, accusing the militia of a number of offenses. The family had been lucky that the man in charge could see through Alex's emotional state and made a gesture for the others to ignore the outburst. Mama Vidal was concerned for his safety and had decided to stay behind until he was able to leave. By this time, future travelers had to request a number and wait until called to receive authorization to depart. Sara's and Alex's opportunity to leave the country was still a few months ahead.

While in Miami, Dr. Vidal would walk to his review lessons for the medical foreign board eligibility exam. He spoke broken English, but he had stayed up to date in his field, reading medical texts written in English. Familiar with the terminology, he aced the exam when the opportunity to take it finally came. Once able to practice general medicine, he agreed to a job at the Western State Hospital in Staunton, Virginia, where Bernie had worked until accepted to do his urology residency in Georgia. The hospital had been known in its early times as the Western State Lunatic Asylum, and Dr. Vidal was to be a general practitioner working alongside psychiatrists to treat the resident patients.

Travel restrictions to leave Cuba became progressively stricter. By the time Sara's and Alex's number was approved, she was forced to transfer their home and valuables to the authorities. The government required an inventory detailing the house contents with each item accounted for. Despite this mandate, Sara decided that since she was going to lose it all, she might as well give away her treasures to loved ones and replace them with less valuable objects. She was lucky to get out of this situation with her life as those caught doing what she successfully did had suffered serious repercussions. In January 1962, Sara and Alex finally got the call allowing them to leave the country. They arrived at Fort Lauderdale International Airport in late January. Seeing Elena quite pregnant for the first time, her mother could not stop crying. After a couple of days, Sara and Alex joined Bernardo in Staunton.

By the end of February, Sara was back in Miami for the birth of her first grandchild, Roberto Fabián Medina y Vidal. Mother and baby were fine, ready to get home as soon as possible and start a new life. It seemed that little Bobby had brought the Medinas' good fortune. Roberto had received a large tip after driving a highly intoxicated man all over Miami. Fortunately, one of the stops included his caretaker-sister whose generosity had helped pay for Elena and Bobby's hospital stay. After their return home, Sara was learning how to take care of a baby all over again. Things had changed so much since her last child, and a grandchild, after all, was quite a different experience. She often panicked at any minor discomfort the baby would show but was loving and patient when Bobby would wake up in the middle of the night. The family was on top of the world with Bobby, albeit too busy to include the outside world into theirs.

Time and history, however, continued its unstoppable march. Between 1961 and 1962, Operation Peter Pan had been organized in Miami to bring children out of Cuba. The United States State Department, the Miami Catholic Archdiocese, and some Cuban exiles collaborated in an effort responsible for the exodus to the United States of approximately 14,000 unaccompanied minors from all parts of Cuba between the ages of six and sixteen. Affectionately known as the *Pedro Panes*, the children became the responsibility of either the Catholic Welfare Bureau or of relatives already in the United States. The bureau often placed the children in foster homes or orphanages spread throughout several states until their parents could join them. Many of the *Pedro Panes* suffered irreversible trauma from the separation, particularly those without the benefit of speaking English or understanding the U.S. culture. Sometimes, it took five to six years for the children to be reunited with their parents. Some did not recognize one another and had to begin the process of getting reacquainted. Pilar's six nieces and nephews were early *Pedro Panes*. The eldest niece, aged twelve, held the little family together, and they were fortunate to have stayed at the home of a retired Cuban physician and his wife who had had a large family but were then empty nesters. Luckily, their parents were able to join them a year later, and the kids claimed to have two wonderful sets of parents.

The project became the target of a great deal of controversy, both in Cuba and in the exile community. To some, the operation was another aggressive move by the United States to spread fear. To others, it meant sparing the children from indoctrination. No one will know with certainty what motivated the project as documents relating to it have remained classified. By 1962, direct flights between the United States and Cuba were suspended, which made it difficult for some of the parents to ever rejoin their children

In a seemingly parallel world, Elena and Roberto were dealing with their own personal challenges. The Vidals had invited the young family to move in with them in Staunton, Virginia, so that Roberto could go back to school and retrain. Bobby was six weeks old, and Elena was thrilled with the invitation. She had sorely missed her parents during their time of separation, and now she had the chance to make up for lost time. The Vidals were generous people, and they insisted on supporting the young family until Roberto found another job. Elena and Bobby arrived at the Shenandoah Valley Regional Airport onboard an Allegheny Airlines prop aircraft that carried only the two of them as passengers. Roberto followed a month later.

Sara was being taught by Bobby how to care for a small child. He became the center of his grandparents' life. If Bobby cried at night, Dr. Vidal would pick him up and, in his off-key bass voice, sing to him the same lullabies he used to sing to Elena. Life in Staunton was enjoyable. The Vidals lived on the lush grounds of the Western State Hospital, which housed several medical families, most of them from Cuba. Close-knit friendships with these families helped alleviate their distress over vanishing memories of Cuba.

ANDREA BERMÚDEZ

The Vidals' home in the grounds of the
Western State Hospital, Staunton, Virginia

The Vidal home was large and easily accommodated Elena and her family. Mama Sara was proving to be a great cook. She surprised everyone, including herself, with new creations. Her recipes were one of a kind as she never quite remembered what she had done before. Once during lunchtime, she served a chocolate pudding dessert she had concocted. Bernardo tasted it, and before he could say anything, his expression gave him away. Alex tried it and was a better actor. Sara took offense at the unspoken criticism, brusquely grabbed the dessert, and disappeared into the kitchen. Everyone was thankful, but the expression of appreciation did not have a genuine ring. In her rush, Sara had forgotten to add sugar to her infamous invention. That evening, the dessert came back covered this time with a layer of meringue. When Bernardo asked what the fancy creation was, she casually responded, "Snowy Mountain." The family laughed at her cleverness and proceeded to consume the dessert with great gusto.

A call from Roberto's brother gave him the chance of a summer job in Toledo, Ohio, as a milkman. Elena was pleased to have an income to tide them over. In the fall semester, Roberto would start his contract with the Staunton Military Academy as a Spanish instructor. His annual salary of $3,700 seemed adequate for the times. The summer, however, turned into a nightmare living in a small home with the brother's big family and the parents-in-law. Roberto had to have a very early start in the morning, which meant Elena and Bobby were up early as well. Her morning duties included fixing Roberto's breakfast, packing his lunch, and keeping the baby quiet so he would not wake up the cranky grandfather. Toward the end of the summer adventure, she had had it with expectations of male superiority in a marriage. Elena was hoping that she had married the best one in the Medina lot, wishing the "I-come-first" genes had skipped Roberto. She was happy to be back home in Staunton with her parents. The Vidals were so different as they did not believe in meddling, or in giving uncompromising advice with the expectation that it would be followed.

In the meantime, after the failed Bay of Pigs invasion, the United States received an ultimatum from Castro that any further act of aggression would be met with the equivalent of a world war. It would have been a case of the mouse that roared if Castro had not had the support of the USSR at the time. In August 1962, the CIA director communicated to President Kennedy his suspicions that Soviet medium-range ballistic missiles were ready for deployment from Cuba. By the middle of October, the United States ordered surveillance flights over Cuba collecting aerial photographs of objects resembling the shape of intermediate-range missiles. President Kennedy and his advisors came to the conclusion that indeed Cuba had missile installations ready to attack the United States and demanded that the missiles be dismantled and removed. A United States-led naval blockade ensued and a nuclear World War III was feared as the relationship between Russia and the United States became even more strained than it had already been during the cold war. Kennedy and Khrushchev finally negotiated removing the missiles provided that the United States would not invade Cuba and would dismantle its own missile installations in Turkey. On October 28, the Russian president announced that the missiles would be removed, postponing the threat of a nuclear catastrophe. A *Washington Post* headline in 1962 described the crisis as "Reliving the World's Most Dangerous Days."

During this time, Bernie and his wife lived in Georgia while he worked on his urology residency. He had married Patricia Morales after he returned from the Bay of Pigs fiasco. Patricia's uncle had been associated with the Batista government, so the whole family had fled to the United States in the early part of 1959. She was about to give birth to their first baby, and the junior Vidals needed help. Bernie worked late hours at the hospital and had become apprehensive thinking of Patricia being alone during the last critical weeks of her pregnancy. She had a very good relationship with her in-laws, so it was only natural that they would invite Patricia to stay with them. Her regular obstetrician had arranged for her to have the baby in Staunton.

Bernie took a leave of absence from the hospital during the last week of the pregnancy and joined his parents who were ecstatic at the thought of another grandbaby. With so many guests in the home, the Staunton house acquired a wild atmosphere. Bernie wanted to show off his recently attained domestic skills and volunteered to do the dishes. For that purpose, he made sure the blinds were closed so no outsider could see him in the act of doing what he considered a woman's job. The opportunity to learn that domestic responsibility did not have a gender requirement came soon, when changing diapers would be a familiar activity for Bernie. Baby Bernardo Justo Ramón Vidal y Morales, BJ for short, was born January 3, 1963. He was Staunton's first baby of the year, and his picture graced the front page of the daily newspaper. A month later, Patricia and BJ left to join Bernie in Atlanta.

By now, Elena was expecting baby number 2. Three days before the baby's due date, a car hit the Medinas' while making an illegal left turn. Immediately, there was an ambulance on the scene, and the paramedics were insisting on loading the very pregnant Elena, but she was fine and so were all the passengers. On October 29, Andrea, a beautiful and healthy baby, was born at the King's Daughter's Hospital in Staunton.

These were difficult times for the United States. In November 1963, the country was thrown into a tailspin with President Kennedy's assassination in Dallas while riding in a presidential motorcade. Shots fired from the Texas Book Depository were traced to Lee Harvey Oswald, an employee in the building. Kennedy was rushed to Parkland Hospital where he was pronounced dead. The next day, and before going to trial, Oswald was murdered on national television. The memory of Lyndon Johnson swearing in as the next president of the United States, with a grieving Mrs. Kennedy by his side, was etched in the hearts of those who lived through those tragic times.

Declassified documents showed that Kennedy had wanted to initiate a secret dialogue with Castro. The president thought that this approach would have more potential for success than all the failed covert operations of the past, but his assassination derailed the opportunity of improved relations with Cuba. Many conspiracy theories regarding the president's death have been argued through the years, some involving Castro and the mafia.

Roberto had been at his new post as high school instructor for a couple of months and seemed to be enjoying the experience. With over a hundred years of history, Staunton Military Academy had a place of honor in the community. An all-male institution, SMA had earned a reputation for its academic rigor and discipline. Elena enjoyed attending football games with Captain Medina, his school-assigned rank, and little Bobby. Learning football rules and trying to follow the games served as the first lessons in acculturating to an American way of life. Connecting with a culture required not only mastering the language but sharing experiences, preferences, and dislikes with others. Attending football games was one of these experiences. Understanding and liking it would have to be a later step. Roberto's students and colleagues embraced her, and that made it easier for Elena to start making friendships and learning the rules of her newfound world. One time, while chaperoning a school dance being aired by radio, the DJ asked her what her favorite song would be. Without hesitation, Elena responded, "This Magic Moment." When played, it was dedicated to her, which provoked a lot of attention from the audience. They probably thought she was not that different after all. At any rate, the incident endeared her to students and fellow faculty alike, giving Elena one of the first feelings of belonging.

Dr. Vidal was intent on helping his children attain their interrupted educations. By now, Alex was commuting to the University of Virginia to complete a master's degree in literature, and he felt Roberto had the potential to advance as well. After he had his first year of teaching under his belt, Roberto decided to work on his next degree. He liked literature as well, so the next semester, he followed in his brother-in-law's footsteps. Driving to Charlottesville after a full day's work was challenging, but he managed well by mixing correspondence courses with actual attendance.

To accommodate their growing family, the young couple had found a modest home on Cole Avenue and was in the process of moving. Elena continued to raise her toddlers as well as take care of her new pregnancy. Her fears of not being able to be a mother were being rapidly dispelled. Two weeks before Andrea turned one, Joey was born. Her mother-in-law came to help with the baby while Elena was trying to figure out how to care for three children under three years old by herself. Elena's mother-in-law had tremendous innate skills to deal with young children, so Elena was grateful when she would come from Miami to help. Her father-in-law was a different story as he would frequently call his wife during those visits to complain about her not being there to do his bidding. Elena thought about the double standard of his repeated indoctrination: "Catholics must have all the children God intended them to have." She figured he meant: "As long as the husband is not inconvenienced."

Disillusioned with the hypocrisy of the religious principles she had dutifully followed, Elena confronted her husband and suggested that Joey be their last child. She also had plans for her education in the future, and she wanted to give her three children the best care she could. Elena felt that this was her decision alone since all the responsibility of the children and the home rested with her. After all, Roberto had never changed a diaper or awakened at night when the children were sick or hungry. To her chagrin, Roberto disagreed, reminding her of her duty as a Catholic wife. Elena was stunned. "Was Roberto really the best of the pack or just like the rest of them?"

Dr. Vidal had been given reciprocity by the state of Maryland, and he was planning to eventually go into private practice there. He accepted a job at the Eastern State Hospital in Cambridge, Maryland, that would allow him to earn his way into private practice. Sara stayed behind to complete her teaching job at Riverheads High School. She was eager to join her husband, but the district could not find another Spanish teacher to complete the academic year. After conferring with the Medinas and getting their approval, Sara suggested to her principal that maybe Elena could finish the year on an emergency basis. She had found a very responsible woman to help her with her toddlers, so when offered the job, she accepted.

Elena was developing new skills on the job but found she had a natural knack for teaching and became readily accepted by her not-always-well-behaved students. She was getting a taste of life on her own. Although called Señora Medina, she was beginning to be recognized on her own merit, and not because she was somebody's wife or daughter. She was a person in her own right, and she very much liked that.

A faculty talent show was being planned, and Elena volunteered to join her colleagues lip-synching a famous tune by the Beatles. She recalled her previous success in elementary school dubbing Al Jolson, so she knew she could do it again. Elena was in character and gave McCartney a run for his money. Her students loved it, and her picture shaking her wig while swinging her guitar made it into the high school yearbook.

At the end of the semester, a representative from the school district came to thank Elena for her outstanding job of replacing her mother and complimented her on her teaching abilities. He told her that unfortunately the district could not rehire her without credentials but offered her a full scholarship at Mary Baldwin College to pursue a degree. How could she decline her family's ticket to a better future? Elena knew it was not a good idea to accept the offer on the spot and promised to call back with an answer as soon as she discussed the matter with her husband. However, she had already decided in her mind that she would not let this opportunity pass by. After all, chances like this should not be missed.

ANDREA BERMÚDEZ

CHAPTER 18

A Taste of Freedom

Life comes with no guarantees, no time-outs, no second chances. You just have to live life to the fullest.

—Unknown

L EAVING CASTRO'S CUBA had only been the beginning in the exiles' search for freedom. Coming from the perspective that humans are powerless to change the prearranged course of their lives did not provide Elena with the skills to question or reevaluate her destiny. If all a person's history and actions had already been predestined by fate, Elena thought that there was little people could do to improve or transform their lives. However, she was starting to challenge the "que será será" attitude as self-determination was becoming a more appealing alternative.

Mary Baldwin College offered Elena an additional opportunity she wasn't aware she needed. Up until this point, she had been a pawn, following Roberto's decision making and spending most of her hours in domestic endeavors. She had not realized she was dying inside, and attending college was just the experience she needed to be revived.

Without Roberto's help at home, she was quite busy adding a study schedule to her life. Roberto had never been exposed to a home in which both parents shared domestic responsibilities. Medina Senior was in the habit of barking orders, which his wife was always willing to follow. Roberto had grown accustomed to this pattern of behavior and did not see any wrongdoing. Changing diapers and waking up in the middle of the night were still Elena's duty even if she had a final exam the next morning.

Elena loved her kids. It was a mutual admiration society. They were little, so she felt that they would not be traumatized by sharing their time with her studies. "Someday," she would say to herself, "they will appreciate what I am doing now." This thought gave her the courage she needed at times not to give up her efforts. Elena was able to take a full-load of courses and even managed to make a few good grades. She was really enjoying the experience although she was exhausted most of the time. In the interim, her husband had finished his master's studies and had gotten a head start on his PhD.

Roberto received an offer at Randolph-Macon Woman's College for the next year, which meant a better opportunity for the family, but it also meant a move to Lynchburg, Virginia. Elena was concerned about her studies but was soon relieved to know that she would receive a full scholarship in addition to a complete transfer of the credits she had earned. It was hard to say good-bye to her many Mary Baldwin friends. She was especially grateful to Dr. Martha Grafton, dean of students, for guiding her through the stumbling blocks she had faced. Elena thought how incredibly wise the dean had been in her advice and counseling. Frequently, she would visit Dr. Grafton to tell her that she was dropping out only to leave her office with a more compatible schedule that allowed Elena to stay in school. The Mary Baldwin experience had been the perfect tutor for future success in schooling. "Life is a series of good-byes, and I am not good at it," she told Dr. Grafton when she went to thank her. "I will never forget what you and this college have done to restore my confidence."

Lynchburg, the land of the seven hills, is a beautiful city south of the James River with rich historical credentials. Founded as the town of Lynch Ferry at the end of the American Revolution, it became incorporated as a city with its current name in 1852. Colonial mansions edged Rivermont Avenue where the Medinas were to establish residence. They moved into a two-story home that had been partitioned into two apartments. Dr. Jones, a professor in the English department, lived upstairs, and the Medina family in the three-bedroom first floor. The home belonged to the college and had been donated by a wealthy alumna, so although old, it had all the modern conveniences. Elena enrolled Bobby in kindergarten at Villa Maria Academy and found a nursery school for Andrea and Joey at Rivermont Avenue Baptist Church. Dr. Vidal was footing the bill, and he wanted the best schooling for their grandchildren. He was not too sure about a Baptist education but figured the kids were too young to be influenced by unwelcome ideas about religion. Elena spent the summer making arrangements for the beginning of the school year for the entire family.

Roberto was to commute to Charlottesville and continue work on his doctorate at the University of Virginia. Everything seemed to be in place for the little family, and Elena felt her life was improving. She was looking forward to her new college experience at Randolph-Macon Woman's College, another top-notch school for women. Founded in late 1893, it had been the first accredited college to educate elite Southern women. From its beginning, it was classified as Division A, at par with Smith and Vassar. Elena was eager and ready to meet the new challenge.

The Vidals were only seven hours away on the eastern shore of Maryland where Dr. Vidal had established his private practice in Hurlock. Weekend trips to see them would be possible in their newly purchased red and white Volkswagen bus. The thought of being near her parents would have been sufficient for Elena to agree to the move, but with the added opportunities for the future of her family, the move was a no-brainer.

At first, Elena felt the gulf between her and her classmates; they all seemed to be rich, single, and quite a few years younger. However, she found nothing but acceptance and a minor degree of notoriety since, after all, she was the wife of Professor Medina. Despite her challenging studies, she was acing her courses. Elena could not sew, but with the help of easy patterns, she had been able to make a few school outfits to avoid looking like Cinderella. She had to ignore the labels that surrounded her and learn the value of being herself without the help of much adornment. Roberto was well-liked by his students, so their time in Lynchburg was mostly undisturbed.

Being two years old when they moved to Lynchburg, Joey was then "a man of few words." Spanish was the language of the home, but it was rapidly becoming a bilingual environment with Bobby attending kindergarten and learning English at the speed of light. On one occasion, Elena heard a loud crash in the living room, only to see the TV on the floor and Bobby pointing at his younger brother. Joey looked pained while managing to point back at Bobby, saying very clearly, "But Bobby pushed." Between cartoons and their brother, the children were making a swift transition to English. On another occasion, Elena had taken Joey on an errand and ran into a curb. She looked back feeling lucky that it was Joey with her and not Bobby or Andrea who would have ratted on her. To her surprise, as soon as they got home, he ran to his dad and, using his hands for emphasis, told him, "Mami went boom boom." With Joey's information, Roberto could tell Elena had run into something.

It was amazing to Elena to watch the ease with which children learned a language. She thought it was a function of their lack of inhibitions since adults were more concerned about social propriety and apprehensive about making grammatical errors. "If adults could only take risks like children do, they would learn the second language at a faster rate," she would tell her father who always hesitated when speaking English.

Her parents-in-law soon moved to an apartment nearby to be close to the children. At first, Elena welcomed the idea, thinking that they might lend a hand, but soon found out that neither in-law was supportive of her pursuing an education. As a matter of fact, they were downright critical. "Women do not need an education," the elder Medina would say. "They only need to be good wives and mothers." Elena was not about to make an issue of the matter and ultimately decided to write it off as a difference of opinion. It was getting to be beneath her to acknowledge the offense.

There was one more thing wrong with their lives in Lynchburg. It was a great place, but it really did not feel like home. Elena and Roberto were constantly invited as guest speakers at various churches and other organizations to discuss life under communism, a constant reminder that they were outsiders. There was even an article in the daily paper entitled "Cuban Refugees Flee Communism," touting their valor in escaping Cuba and making a life that included their pursuit of higher education. The picture accompanying the article showed Elena, Roberto, and the three smiling children. It was the picture of total bliss, or was it?

The two years spent in Lynchburg went very fast, and soon it would be time for Elena's graduation from college and Bobby's from kindergarten. Elena could not decide which of the two excited her most, the completion of her baccalaureate studies or little Bobby's beginning of his own educational journey. On a Saturday, while sitting on her porch preparing for her comprehensive exams and babysitting her children, a car passed by blowing the horn. It was Roberto taking his parents for a ride to the country. "Why didn't they take the children?" she wondered, beginning to feel angry at their lack of sensitivity but more determined than ever to follow her dream despite the lack of support.

Bobby's kindergarten graduation ceremony came the weekend before Elena's. Dr. and Mrs. Vidal were present, and so were the Medinas. Everyone was beaming with pride at the sight of Bobby in his white cap and gown. One would have thought it was a PhD graduation from the excitement shown by the two families. The Vidals stayed the week to be able to attend their daughter's graduation. The day came and Elena could not stop smiling. She and her kids had made it. She felt the children had been a part of her dwindling support system. They had managed not to get sick or have any childhood-related accident, which would have prevented her from achieving the first leg of her educational plans. Whatever today meant, the children knew it was important, and they seemed proud of their mother. Mrs. Vidal had bought them beautiful clothes to wear on that special day. The boys in coats and ties, and Andrea dressed as if she were a flower girl. She was a beautiful child, and being the middle child and the only girl, she was the peacemaker. That day her job was made easy; all three were on their best behavior.

The ceremony went on forever, but to Elena, it did not go long enough. She was hanging on to the first moment in her life when she had achieved something important on her own. To top it, she graduated cum laude with special honors in Spanish, so on this day, she felt the sky was the limit. After the ceremony, congratulatory wishes were exchanged. When she saw Roberto looking smug sharing the credit, she could not resist whispering in his ear, "I did this in spite of you, not because of you." She could not believe her own daring words and the ultimate confidence they revealed. She had not realized the resentment that had built inside of her. She was not a victim and did not need to act as one anymore. The moment of tension between Elena and Roberto soon dissipated, and the couple was able to enjoy the rest of the celebration without any further show of hostility.

The plans for the next academic year included a move to Charlottesville where both had been offered teaching assistantships to further their education. Roberto had a dissertation to write, and Elena was pursuing a master's degree in Spanish literature.

That summer she was accepted to a six-week language institute in Tulane. The children would stay with the Medinas while Elena completed her program. They would use the remainder of the summer to prepare the move. Elena was invited to stay at the home of Dr. and Mrs. Cerda, friends from Cuba, who had made New Orleans home. Although she enjoyed her studies, life at the Cerdas was stressful since the couple was on the verge of divorcing after more than twenty years of marriage. Elena heard, at a later time, that the good doctor was eager to shed his better half. Fortunately, the summer program had come to an end before the fireworks really started, and Elena left to prepare for the move to their new destination.

Charlottesville, located at the foothills of the Blue Ridge Mountains, enjoyed a vast historical tradition as well. Thomas Jefferson, author of the Declaration of Independence and third president of the United States, was from Charlottesville and had designed and founded the University of Virginia, one of the first state universities in the nation. Its design followed the style of Jefferson's splendid home, Monticello. Presidents James Madison and James Monroe had also been part of its history. The buildings were on property formerly owned by Monroe, and both men had been members of the original board of visitors.

University of Virginia, Charlottesville, Virginia

As soon as they arrived in Charlottesville, Elena took a tour of the magnificent terraced lawns bordered with huge magnolia trees in bloom. The academic village, as originally conceived by Jefferson, could not have been a more perfect setting for someone as hungry to learn as Elena was. To her, an informed mind offered unlimited possibilities, and UVA was going to be another excellent opportunity to expand her horizons.

The Medinas moved to Copeley Hill, student off-campus apartments, with plenty of open space for the children to play safely. Schooling was arranged for the kids, and teaching schedules for the couple were assigned by the university. John and Dolores Garcia, old Staunton friends, lived now in Charlottesville where Dr. Garcia was a practicing psychiatrist. Picking Bobby up from school was not going to be an issue since Elena and Dolores would take turns. Once more the stage was set to let life decide what was to be next. The Vidals bought a big color TV as a house-warming present, and the whole family was excited with the prospect of their new life.

Elena was assigned two sections of Spanish I, and she felt that being a native speaker would ease her preparation. *Wrong*! She had not considered that native speakers acquire the language from hearing it spoken by significant adults around them, while second language learners have to know what rules apply before they can construct speech. She found herself having to spend time studying how to teach her own grammar. That was still the easy part. What took some adjustment was the nature of her students. Elena had a class full of young white Southern gents in coat and tie! She had to get out her easy patterns again and build herself a better-looking wardrobe. The students were most respectful, and early in the semester, Elena had built a great rapport with them.

She enjoyed all her courses, especially Dr. Valverde's poetry course. Elena enrolled after both Alex and Roberto had justified their B grades by saying it was one tough experience. Elena sailed through the course with flying colors and could not help but grin at the thought that she had made an A. During this year, she fell in love with Dr. Wolf, her thesis director. Theirs was a platonic relationship since he was openly gay and most respectful of his student. At a party, he told Roberto, "If I weren't gay, I would give you a run for your money with Elena. She is truly a great person." Roberto did not appreciate the quip, which may or may not have been true. At any rate, he became a close friend of the family.

Graduation was set for August for both Elena and Roberto, so it was finally time to look for a permanent job and settle in one place. By this time, Elena was seriously reevaluating her relationship with her husband. She felt that he expected much more than he was able to give. She was proud of what she had been able to accomplish without having overlooked her children's needs. Elena had managed to complete her studies with a straight A average while still cooking and cleaning for everyone. Actually, her brother Alex had been more helpful than Roberto.

Elena thought that the next move was a perfect opportunity for them to part ways, even if it was temporary. Roberto had had three job offers in Tennessee, North Carolina, and Texas; and Elena fretted at the thought of being so far away from her parents. However, the idea of separation and divorce seemed insurmountable, and she was too tired mentally to make such a serious decision now. Taking these feelings into account, she decided to give their marriage another chance, so she started preparing the family's next move, although a decision had still to be made as to where their next home would be.

Thanks to the Vidals, Elena and her family could witness the first man on the moon on the color TV. On July 21, 1969, they watched Neil Armstrong exit the *Eagle* and take a few steps on the surface of the moon. She was amazed thinking that it had taken only a few generations to go from the invention of the radio in the 1920s to this incredible event! Armstrong's words rang loud and true: "One small step for man, one giant leap for mankind."

August 20 was graduation day for the Medina couple. It was also a celebration of Dr. Vidal's saint's day and the ninth anniversary of their arrival in the United States. It seemed so much longer than nine years to Elena. The saying "Ha llovido mucho" (It's rained a lot since) applied here after three babies and two degrees each for Elena and Roberto. Maybe if she slowed down, things would get better between them, she thought.

The day was a joyous celebration. Bobby wore the same suit as he had for last year's graduation ceremony, except it did not fit as well. He had grown a couple of inches but looked dashing in his three-piece suit, albeit with shorter pants. Grandpa Vidal had given him a pocket watch that looked humongous on Bobby, but he insisted on wearing it. Andrea and Joey fit better in their old outfits, so all three looked well-groomed and happy. Elena felt a bit distressed, in the midst of the festive occasion, as they had settled on Houston as their new home. The Vidals assured them that distance was no obstacle, and that they would make the effort for the family to see one another frequently.

On moving day, Elena finally had the opportunity to meet her upstairs neighbors. It had been a busy time and a rough winter, so everyone had kept a low profile. She thought again, how strange all these experiences would have been back in Cuba. "Actually, they would have never happened," she thought. Mobility was not a common occurrence of life on the island, much less the experience of having lived in three cities in the last four years as the Medinas had. This happening was excessive even by the standards of a mobile society such the United States.

ANDREA BERMÚDEZ

CHAPTER 19

Embracing the New Culture

Be who you are and say what you feel, because those who mind don't matter, and those who matter don't mind.

—*Dr. Seuss*

E LENA WAS BROUGHT up with the skills and value system appropriate to an environment in which she never lived. She had the important responsibility to raise her three children but lacked the insights about the culture to which they were born. Fortunately, she was a quick study, so she was able to learn on the job once again. This time she was mostly learning from her own kids who, if listened to, could be the best teachers.

When Elena and Roberto arrived in the United States as political exiles, they never thought that their decision was to become permanent. Once they realized that their homeland was lost, at least for the moment, they needed to figure out what the world out there was like. Most importantly, they needed to determine what the rules and expectations were now that they were to make the United States their new home. Elena had attended American schools in Cuba and had lived in the United States for a year when she was fourteen. She had learned English, but now she realized she had learned words and phrases but lacked the context, the cultural knowledge, to actually communicate. She and Roberto had left behind a cultural system they understood, and now was the time to figure out an unknown environment that was to be home. She found herself at a loss. There had to be an easier way to reach out to life other than through tears of frustration. If there was method to this madness, she was going to find it.

Not feeling sorry for herself was her first step so that she could use that energy to try to decipher the world around her. Elena had heard of the American dream but was learning that it came at a high price. When she thought of the friends she left behind, she realized she had no idea what happened to any of them. It was time to make new friends. But how do you do that in another world? She had never had American friends before. At school in Cuba, she had been friendly with her Anglo peers but not friends with them. They had responded in kind. She explained this disconnect as lack of fully understanding what the others stood for and what they really meant when something was said or done. It was amazing how large the gulf between words, intentions, and actions could be. Elena had only managed to learn empty words devoid of soul. She could certainly conjugate a verb to death, but she lacked the understanding of the value system that determined the deeper meaning of those words. Until she managed to comprehend that dimension, Elena knew that friendships would be difficult, an awareness that would not stop her from trying.

Her first attempts at making friends were clumsy. She would call her new acquaintances two, three times a day just like she had done back home in Cuba. She soon realized that this was not acceptable. Marsha, a classmate at Randolph-Macon, taught her so. She would tell Elena she needed "space" but did not explain what she meant. That was not a concept she had experienced before. To Elena, space translated into distance, and that was not something you wanted between you and your friends. However, this was not Elena's reality anymore. She had to play by someone else's rules, and she could not move forward until she could figure out what those rules were.

Since all aspects of life wrap around a particular concept of time, Elena was determined to figure out its new definition. She had been accustomed to a timeless approach to life. If you were having fun at a party, for instance, why leave? However, she knew better than to challenge well-established mores, so she set out to learn how to schedule her life in chunks of specific times. Elena had come to this realization when she was invited to a birthday celebration that, according to the invitation, was to take place from 4:00 to 7:00 p.m. She had found it odd but complied. Elena even got there early for fear of being late but decided to go around the block a couple of times to avoid arriving too early. She found a number of cars driving in a circle, probably doing the same thing she was. Four o'clock arrived, and everyone showed up at once. Elena was having such a good conversation by 7:00 p.m. that she did not know whether to stand up and leave or to stay and

ANDREA BERMÚDEZ

enjoy her chat. She didn't have to worry too long since, as if rehearsed, everyone stood up and said their good-byes. Elena, of course, did too. She was still chuckling at the experience when she remembered Andrea's seventh birthday party when Marta, her Argentinean friend, arrived with her three kids after the partiers had left. She was beginning to understand why a time limit had to be set. Marta had put her through two birthday parties on the same day, and eight hours of a children's party was a bit too much!

It was great that she had Marta who was going through the same adaptation process as Elena was. They laughed at their awkward efforts to do things in a different way. Marta told her of a time when she was invited to a party, and she only knew the host. She arrived at the address she thought was on the invitation and joined a nice group of partygoers. She introduced herself to everyone since the friend who had invited her was nowhere to be found. Marta had a grand time only to find out later that she had crashed one party and been absent from another! Elena felt her friend was flunking Adaptation 101, but they were not about to give up.

Elena realized how unusual it was back in Cuba to attend a party where everyone was new to her. Back home, she was used to knowing, and being known to, all with whom she socialized. It would have been so unusual for Elena to come into a place having to introduce herself. Someone was bound to respond, "Are you crazy, we have known you since you were born," or something to that effect. At that very moment, it occurred to her that one important difference between the two cultures was the issue of mobility. In the States, it was quite unusual to stay in one's place of birth for an entire lifetime. Generally, people followed opportunities to determine the next place in their journey. This epiphany made Elena understand some of the cultural dissimilarities between her old and her new homes, including the issue of "space" that her classmate, Marsha, had left unexplained.

People's reactions to her ways made Elena feel very sensitive, but with lots of discipline and practice, she eventually learned how to function in both worlds. She new deep inside that adopting new behaviors did not mean totally giving up what had made sense to her for a lifetime. If she could figure out what to do when, she would have the best of all worlds. So Elena set out to do just that. To a certain extent, she developed a "new personality." There was nothing wrong with her old one, she thought to herself. It worked in some instances rather well, and at any rate, it was a part of her she would not want to give up. The "new personality" took some adjustment, but she thought it worked better in her new environment. Her love of life and sense of humor were the bridge between both, and she became quite adept at learning to communicate in different ways while remaining true to herself. If she were speaking Spanish, her hand gestures would immediately reinforce the animated verbal message. When she switched to English, a more restrained nonverbal behavior would seamlessly take over. This swap became routine as she switched from one language to another. One time, while she was visiting with a couple of Anglo friends, her phone rang, and it was Marta. They chatted for a short while, and when she hung up, her friend Margaret seemed startled. She asked Elena, "Wow, you sounded mad as hell, what happened?" "Oh, nothing!" Elena answered, "We were just having a friendly chat." To this Margaret responded, "But when did your friend have a chance to say anything?" They burst into laughter as explanations became unnecessary.

That experience made Elena think of the time she took Bobby to a party at some of her Cuban friends. They were chatting in a circle, and to an outsider, it seemed that everyone was talking at the same time and that no one was listening. However, those in the circle had no trouble communicating. Elena noticed that Bobby's head was moving right and left as if in a tennis match. He suddenly asked, "Mami, who are you really listening to?" It was funny at first until she suddenly realized the link had been broken, and her own child was an outsider who could not relate to her culture.

It was clear to Elena that she would always be judged by mainstream standards, and she became aware of how many times actions and words could be perceived quite differently from how they were intended. She could think of the time when she was living in Staunton with her parents on the grounds of Western State Hospital. One of the patients, who was well enough to do odd jobs, had come to fix the sink. After he had left the house, Sara Vidal realized that the problem persisted. She tried to call him back using a hand gesture, which in Cuba meant "come here," but she had forgotten it actually meant the opposite in the United States. The patient-plumber looked and waved back, probably thinking that the Doc's wife was the one who needed help. She realized a bit too late what had transpired and felt rather embarrassed. When she told her husband, he responded, "Well, Sara, today I can top your story," and proceeded to tell her how he had made a fool of himself that day. He told her that his nurse had called his extension to get some information about a patient and had asked him, "Doctor, please hang on." He had hung up. She came in person and said, "Sorry, Doc, *hang on* means stay on the line." They both laughed. She had to call back at a later time, so at the end of the conversation, she jokingly said, "Now, Doc, you can hang up." Dr. Vidal stayed on the line while the nurse repeated, "Hang up . . . hang up . . . . . ." He finally got it.

Elena was conscious of the fact that many times she would have to allow fumbles like these to take place without becoming embarrassed or inhibited. She knew that taking risks was part of learning a language and understanding its culture, although she also knew how these experiences were being judged. Since the United States was largely a monolingual country, it was very difficult for Americans to develop cultural empathy for those who navigated between two or more languages. In most situations in the United States, having more is better than having less, except when you are dealing with foreign languages and bilingualism. Once Elena heard someone quip, "If you speak three languages, you are trilingual. If you speak two, bilingual; and if you speak one, you are an American." That was a sad commentary, but it was, unfortunately, pretty close to the truth. She could not count the many times a teasing comment had been made about her accent as if bilingual speakers were unique in having one. She asked her class once, "If you think you have an accent, raise your hand." She chuckled when none of her Texan students were aware they did too! Elena went on to tell her students, "Accents are a connection to one's roots. Sometimes they are great reminders of your own history. Since they are distinctive of an area, the minute you travel outside your region— bingo! You have an accent." She realized that in the United States, languages other than English were a political issue, not a cultural one.

Elena grew accustomed to dealing with this barrier and used every opportunity to educate her friends. She could not help but feel proud of being able to communicate in two cultures. She had made the transition and could now afford her pride. She remembered her sister-in-law telling her about her nephew BJ coming from school crying. He had just started kindergarten, and the other kids were making fun of the way he spoke. It took him no time to lose his "accent," but the trauma took a bit longer to dissipate. He would be embarrassed if his mother spoke Spanish in public. BJ was already an adult when he finally came to appreciate his parents' culture.

Elena had had a brush with prejudice many times herself and had grown tired of people telling her "My best friend is a Cuban," probably meaning "I am not prejudiced." Elena knew better than to let these experiences upset her. She had finally learned that, oftentimes, they were a product of ignorance, not hurtful intent. However, she was pained for those who believed the negative messages or for young children whose traumatic experiences with prejudice made them feel inferior for life.

Prejudice, thought Elena, stemmed from fear of the unknown. In such cases, she was convinced that people substituted the reality at hand with preconceived notions and feelings. Elena would tell her students, "What's unfortunate is the fact that prejudice is universal and cuts both ways." She had shared with them an incident that took place late one night after class, when she was driving on the Gulf Freeway in Houston and had a flat tire in a sparsely populated area. At that time, there were no cell phones, so she decided to walk to the nearest apartment complex and seek help. That was not the smartest thing to do at ten thirty at night, but she could not think of a better solution. She removed her jewelry and stuffed it in her purse and, in her mind, bid farewell to her kids and family. Elena knocked on the first door, and a long-haired, disheveled young man who seemed to be under the influence of something, opened the door. Her heart was racing, but this was a point of no return. She explained her predicament, and the young man, without missing a beat, offered to help. He called a friend who was in the next room, and another long-haired, disheveled man joined them. They walked to the car in the dark Houston night, and Elena could not stop thinking that this was her end. To her surprise, the young men got to work, changed the tire, and refused a tip. One of them turned to Elena and said, "Next time you see punks like us, you may think they are nice guys. You were lucky to have knocked on our door because we have Mexicans living next door." She thanked them for helping her and said, "By the way, I am Cuban, maybe next time you see your neighbors, you may think differently about them."

An officemate, a PhD Texan, was ordering lunch for a few of them and said to Elena, "I assume you like tacos." To which Elena responded, "I sure do, but I am from Cuba where we don't have tacos. I learned to eat them here in Texas." Her colleague seemed confused and not too sure she had said something wrong. Later, Elena told someone who came to apologize for her friend's comment, "You know, stereotyping is not always intentional. People categorize because they just don't have enough information."

The rules of the new environment were slow in coming. However, with effort and determination, Elena learned how to navigate. She also learned many valuable lessons that helped along the way, particularly when she decided to divorce Roberto. The one message that allowed her to become a participant in her own life was understanding the value of being an individual and the freedom inherent in becoming one. She did not need

ANDREA BERMÚDEZ

permission from others to think or act. She only needed to rely on her own courage and skills and accept the responsibility for her acts.

Elena enjoyed her life in the United States, except she felt at times she was more an observer rather than a participant. There were so many experiences she had not shared with her American friends that at times she would miss the context of jokes or entire conversations. She would tell Marta, "It's so easy to '*perder el hilo de la conversación*' (miss the thread of the conversation)." Marta agreed and even shared a recent example of what had happened to her when she and her husband, Héctor, visited an Anglo couple who were friends of his. Somehow in the midst of the conversation, the wife had said, "You have to be careful with what you say here. These walls are paper thin." Marta could not keep herself from touching the wall since she was not familiar with the expression and had taken it literally. Héctor could have killed her! She also mentioned her mother's recent embarrassing experience when she had barged into the men's restroom at a restaurant after asking Marta which restroom she should use. Since her mother spoke no English, Marta told her, "Go to the one where the sign has the most letters," expecting the sign on the other door to read "Men." Marta's assumption was wrong; the door had read "Gentlemen." These are funny experiences when travelling but not so funny when you are already home.

Education facilitated Elena's opportunity to function in both worlds. She realized that it had made a great difference that as a child she had experienced schooling at home where she was not considered a member of a minority group. As a result, she had missed the negative messages other culturally different children are exposed to when they attend school in the United States. Unfortunately in trying to assimilate children to the value system of the mainstream, American schools tended to disregard the students's culture. Elena also recognized that home languages were treated as disposable commodities that needed to be shed as soon as the student mastered enough English. It was her experience that those who couldn't assimilate were ferreted out and became marginalized. Elena felt fortunate to have arrived in the United States with a wholesome sense of self, undeterred by the trauma of prejudice. Her American college education had been a key to her successful adaptation to her new life, but she realized that for others it had not worked out the same way. If schools were more responsive and better informed on how to incorporate cultural differences in their educational practices, these children would be as fortunate as she was. Elena felt that education could break down the cycle of poverty, only if and when schools stop the trauma culturally and linguistically different children suffer while attempting social adaptation.

Elena had decided that as long as she felt like an observer, she would postpone applying for citizenship. She would become an American when she felt like one, and she needed more time developing her new identity as a Cuban-American. It took her the better part of ten years to feel she had finally attained enough cultural competence to lead a complete and joyful life in the United States. Maybe there was an American dream, after all. It was definitely not like the welcoming Statue of Liberty had the power to summarily grant a place at the table. You had to earn your place in the culture, and this process took time and determination.

Statue of Liberty (*www.romanvirdi.com*)

The decision to become a naturalized American citizen came upon her return from a six-week study trip to Spain. Elena loved visiting the places from which her Spanish ancestors had come. There were little towns named after someone she knew and memories of the past in places she had never visited before. Elena had fallen in love with the country's splendid culture. She shared with its people a common language and history, but at the same time, she realized how much she had changed in the last ten years. Elena was having a good time, but this was a vacation. While she loved her stay in Spain and loved the beauty and generosity of its people, it was her ancestors' home, not hers. Ten days after returning from Spain,

ANDREA BERMÚDEZ

Elena applied for citizenship. She was finally ready to call the United States home. This decision did not mean she had to renounce her homeland or disavow her roots. The island would always be an integral part of her, but she needed a home. She was tired of not having roots anywhere. On July 4, 1971, she became an American citizen in a very touching ceremony that made her remember her father's words when he was naturalized the year before. "I was married to a beautiful woman, Cuba, but she is no longer. I am now remarried. The United States is my new bride. She is also beautiful in a different way. There should be no comparisons made as each has a unique place in my heart," he told the guests that had joined him and Sara for a celebration. What truth his words had! To Elena, that's what it meant to be a Cuban-American. You could love both countries without taking anything away from either one.

CHAPTER 20

D-I-V-O-R-C-E:
The End of the World or a
New Beginning?

*Some people are always grumbling because roses have thorns; I am thankful
that thorns have roses.*

—*Alphonse Karr*

THE FIRST FEW years in Houston told Elena the whole story of
what her life would be like if she and Roberto stayed together.
When Roberto's mother came for a visit right after the move in late August
1969, it was clear to Elena that they had been scheming to convince her
to stay home now to be a full-time wife and a mother. Mrs. Medina had
already told Elena in her no-nonsense-do-as-I-say style, "This is a good
opportunity for you to stay home. Husbands need a lot of attention and
care to stay happy." These words had made Elena so angry that, for a few
seconds, she thought she had lost her ability to speak. She surprised herself
by responding, "I am sorry, but I did not spend endless hours going to
school, taking care of the kids, taking care of Roberto to give it all up now.
I went through that much sacrifice to make a future for the children, and
what's more, I am not done." Her mother-in-law's face turned ashen. She
was probably thinking how Elena could have the gall to challenge tradition
in such a way. In her world, women were supposed to "serve and obey" their
husbands, so there was no room for understanding or accepting Elena's

stubbornness. Although no more words were exchanged, it was clear that a line had been drawn in the sand.

Roberto had been hired as an assistant professor of Spanish at the University of Houston. They were finally able to get a few extras, such as a new car for Elena. She was ready to give up her old Chevy that she had loved so much. It had performed its job well, but it was in great need of retirement. That semester, Elena was able to get two part-time teaching jobs. She was to teach two courses at Rice University during the fall and spring semesters and two at the Universitry of Saint Thomas. Her plans had been to continue working toward a PhD, but she would have to drive to the University of Texas in Austin, and she had too much on her plate for now. That part of her plan would have to wait.

View of the Houston skyline

Bobby was enrolled in second grade at Holy Ghost, a parochial school that had come highly recommended, while Andrea and Joey would be at Saint Peter and Paul's preschool. Elena and Roberto found a spacious apartment near the schools and settled in. Life was falling in place once again in yet another location. The children, however, seemed to thrive in the family's new routines, such as the afternoon visits to the apartment's swimming pool. Andrea was a natural who, not being afraid of the water, taught herself how to dog-paddle. Bobby was a bit more cautious but comfortable. Joey was petrified, so they kept a close eye on him. That was fortunate because one day, when Roberto and Elena looked his way, he was struggling to stay afloat. Both parents jumped in unison, but it was actually six-year-old Andrea who pushed him toward the steps. It was a close call, so all three children started swimming lessons right away.

Andrea had shown her athletic side early on in Charlottesville when she was watching her dad teach Bobby how to ride his bike without training wheels. Bobby did the usual. In trying to maintain his balance, the bike would go right, left, left, right— crash. After a few tries, he did pretty well. When he was done, both Elena and Roberto praised him for his efforts when out of the corner of her eye, Elena saw Andrea get on the bike and ride forward. The only problem was that she did not know how to brake, forcing her to aim at the trash cans, which, fortunately, did the trick. Andrea was safe and sound. The bike had a small scratch. The trash cans had seen better days, but Andrea had shown how self-sufficient and brave she could be. Those were three fine kids, and both parents were crazy about them.

After just a few months in the apartment, Roberto's boss, Dr. Nieto, called to tell Elena that the house next door to hers on Darnell Street was on the market. It was a good buy, so Dr. Nieto had decided if the Medinas were not interested in the purchase, she would buy it as an investment. Dr. Nieto insisted that they come see it, and Elena and Roberto agreed. The couple became excited at the possibility of owning their first home. The three-bedroom house was in a safe middle-class neighborhood, and Elena fell in love with it. The backyard was big enough for the kids to play and, maybe, for a future swimming pool when they could afford it. Elena and Roberto decided not to let the opportunity pass. Dr. Vidal loaned them money for the down payment, and after signing what looked like a huge stack of papers, they closed the sale and moved in. Very soon the kids had made lots of friends and were really happy in their new home. Elena loved the house and, especially, an area where bikes could still be left outside and found in the same place the next morning.

While teaching Spanish at the University of Saint Thomas, she had met Marta with whom she immediately clicked. Beyond sharing similar backgrounds, both women seemed to want more from life than what they had. Marta's three children were contemporaries of the Medinas', and they also became fast friends. Her husband, Héctor, was an engineer, so he and Roberto had little in common except for their love of sports. Marta was very sociable and enjoyed attending all the cultural activities the university offered. One evening she invited Elena to a student jazz festival on campus. It had been fun, but when it ended around ten p.m., Elena rushed home. Standing at the front door, she was having a hard time pushing it open when she heard Roberto's angry voice. "What kind of late nights are you keeping?" It was 10:30 p.m., and he had placed a sofa behind the door to block her entrance. The wonderfully innocent evening with friends had been ruined in one swift move, but that was not her concern. She needed to stop the distasteful scene before the kids could witness it. With more patience than she felt, she was able to convince Roberto to let her in, knowing that this very moment had irreversible consequences. The thought of the children muted her, so she entered her home without excuses or accusations. If looks could kill, Elena would not have been able to tell her story.

She kept her feelings to herself although there was little she could do to repair the damage. Elena was not ready to make a final decision; life was still too complicated at this time in her life. Fortunately, a few months later in the summer of 1970, Roberto received a six-week scholarship to conduct research in Madrid, Spain. The Vidals offered to take the children so Elena could join him. They had a feeling that all was not well between the couple and were hoping against hope the trip might work a miracle. Elena had just been accepted as a doctoral student in Foundations of Education at the University of Houston and knew that after starting the program, there would be few opportunities for a trip of this nature. She had never been to Spain, the land of her ancestors, and was eager to experience life there, even if it were only for a short time. Elena was going to miss her kids, but they loved being with the *abuelos*.

She planned a study trip for herself that included places she only knew through books. Elena would spend time at the famous Prado Museum in Madrid and learn all she could about the most famous artists in the world, among them her favorites, El Greco, Velázquez, and Goya. She had always wanted to paint, and now she had the opportunity to meet the masters whose work had made them immortal. She was not disappointed. The Prado visits were a powerful experience. Elena later remembered encountering Velázquez's seventeenth-century *Las Meninas* (*The Maids of Honor*) and feeling a direct connection to the times. The painting, displayed in a room to itself, portrayed the Court of Philip IV as in a captured snapshot. The realistic nature of the painting made Elena feel as if she were interacting with the royal characters depicted. When Roberto got home from the library, she could not stop talking about the painting. "I was almost spooked," she said. "The characters seemed three-dimensional and made me feel as if I were one of them."

Elena also planned daily trips to various historical places. That was one of the things that captivated her about Spain. Every site was steeped in lessons from the past, a common past she shared with its people. A trip to the municipality of San Lorenzo del Escorial, near Madrid, took her to El Valle de los Caídos (The Valley of the Fallen), a monument built by then dictator Francisco Franco to commemorate the death of his forces during the Spanish Civil War. Not too far from the monument, Elena visited the Escorial Castle, a blend of museum, royal palace, and monastery. It was built in the sixteenth century as a symbol of Spain's grandeur by King Philip II, the leader of counterreformist efforts in Spain. She could not forget the sharp contrast between the opulent basilica with its extravagant main altar and the austere residence of the king with a small window over his bed from which he could attend daily mass.

A visit to Toledo, a city located about seventy kilometers south of Madrid, was most enjoyable. Present throughout the city, a former capital of the Spanish Empire, was the complex mixture of Christian, Moorish, and Jewish influences on its unique architecture. While enjoying the visit immensely, Elena also had an embarrassing experience when she went into a store looking for a specific request from Dr. Nieto. She collected artwork and was looking for a bell shaped in the form of a turtle showing the typical work of Toledo on its carapace. It was getting late, so Elena entered the store in a bit of a hurry and asked, "¿Tienen jicoteas?" (Do you carry turtles?) The man looked puzzled and directed her to the restroom. Elena instantly realized her mistake. She had used a word *jicotea*, indigenous to Cuba but not commonly understood elsewhere. She went ahead to the restroom not to cause the man further embarrassment and to give herself time to think of the word used in Spain. She found the *tortuga* for Dr. Nieto at that store while living through an anecdote worthy of telling upon her return.

For Elena, the trip reinforced the knowledge she had acquired through study. The visit to Spain made her realize what had preceded her own history and to witness first-hand the cultural contributions Spain had made to architecture, literature, and the arts. The experience also provided her with the opportunity to think about the future of her marriage. "Was there really a future for them?" she had been asking herself. While Elena enjoyed her self-planned journey, Roberto had been busy with his research project. They were physically in the same place but could not have been any farther from each other in spirit. Elena and Roberto were living in different worlds at this time of their lives.

As soon as they returned, Sara travelled to Houston to bring the three children home. It was such a happy sight. The children had had a great time at the *abuelos*, and Elena noticed how good their Spanish skills had become. The Vidals used Spanish as the language of their home, and the grandchildren had had no difficulty adapting. Sara stayed with them for a few days, enjoying the conversations about the trip to Spain and watching the hundreds of slides her daughter had taken.

Once again, it was time for Elena to prepare the family for the new school year. The University of Houston was a great place for Roberto. He was really happy with his job and loved his boss and next-door neighbor, Dr. Nieto. She had never married, so she adopted the Medina family, particularly the children. Joey was convinced she was a dentist when she once helped him pull a dangling baby tooth without much pain. Dr. Nieto also followed Elena's progress at school and was always ready with valuable advice and support. She had been instrumental in getting Elena a scholarship from a foundation she chaired so that the Medinas would not have to sacrifice their income. School had increased Elena's previous responsibilities, which included two part-time jobs and three kids, four if one counted Roberto. In contrast, he had a job. Nothing much had changed.

As summer approached, the Medinas decided to build a swimming pool for the children. The kids had been begging to go back to Maryland and spend part of the summer at the Vidals. That was fortuitous for Elena and Roberto to be able to surprise them. The children were enrolled in swimming classes and had another terrific time with the grandparents. When they returned from their trip, the pool had been finished. As soon as they got home from the airport, Elena turned on the pool lights and opened the shades. The kids stared in wonderment, delighted at the sight. It was 9:30 p.m., and the whole family went for a dip. It was a much needed family fun experience. Elena and Roberto were having another opportunity to start anew, but unfortunately it was not to be.

Their relationship had been withering for lack of attention. Elena had once believed that marriage was for life, so ending it made her feel like a failure. If both had tried to meet in the middle, the marriage could have worked out, but Roberto had no intention of changing, and she had no more to give. It seemed that any efforts now were too late to save the marriage. She could not remember a single time when Roberto had not put himself ahead of the rest of the family. Elena dreaded the fact that the role model might stick, and the children would turn out to be like their father. She was dying inside and needed desperately to be out of her misery.

When Elena finally approached her husband, he seemed surprised, unaware that his wife could have been so unhappy for such a long time. "I have provided for the family, haven't I?" he kept repeating as he had no idea what else he could have done to prevent the disaster. Roberto was also unaware of the fact that he had been duplicating the pattern of his home. Like a tree whose roots overpower the surrounding environment, he had not learned to grow without taking away from others. Soon after, the couple separated, and Elena filed for divorce alleging irreconcilable differences.

One of the mistakes Elena believed to have made in her relationship with Roberto was that she never told him how miserable and lonesome she felt most of the time. Roberto had been taught by example that life was for men to enjoy and for women to endure, so the marriage had left her cup empty. Once she realized that she was really in command of her destiny, it was too late to salvage the relationship. The Vidals' reaction to the news of an impending divorce was almost as theatrical as a stage tragedy. Sara dissolved in tears while Bernardo, in trying to understand the high emotions of the moment, did not realize his voice was betraying his level of frustration. Neither one was brought up to understand that choices and rights are not obliterated by a marriage vow. Elena had to give credit to her parents as both were eventually persuaded by her argument that most times divorce was not the problem, but a bad marriage was. "Night and day we have been," Elena sadly mused. "Life brings enough challenges without adding a daily struggle to keep my dignity," she told her parents. Once they recovered from the shock, they suddenly remembered numerous stories about a Roberto they did not particularly like. Those memories had been suppressed, hoping that things would work out for the sake of the family. In time, they became Elena's strongest supporters. However, neither Bernie nor Alex was ever able to forgive her.

ANDREA BERMÚDEZ

Elena could not remember when she had stopped loving her husband and even wondered if she ever did. Elena had wished for Roberto to be like their friend Brent, attentive and willing to lend her much needed support. Brent was an associate professor at Baylor University Medical School, who had an undergraduate degree from the University of Houston, and was a rabid supporter of the Cougars, their basketball team. They had met at one of the games, which Elena and Roberto faithfully attended. Although Brent was a few years older and a widower, they all became best of friends. Elena realized how easily it would have been to fall in love with Brent, but she never let this happen.

After the separation, Elena felt as if shackles had been removed. She knew it was not easy to be a single mother but had felt like one even while she was married. Her task now was to help the children understand what had happened. Elena felt she had to stay away from saying anything negative about Roberto, but that made her explanations more difficult. As a matter of fact, it was impossible to find words that would make sense to the children as she soon found out when Bobby made it clear by asking, "If you liked him that much, then why did you divorce him?" It was obviously confusing to the children if she only had nice things to say about Roberto, so she settled on, "I loved him, but I did not like him." That gave her an opportunity to offer her children more reasonable answers to their questions.

When the divorce became final, and Roberto accepted Elena's resolve to end the marriage, he turned his attention to dating. His parents were not happy with the prospects since the Catholic Church does not recognize remarriage. Soon Roberto met the woman who would become his second wife and proceedings to annul the marriage to Elena began. She thought they had lost their minds, but it did not surprise her that their *religión mal entendida* would compel them to do so. After letting Roberto know her thoughts about the matter, Elena decided to cooperate. "What hypocrisy!" she told her friend Marta. "How dumb is it to believe that God cares one way or another? These people are going to pay money to obtain peace of mind when peace of mind comes free from just doing the right things." Three children and twelve years of marriage later, the nuptials were annulled. Roberto married his Argentinean bride, resigned from his university post, and left for Buenos Aires.

Elena had found a live-in caretaker that would help with the children and the care of the home. By now, she was almost finished with her studies and had finally been offered a full-time position at the University of Saint

Thomas. She still had to add part-time work at other places to make sure the family remained solvent. These were tougher times financially but, to her, much happier ones. At one of her professional conferences in Arizona, she bought a T-shirt that read, "Bilingual, bicultural, and by myself." She was ready to meet life head-on.

PART VI
Surviving the Odds

CHAPTER 21

Coping with Loss

We must embrace pain and burn it as fuel for our journey.

—*Kenji Miyazawa*

S ARA VIDAL HAD had a congenital heart condition, and her mitral valve was failing. Dr. Vidal had kept her alive through medications, but even these were beginning to block his efforts. As a physician, he knew her time was near unless surgery was performed. In 1976, Houston, Texas, was the place to take Sara. With at least two world-renowned cardiovascular surgeons to choose from, it was regarded around the world as an avant-garde medical center. Preparations were made for Sara to be evaluated, and the surgeon chosen was Dr. Denton Cooley who, by that date, had performed with his team in excess of ten thousand open-heart surgeries, including transplants and valve replacements.

Since Elena already lived in Houston, she offered her home as a base of operations. Valve replacement was still in its infancy, so Dr. Vidal's hopes were not set very high. The date selected for the surgery arrived, and Sara felt confident. All four children were at Saint Luke Hospital by her side. Looking at Bernardo and their offspring gave her courage to go through the risky procedure. Everyone was trying to sound strong and optimistic although they knew the odds were against her.

The wait was intolerable. Elena knew that her mother's heart would be stopped, and her life maintained by a mechanical contraption while the surgeon replaced the ailing valve. She was terrified by the thought of her mother's life dependent on a machine to do its work. Little was said while they waited since the Vidals were preoccupied with thoughts of mortality. After several hours, a smiling nurse appeared to share good news about the surgery, and that details would follow as soon as Dr. Cooley was able to visit with them. This time, the wait was not as unpleasant. The good news perked up the family's mood, allowing moments of levity, while they waited for the surgeon. When Dr. Cooley finally arrived, he assured the Vidals all had gone well but warned the family that it would be a slow recuperation. Dr. Vidal was relieved, and the children overjoyed. After a few days in intensive care, Sara was moved to a private room where the family could visit with her more often. Every day seemed to make Sara look stronger as medical signs were optimistic. A day short of two weeks, she was released to go home with Elena. As the surgeon had predicted, recuperation was slow, but by August she was building up her strength, taking longer walks and able to enjoy visits with her friends and family.

The Vidals fiftieth wedding anniversary was coming soon, and Elena was preparing a surprise celebration for them. She had been able to approach her colleague, Father John Hanes, to say a mass in Spanish so her parents could renew their wedding vows. Elena had a friend with a beautiful soprano voice who was happy to sing the "Ave Maria" just like in the Vidals' wedding in 1926. She invited her parents' siblings and a host of family members to come to Houston and commemorate the special day. The beautiful private chapel at the University of Saint Thomas was bursting with flowers. Behind the altar, there was a large glass window from which you could see magnificent trees and beautiful lush gardens. Sara looked radiant dressed in purple, her favorite color, and handsome Bernardo was beaming at the sight of his happy bride. In perfect Spanish, Father Hanes asked the audience if there were any witnesses to the original wedding ceremony. To his surprise, two hands were raised. Sara's brother and sister were asked then to stand by the Vidals while they reaffirmed their wedding vows. It was a very touching moment for all, and Elena could not stop sobbing seeing her mother's radiance. The celebration was a success, and Sara managed to enjoy every bit.

The Vidals' golden wedding anniversary

As a matter of fact, Sara felt cured being able to breathe gain. She had gradually recaptured her vivacious demeanor. The Vidals were planning on returning home to Hurlock to continue her recuperation. Having been with Elena and her children during all this time had been a wonderful experience for them, but she was adamant about returning to her home routines as the final step in getting well. As soon as her cardiologist authorized her to travel, Bernardo took her home. Those were the happiest months of her life. For the first time, she was living in the moment, enjoying her stamp collection, her TV game shows, and visiting with her many friends. By late November, however, Dr. Vidal realized that something was not going well. He could detect an irregular rhythm in Sara's heart. They immediately returned to Houston to face the grim news. The operation had not been as successful as they had originally thought, so Sara had to remain in Houston close to her cardiologist.

During this time, Elena became fully devoted to Sara's needs. Frequent visits to Sara's physician required that she kept her mother's ID cards on hand. Her mother had been so protective of her real age all her life that her own children had not even known her birth date. Sara had kept the cards that showed her age hidden in a small envelope that read in her stylish handwriting, "Prayers to Saint Jude." She thought this would discourage the "curious" from digging further. Sara was seventy-four, two years younger than her husband. The present circumstances had forced her to break down and share the big secret with Elena who promised her she would not divulge her age.

On December 6, Sara was hospitalized for the last time and, two days later, sent home to wait. Nothing more could be done to extend her life but to keep her comfortable. Her husband, children, older sister Julia, and brother Ray were by her side when her moment of transition arrived on December 11, 1976. A peaceful silence surrounded Sara's passing. Everyone reflected on a prayer of thanksgiving for her presence in their lives and for the many sacrifices she had unselfishly made for her family. Her suffering had come to an end. Sara had gone to a better place. Her passion for education was reflected in her obituary, with the title of "Dr." preceding each of her children's names.

Despite his grief, Bernardo soon returned to his work in Hurlock while everyone else rejoined their respective families. Dr. Vidal's work had been the anchor that had helped him overcome the many challenges in his life. His work had to rally around him one more time. Elena was left to grieve her loss alone and to realize that she was now expected to take her mother's place. She was not as good as Sara had been at holding the family together, so it fell to Dr. Vidal to remember birthdays, anniversaries, and to call his children with reminders. He also learned how to care for himself. Learning to cook at seventy-six was quite a feat, which he accomplished fairly well with minor exceptions. One time, when Elena visited him, he showed her with pride the pantry full of his successful grocery shopping spree. With a twinkle in his eye, he said to Elena, "I can fix a dynamite tuna sandwich. Would you like one?" Thankfully, Elena looked at the can of tuna and realized it was for cats not humans!

Not long after, a call from Dr. Vidal brought on mass hysteria among his four adult children. Doctors had found a blood clot in his left leg, and his offspring had panicked. When Elena arrived in Hurlock, she found her father impeccably dressed with his right leg resting on an ottoman. After greeting him, she observed that she had thought the problem had been with his left leg. He smiled in agreement, switched legs, and remarked, "They look just alike." She returned home knowing for a fact that he would beat his condition with his uncanny ability to play down life's travails.

The respite did not last long. On August 14, 1982, a phone call in the middle of the night would change everything. Elena had agreed to spend the night at her friend Carmen's following an outing to the theater. Andrea and Joey were old enough to fend for themselves, so they had agreed that driving alone at night in Houston was not a safe thing to do. When the phone rang and it was Andrea's voice, Carmen knew it could not be good news. She tried to wake up Elena without alarming her, but a gut feeling made Elena shiver with fear. She knew something terrible had happened. With tremor in her voice, she took the receiver only to hear Andrea say, "Mom, Bobby is dead." His young life had been taken in an automobile accident while visiting his grandfather Bernardo. All four teenagers in the car had been killed instantly.

Life had been sucked out of her. How could this be? It had to be a nightmare. It was indeed a nightmare from which Elena would never wake up. Her friend had to drive her home in the middle of the night. She had to be with Andrea and Joey. They had lost their older brother— their hero. For a few days, Elena was in a trance. A part of her was functioning so she made all kinds of arrangements and phone calls. The other part of her was mourning so intensely she felt numb, like walking on very dark clouds. The family congregated to offer some support. Elena, Andrea, and Joey were inconsolable. Joey was angry, kicking doors, walls, trying not to cry. Andrea was wondering about death for the first time. During the funeral, she told her best friend, "I am sitting here wondering who would be next," too grim a thought for an adolescent. Young people hardly ever think of death, much less their own. Elena, on the other hand, was giving into her grief. After the interment, she requested privacy. She just wanted her surviving children around. They all needed to understand what had happened and figure out a way to survive. Elena spent several days staring at the wall, only interrupted by hysterical sobs. Each member of the family was dealing with their grief separately. Elena suddenly realized what was happening. It was wrong, she thought. Her surviving children needed her, and she had selfishly isolated herself. She needed to function, to be there for her children and move what was left of the family forward.

Elena thought of what her father had done in the past to cope with loss, and decided that returning to work might help her and her children get back on their feet. However, all she could think about was all that had been left unsaid between her and Bobby. As a mother, she felt guilt and responsibility for not being able to avert the tragedy. Elena pushed herself hard, and two weeks later, she was walking down the hall leading to her classroom. She was not sure she could do it, but when the classroom door opened and she saw her students expectantly looking up to her, she knew she had to. The first time, she went through the motions. As time passed, she concentrated on the moment and was able to perform her duties. Her children slowly recuperated with her help, and that of their friends. For the longest time, she felt Bobby's presence every step of the way. When grief was too much to bear, she felt the strength of his arms and mischievous smile consoling her. As months passed, Elena was steadily growing more resilient. She recalled one day mentally communicating to Bobby that it was time for him to continue with his spiritual journey. His presence had invigorated her, and now she could go on strengthened by his many memories. Elena told a friend that at that very moment, she had felt as if a dove had flown away from within her, leaving her with a soothing sense of peace and the certainty that she would survive their loss.

Bobby became an inspiration for all of them. The three learned to relate to his memory rather than to his physical presence. Elena knew that a part of Bobby would always be with her. A year after his death, on the exact date, she received another gift from him, a federal grant to help her students with their graduate program. For many years, on the anniversary of Bobby's death, something positive would happen to Elena or her children. Many times, she would wake up with the feeling she had communicated her love to Bobby directly. It was a comforting sensation that allowed her to go on. Elena and her children had survived. The family of the young man who drove Bobby's car, however, was not so fortunate. His mother had not been able to come to grips with the tragedy so she had overlooked her youngest son's grief. Exactly a year after the death of her oldest son, her youngest crashed his car into a tree not too far from Bobby's accident site. This horrific episode taught Elena that her efforts to remain sane had paid off in helping Andrea and Joey cope with their irreparable loss.

Seven years later, in June, a González-Vidal family reunion was well attended. Bernie and Patricia served as hosts in their beautiful home in Georgia. Elena came alone and found herself the target of her brothers' jabs, particularly Alex's. Her older cousins were still married to their spouses; some perhaps not so happily but together, as was expected of their generation. The men boisterously entertained one another while the women formed their own little groups. Being divorced and younger than the crowd, Elena felt like a fish out of water.

Elena started a conversation with her second cousin Mike, who was just a few years younger, and had always liked her. The natural thing was to ask him about his siblings. Were they coming? He seemed taciturn and abruptly responded. "Olga will be coming later, but Jack won't. He died

ANDREA BERMÚDEZ

last Monday of AIDS." Elena was stunned. It took a few seconds for her to react to the shocking news, such an agonizing death for such a nice young man. They hugged and cried and remembered Jack very much alive and healthy. There were no words Elena could say to make things right, so she said nothing. Both parents were at the reunion, and she had to at least convey her sense of sorrow.

The news travelled fast through those present, but no one was discussing the matter. At the end of the day, Bernie drove Elena and Alex to a nearby hotel where they were staying. Dr. Vidal went along for the ride. The conversation turned to Jack's death. Elena was distressed to witness no sadness in their comments, only contempt and condemnation for Jack's lifestyle. She had had enough of these guys' homophobia and was quick to remind them, "Jack had a mother, your cousin, and her heart is aching for the loss of a son. I know well how much. This is not the time to condemn Jack. He is gone. This is the time to embrace his mother who is mourning an irreparable loss. She needs comfort, not condemnation." Silence followed Elena's words, and right then she knew, without a doubt, that she was not one of them.

It was clear Elena did not want to be like them. She realized that she had kept a semblance of having a family, but she knew deep in her heart that family meant support, love, and acceptance. Instead, she had met with rejection, indifference, criticism. Elena understood, at this instant, that she had to wrestle life on her own. Her new family was her children and her friends. Jack's agony and death had given her the strength to pursue life as she understood it. He had become a symbol of what rejection and contempt can do to the soul. Coincidentally, there were no more family reunions.

Dr. Vidal and Elena remained close despite the distance that was intensifying among the siblings. Notwithstanding his age, he had the ability to adapt to changing times and made a concerted effort to try to understand Elena's generation, her needs, and her concerns. He still had a hard time acknowledging Elena's professional successes. To be honest, he really did not even know what she did for a living, but he was still proud of her. She had borne three of his favorite grandchildren and had dealt with life's blows with dignity and strength. "She is quite a woman!" he always said about his daughter. "Just like her mother was . . . a hell of a woman . . . . . ."

For his 101st birthday party, the whole family, including its extended members congregated at his home in Hurlock.

Dr. Eloy Vidal at 100 years of age

He was having a wonderful time during the several days' celebration when suddenly he felt short of breath and nauseous. His three boys were all thumbs. Even Bernie, the physician son, had no idea what to do. Elena and Joey were clearheaded and could see this was a serious crisis. Despite Dr. Vidal's protests, Joey called an ambulance. While they waited, Elena put a protective arm around her father to try to assure him that everything was going to be all right. At this point, she was the parent, and Dr. Vidal her little boy. Her words did not deceive him, and in a firm and clear voice, he said to her, "This is it, *mi hijita*, you know that." Since Elena could not diffuse the situation, she just held him tight. He was lucid and was still trying to be the strong family anchor. He added, "Don't worry about me. I am really excited about the next step. I have dealt with death all my life. Now it's my turn, and I am not afraid." He may not have known how much courage his dying words had given his daughter. His message stayed with Elena the rest of her life. He passed away three months later with total acceptance of the next chapter in his journey.

ANDREA BERMÚDEZ

Elena was numb to any other bereavement, having experienced the ultimate loss. She accepted her father's passing with the realization that she no longer had an older generation to rely on for answers in times of trouble. She had become the older generation. There was no way out of accepting the responsibility passed on to her. She would have to rely on her own wisdom and experience to help her young ones. Elena was able to let go of her parents by thinking that they had lived full and meaningful lives, and that it was their time for a reward if there was to be one. Her relationship with them was through the many memories they had left behind. Their legacy was their courage to accept the cards that were dealt to them and to do the best they could at every turn.

A few years after both Vidals had passed away, Elena had a phone conversation with Alex, which she hoped would be their last. During the course of the conversation, Alex questioned Elena about her life. "People are suspicious of your relationship to your friend Jamie. It's embarrassing for me to face the rumors," she recalled him saying with righteous indignation in his tone. Elena stopped him in his tracks: "My life is none of your business. I am fully responsible for mine, and you should go about living yours." For the first time, Elena felt free to speak her mind. Alex had taunted her all her life, and for fear of hurting her parents, she had not put him in his place before. She was now a woman in charge of her life, and no one had the right to tell her how to live it.

Elena had lost her much-loved motherland but had survived the experience by finding a home that had accepted her without reservations. She had been through the loss of her Bobby and now lived inspired by his memory. Her relationship with her brothers Bernie and Alex was distant. Elena loved them but being around them required a restraint she did not have. She did not owe them an excuse for not becoming the person they expected her to be. The brothers would always be welcome back, but, this time, on her terms. She had kept a spiritual connection to her family and friends from Cuba even though geographical distance made contact difficult. With time, Elena had gained a very loving and supportive extended family, which included Jamie, Andrea, Joey, their families, and a host of good friends. She was blessed.

CHAPTER 22

Life Goes On: A Tale of Survival

When life gives you a hundred reasons to cry, show life that you have a thousand reasons to smile.

—Unknown

E LENA CONCEIVED OF survival as a pyramid, with spirituality as its base and support systems —such as family, friends, and gratifying responsibilities— buttressing the sides. She felt that these two forces, spirituality and support systems, fueled courage and confidence for an individual to move on. Spirituality, as she defined it, was personalized and inclusive. It did not require that rules be followed even when they did not fit, nor did it threaten spiritual extinction if one should fall short. Support systems, on the other hand, were a mechanism that allowed her trial runs for decisions she was inclined to make. She could discuss ideas with friends and family before these decisions were executed. Fortunately for Elena, her professional activities had helped her expand her mind, gain confidence, and enjoy what she was doing. She was aware of her good fortune, as for many, their professions become a source of stress and frustration. As had been for her father, her profession, although not her chosen one, had proven to be satisfying.

Understanding life and death was a personal matter to Elena, and off-the-rack answers did not satisfy her curiosity or her needs. She remembered her father's words: "Just don't worry about the things you can't change." Words that at first glance seemed simple, but they truly captured her acceptance of life and death as a matter of fact. She would agree with her friend Lynn whose mantra was "to make everyone who comes into contact with me a little better, a little happier." Lynn's words summarized spirituality for Elena as they clearly focused on the responsibilities we have for each other. She also agreed wholeheartedly with Jamie who believed that "nature is my god and the wilderness is my church." In time, Elena had learned to make a distinction between religion and spirituality. She had come to believe that established religions left very little choice and disrupted the direct communication she wanted to have with God, her "maker," whatever or whomever this maker was. She was grateful for all the gifts of nature and felt closer to God when she saw that natural beauty could not be created by humans, only destroyed or changed. Elena felt it was an irony to create an individual only to judge his or her sins and condemn them to eternal rebuke. What kind of god would do that? She believed in a god of kindness, not a god of wrath. Her god was one who knew that life could be a valley of tears and that individuals did the best they could with the benefit of whatever gifts or talents they had been granted.

She could not believe that man-made rules created to ward off infinite punishment were the road to any type of "salvation." Elena's strict adherence to Catholic dogma had only worked for a while. During her early teenage years, she attended mass regularly, joined spiritual retreats, and took any other opportunity to make a spiritual connection. She even thought she might have the vocation to become a nun but, fortunately, found out in time that her aspirations were incompatible with life in a convent.

Elena never forgot the many silent retreats she attended with her friend Isabel. She could not help but smile at the memory of the time when she and Isabel got the munchies in the middle of the night. Although they had to remain silent, they managed to convey to each other that they would like to get a snack. After everyone had retired for the evening, and the convent was dark and quiet, the girls put their plan in action. Both tiptoed down the stairs, hiding behind anything they could find to finally make it to the kitchen. "There's the fridge. We made it," briefly crossed their minds. However, a tall angry-looking figure dressed in black was standing next to the refrigerator. An arm, extended across the door, stopped them cold. Their hearts were racing as they were not sure if this ghostlike figure was real or not. Unfortunately, the figure was real. It was none other than Mother Superior, angry as the dickens at the girls for breaking the silence and for breaking into the kitchen to grab a nibble. Instinctively, Elena and Isabel tried to run to no avail. They were in serious trouble, but they could not stop laughing. "What was so funny?" Elena thought, but her laughter betrayed her thoughts. The girls' nerves finally calmed down, and Mother Superior gently pulled them by their pajama tops and directed them to their rooms. The incident did not escalate any further, except to become a hilarious memory.

Elena became further disillusioned with the established church by the ongoing sex abuse scandals of the priesthood, which finally came to light toward the end of the 1900s, despite the fact they had been happening much earlier. Even the Catholic pontiff finally acknowledged the issues in 2010, too late to offset the damage done to the victims and their families. The harsh denunciation of the Catholic establishment against issues such as same-sex marriage, abortion, and divorce, while protecting pedophilia, seemed hypocritical to Elena. She had quite a few heated arguments about these matters with Alex who blindly took the side of the church. He regularly reminded her of how wayward it was to disagree. Elena, not persuaded by Alex's unsubstantiated arguments, would counter, "Es la ley del embudo: Lo ancho para tí y lo estrecho para mi" (figuratively translated: what's good for the goose should be good for the gander). Sometimes Dr. Vidal would join the fracas only because he seemed to appreciate Elena's independent thinking. However, he would frequently signal to Elena to avoid these conversations with Alex since his religion was all he had.

With spirituality came acceptance of things that she could not change, for example, the passage of time. Attending class reunions had always been a mixture of joy and disappointment for Elena. After all, the "most likely to succeed" from her high school senior year had been run over by a bus in Spain, and the "most handsome" had lost all his hair and had let extra weight cover his once well-defined muscles. She was fearful about what all else time had concocted against her classmates. Notice that she never included herself in this picture since she felt as if she were still young and vibrant. Elena often wondered who the aging person staring back at her in the mirror was. She recalled how her mother had hated mirrors, and now Sara was right there reminding her not to look too closely. Other than these thoughts, Elena did not dread aging like her grandmother or her mother had. She was more like her dad, always considering the alternatives.

Dr. Vidal, at 101 years of age, had always been positive about life and its challenges. Elena had often asked him what was the secret to his longevity, to which he would reply by quoting Mark Twain: "Age is an issue of mind over matter. If you don't mind, it doesn't matter." Elena thought that a positive attitude and a sense of humor were his weapons against time. Dr. Vidal tended to turn life on its humorous side. On one of Elena's visits to Hurlock, he had left a note embellished by one of his celebrated caricatures, this one of a hunched old man carrying a medical bag. The note read, "Gone to the nursing home, as a doctor, not a patient."

As a matter of fact, she thought she had resolved the issue of aging after the near panic attack she had when she turned fifty-five. Elena had recovered swiftly upon recalling her daughter Andrea's similar reaction to turning thirty and Dr. Vidal's comments to her: "Don't worry, dear one. I have already been there three times." Aging was hardly a piece of cake, but admitting that there was nothing she, or anyone else, could do to stop the clock at the place of one's choice made it much easier to accept. Elena also felt that aging had some advantages for her. For one, money had ceased to be a problem, and she was able to plan a comfortable retirement.

Living in the moment had been a significant message Elena had turned into a philosophy of life. She had pretty much figured out how to survive in a world chock-full of surprises by hanging on to the present and making the best out of it. Elena often told Jamie, "If we concentrate on the now, the sadness of the past and the fears of the future do not come to haunt us. The moment is eternal. We are always in the now." She was very determined to practice what she preached. If there was a problem for which she could not provide an answer, she tried to let go or, at least, set it aside so she could concentrate on the now. Her constructive attitude was self-inspiring and allowed her to manage her expectations about life.

Elena viewed sanity as a byproduct of spirituality. "In order to survive, I have to stay sane." Pursuing sanity through humor worked hand in hand, and she believed that in her family, the sane and funny ones were the same people. Elena was convinced that doing something crazy, like trying to get food in the middle of the night in a dark convent, was a release valve that kept people from actually going crazy. Humor was a more reliable weapon to deal with her inadequacies than drugs or alcohol, which only served as temporary escapes. She had tried the alcohol route, and it had not worked. Self-anesthetizing night after night only created more problems when the effects were over and done. It finally dawned on her that she had a problem, and she definitely could do something about it. With the help of intense therapy and her loving and understanding children, the excessive drinking episodes became a thing of the past. Elena was lucky she could stop when she did. She had been spared one more time, and this time she had been rescued from herself.

Support systems meant survival to Elena who believed friends, family, and activities of interest had helped fill her cup. She had met Jamie Baxter, a medical doctor, who had cared for her when her regular physician had gone on vacation. They hit it off right away when Elena shared stories about her father's plans to never retire from practicing medicine. Jamie was impressed, but was fast to make it clear she was not planning to wait that long for her retirement. The ear infection was gone, but their friendship blossomed as they found how much they shared in common. Jamie had become a great sounding board since she could listen attentively and offered advice only when asked. She was quiet and disciplined, a good balance to Elena's vivacious and always-on-the-move personality. Their friendship was a growing experience for both, and they soon decided to move in together.

Elena cherished her friendships but always lived with the fear that they were a fleeting experience. After all, she had never seen her Punjab friends again, except for Ofelia with whom she reconnected after forty-five years of separation. Elena had to tell herself that the devastating aftermath of the Castro revolution was a once-in-a-lifetime dreadful experience, and that now she could rely on the permanence of good friendships.

Meanwhile, Elena's youngest son Joey had met Marie while at the University of Texas, and the couple's relationship turned into a full-fledged romance. They were now planning a fall wedding. Elena was excited that her adult children were in the process of making lives for themselves. She was selfishly thinking of the possibility of grandchildren, and the thought thrilled her. On October 1994, Joey and Marie tied the knot in a Catholic ceremony officiated by Father Green, who had been Joey's principal at Saint Thomas High School. The wedding reception was a bit of a circus as it included her ex, Roberto, his wife, their child, the rest of the Vidal and Medina older crowd, Jamie, and the bride's family. Joey was happy he had found his soul mate. When he had a chance at his first dance, he asked Jamie. That was a most extraordinary moment for Elena. The silent statement had said all that needed to be said.

Although Andrea enjoyed the wedding party, she was thinking that when she and Charles would marry, they would not have an extravagant ceremony. She preferred to honor the special relationship they had developed with a more intimate celebration. When it happened a year later, it was really private, just the two of them. They had eloped, calling Elena after the fact to share the happy news. It was fine with Elena. She had learned to respect her children's decisions and not make them feel guilty for thinking their own thoughts and acting accordingly. In one respect, she was sad that an era has ended, and now her kids were grown-ups facing the responsibilities that come with marriage. She was hoping that they had

ANDREA BERMÚDEZ

learned on their own how to make their relationships last, as her divorce from Roberto had brought so much pain to the whole family. The feeling of sadness was mixed with a sense of relief. She now had her children's spouses, Marie and Charles, as allies in supporting and loving her children. It had been a difficult road to raise the three as a single mother. Having lost Bobby, she had felt like a failure. Seeing Andrea and Joey happy in their marriages made her feel she had not been such a dreadful mother after all. At the end of 1997, Elena received the happy news that Andrea was expecting.

While her immediate family was growing and becoming very close to her and Jamie, Elena's relationship with her brothers had become more distant. Bernie had retired after a successful career in urology, and he and Pat had become empty nesters. He would occasionally send e-mails to Elena and never forgot a birthday. From a distance, his communication was loving, and the two seemed to genuinely appreciate the other, although there was no mutual understanding. There was no communication with Alex or David. She knew that eventually she would reconnect with David who had always been her favorite. His life had been a living hell confronted by his own ill health and the presence of two ex-wives. Alex never married and hung on to religion as his only ally. He made it his mission to try to reconvert Elena who resisted by reminding him, "If God wanted me to hear that message, she would come to me directly, not through you." Alex considered it a blasphemy to refer to God as "she."

In 1998, Charles Paul, Chuck, was born to Andrea and Charles. Elena was beside herself with joy. Her first grandson gave her a taste of the perfect relationship: spoil the baby rotten and then send him home to his parents. Elena was great at that as she doted on the little blue-eyed masterpiece. When Chuck was three years of age, he had already shown a remarkable ability to communicate in sophisticated adult language. He was delighted with his baby sister, Milly, who was born a year earlier. Joey and Marie waited till 2000 to start a family. Once started, they didn't seem able to stop as they produced four beautiful children: Heather, Bobby, Elena, and Joey Jr. The six grandchildren were Elena's pride and joy. When she was with them, she reverted to her childhood and realized the beauty of innocence. Elena would not dwell on her concern about what kind of destiny each would have. Being a grandmother was an amazing experience, a privilege, which she had decided to enjoy with abandon.

Professionally, Elena had continued to succeed as a well-liked university professor and prolific writer. When she was presenting her research at a conference in San Francisco, an editor from a well-known publishing company approached her with an offer to participate in writing a textbook series. She flew to New York, and the offer turned into an incredible opportunity she could not refuse. The textbooks became one of the most successful projects in the history of that publishing company. Other professional experience included administration, which actually had not been part of Elena's career path. She took a year sabbatical to finish one of her book projects with plans to return to her faculty job when completed. She decided to spend the year in New Mexico where her friend Lynn lived with her family. Elena had visited them on several occasions and had found the high desert landscape inspirational for creative work. Before the year was up, she had agreed to go to Atlanta as a guest speaker in a professional convention. When her plane arrived, she waited for the passengers from the previous flight to deplane, and as luck would have it, her boss was one of them. They greeted each other warmly as he was one of her favorite people at her university, and he shared the sad news about his associate provost who had unexpectedly passed away. What he said afterward surprised Elena. He wanted her to consider the post as an interim. She did not take the offer seriously, but she did not deny having thought about it a lot. Elena was back as faculty, and for three months, there were no calls from the provost. When the call came, she had had time to think about it, so she accepted.

Elena never thought she would enjoy being a university administrator, but the job gave her a chance to see higher education from another perspective. Teaching had been a venue to make a difference in her students' lives, and for them to do the same for her. She had thought administration was mostly a bureaucratic experience but found this not to be the case. With her first administrative experience, she had an opportunity to work directly with faculty issues and university curricula, two of the most critical building blocks in education.

After three years as associate provost, Elena was offered the job of academic vice president at a small college in Santa Fe, New Mexico. She and Jamie had loved their visits to Santa Fe and decided it would be an exciting new beginning. Jamie was able to reestablish her medical practice in New Mexico. It was hard for Elena to leave the institution where she was loved and respected to accept a post in an unknown environment. She had spent her best years there, and although she would be leaving many friends, the decision to accept the new job seemed to be the right one. Her retirement party was attended by hundreds of people, from custodians to the president. Each brought presents and good wishes for her future success.

ANDREA BERMÚDEZ

It was a heartwarming event. When Elena stood up to speak, she summed up her feelings of gratitude by saying, "Few people have the opportunity to enjoy such a substantial expression of love and support other than at their funeral. I am glad to be alive to thank each one of you for being in my life."

Moving to New Mexico was quite an elaborate enterprise. After being in Houston for thirty-one years, there was a lot to move. They found a wonderful adobe home with magnificent vistas of the Sangre de Cristo Mountains. Sunrise and sunsets were magical, and so was the beauty of the clear skies. At night you felt you could touch the stars. What an incredible place! Elena would say, "God lives here. She may or may not vacation in other places."

Elena had planned to stay at Santa Fe Community College until retirement. It seemed like the perfect job in the perfect place. She was impressed with how passionate faculty and staff were about their work and felt a connection to them. However, Elena's immediate supervisor was a different story. His inability to articulate a clear vision for the college did not allow for a productive working relationship to develop. She decided that retirement would be a better alternative, but an offer from Miami Dade College in Florida gave her an opportunity to delay the decision for a couple of years.

Jamie decided to stay in New Mexico during that time, since exporting a medical practice to another state was not an easy endeavor. They both loved Santa Fe, so they agreed that it would continue to be their home.

Miami Dade was an incredible experience. Her new president could not have been more welcoming and organized an elegant campus-wide reception where she met most of her future coworkers. There was warmth and excitement in the air, and Elena felt she would be a good fit for the campus. She was not wrong. From the administrators, faculty, and all levels of staff, Elena felt as respected and well-liked as she had been in Houston. Every morning at ten a.m., her secretary, Peter, would come in with a *colada* (a shot of Cuban espresso), saying, "Doctora, la medicina" (Doctor, here's the medicine). The first time Peter brought her the *colada*, Elena had not realized that she was to share it with others in the tiny paper cups that came with it. She drank it all herself. Cuban coffee is not for the faint of heart, so when Peter realized what she had done, he said laughingly, "Doctora, you've been gone too long." He was right. The Miami experience was very satisfying professionally and personally. She was sorry that it had come so late in her career as she thought this place really had it all.

Dr. Elena Vidal Medina addressing the faculty at
Miami Dade College, Kendall campus

Elena felt grateful to have had the opportunity to live in Miami and reconnect with her roots. For the first year, she gorged on Cuban food and immersed herself in Cuban music. Her staff was tickled when she returned from the cafeteria for the first time, overly excited to have eaten a *papa rellena* (breaded mashed potato stuffed with ground beef) after not having even seen one in over forty-five years! Elena realized how many times she had taken for granted the little things in life, and how important these had become when no longer available.

During 2006, the rumor that Fidel had died spread like wildfire all over the United States. *Calle Ocho* in Miami, the heartbeat of Cuban life, was in a celebratory mood. People in the streets carried Cuban flags and lived a few days in the hope that Castro was finally gone. To everyone's disappointment, it had been a false alarm. "Bicho malo nunca muere"

(Bad insects never die), she was thinking when her office phone rang. The voice from the other end was a reporter from the *Santa Fe New Mexican* wanting to know how she felt about the news. She had to control herself to sound objective. New Mexico was calling her to ask for her opinion. How appropriate was that! The place she had called home actually felt like one.

Elena was so touched by the many gestures of appreciation she received during her tenure at Miami Dade College. It was hard to leave the college, however she realized that she had spent most of her life working, and it was time to be good to herself. She was sad to go, but she was closing her career with *un broche de oro* (a gold brooch). She missed Jamie, and Santa Fe was home. She had retired twice before, and the third time was a charm.

CHAPTER 23

Two Worlds Apart: Cubans in Exile and in the Homeland

A journey of a thousand miles begins with a single step.

—*Laozi*

AFTER MORE THAN half a century of communism, Cubans on the island have become isolated from the rest of the world. Not so for Cubans in exile who, along with the separation from the homeland, have experienced a different set of circumstances. Cubans have arrived on U.S. soil in several distinct waves. Overcoming language and cultural barriers was not effortless or uncomplicated for any of them. For most immigrant groups, the road to the American dream was fraught with discrimination and prejudice as a result of differences in religion, language, and ethnicity. The earlier the wave of exiles, the easier it was for them to find acceptance and help in navigating their new lives. These first groups had the empathy of the American people as they were viewed as heroes escaping communism. Elena recalled the notoriety she and Roberto had gained while in Virginia as anti-Castro crusaders, often being invited by various organizations to share their experiences. However, exotica had its limitations. On the one hand, they experienced the warmth of a welcome, but on the other, they felt they were guests and not hosts.

Until the mid 1980s, there were no quotas restricting Cubans exiles entering the United States, so the most serious challenge was to be able to leave Cuba safely. The first group comprised mostly of white Cubans, professionals, displaced business owners, and political figures who spoke, at least, some English. If they were not able to bring their fortunes, they looked for work. No job was beneath them. It was not uncommon to find physicians and lawyers parking cars or teachers doing the most menial jobs. They attended night school, job permitting, and plowed right ahead. The early group included the fourteen thousand unaccompanied children sent to the United States under Operation Peter Pan, sponsored by the Catholic Church and American taxpayers. Most children went to foster homes until they could be reunited with their parents. In the early days, this was a mass exodus, and soon Cuban exiles in the United States neared two hundred thousand people. The special immigration status granted to the early groups made it easier for them to gain permanent residency and eventually citizenship.

Freedom Flights started around the mid-1960s until the early 1970s with the purpose of reuniting families. A vast majority was relocated outside Miami. The Castro government established emigration restrictions that included political prisoners, younger Cubans of military age, and professionals needed in Cuba. These restrictions defined the demographics of the second wave, making them older and less educated than their predecessors. After the Freedom Flights ended, the exodus continued via other countries, principally, Spain, Mexico, and Venezuela. Most became parolees, which was the most common status assigned to Cuban émigrés after this time. Their adjustment to life in exile was that much harder when considering the negative attitudes that emerged due to large unemployment rates and opposition to the use of Spanish evidenced by an "English Only" policy approved by Florida voters in 1980. It was an uphill road to start a life with the stigma of being a parolee and of speaking a language other than English when the only "broken rule" had been to seek freedom in self-defense.

From April to October 1980, Castro lifted restrictions and declared the Port of Mariel open to Cubans who wanted to leave the island. Hundreds of boats left from Miami to rescue the refugees seeking asylum in the United States. Despite the coast guard vigilance, the Mariel Boatlift included almost one thousand successful operations responsible for bringing more than a hundred thousand undocumented Cubans, the Marielitos, to U.S. shores. The lives were saved, but now the Marielitos and the boat owners were facing prosecution for suspected illegal activity. However, the alleged criminality was not found to be punishable by law. The very small percentage of refugees that had previous criminal or mental history was placed in custody by the Bureau of Prisons since Castro refused their repatriation. South Florida, almost single-handedly, absorbed the great majority of the mostly working-class Marielito population without any lasting negative consequence. Rumor had it that the Marielitos were all escapees from Cuban prisons and mental asylums, but this myth has been proven false as a large number have become productive members of their respective communities. Gone was the empathy for Cuban migration, and this group, as well as subsequent ones —who came largely for economic reasons rather than political— met resistance rather than welcome.

In the early 1990s, when the Soviet Union collapsed and stopped subsidizing Cuba, thousands of Cubans, the *balseros*, fled the island in their rudimentary man-made crafts, seeking political asylum in the United States. Those who were repatriated risked retribution, and those who were able to stay joined the struggle for cultural adaptation. Some have stayed in Miami and have helped to turn the city into a burgeoning Latinized metropolis, a symbol of economic, social, and political power of Cuban-Americans in the United States. A number of *balseros* relocated to already existing Cuban communities mostly in Texas, New Mexico, New York, and California.

Although exiled Cubans are referred to as *meringues* (softies) or *gusanos* (worms) by those who stayed behind, their lives have been anything but easy. Giving up the homeland was a difficult experience that had led many to a variety of posttraumatic stress disorders. Exiled Cubans have given up what was familiar and valued and traded for a world unknown filled with challenge and, at times, despair. The hopelessness of ever reuniting with loved ones or of seeing their native soil has caused much sorrow for expatriate Cubans. The first ten years Elena spent in exile were the most difficult. Aside from the financial and emotional struggles of starting a new life with rules unknown, the thought of not being able to be by Tata's side when she died or of never seeing her friends again haunted her.

She believed that if anyone left a place by choice, there was the possibility to return or visit. It would not have the same finality as the decision to become an exile, which carries with it permanent banishment from the island as confirmed "enemies of the state." When Cuban exiles were stripped of their nationality, they became homeless, adrift. If the decision to leave is made to escape persecution and fear, the loss of the country is excruciating and definitive. Years later, Elena confessed to a friend that every single night, she cried herself to sleep disturbed by thoughts of a past that could never be revisited.

After 1959, Castro imposed the Agrarian Reform, which contained a series of laws seeking the division and redistribution of large landholdings.

ANDREA BERMÚDEZ

The Agrarian Reform sought redistribution of large landholdings

At the same time, the laws forbade outsiders from owning sugar plantations. In an effort to reduce the extremes of poverty and wealth, Castro's policies had managed to create an impoverished majority. After the fall of the Soviet Union, Cuba entered what the Castro regime called a special period of scarcity and rationing, a time that has been extended in perpetuity. The *Libreta de Abastecimiento* (supply booklet) has determined the amount and quality of the food Cubans on the island can consume. Despite hardships, they continue to survive and make the best out of so little ("hacer de tripas corazón").

Not too many countries experience scarcity as much as Cuba has. Two fundamental needs of modern society are running water and electricity, which many Cubans do either without or with less. Water is distributed every other day to the households and stored in cisterns built on the roof. If electricity is cut, which is a common happening, the water distribution is skipped for that day. No electricity means no fans and no air-conditioning for the tropical-island summer days. Housing is also a serious issue among Cubans on the island. A great majority live in overcrowded dwellings, sometimes more than a few families, and many times, several generations in the subdivided crumbling mansions that no longer reflect their illustrious past. It is a difficult life, but fear of retribution keeps Cubans from complaining about their living conditions.

Dilapidated apartment building in Havana

The peso economy has also created a dual caste system based on those who have access to dollars and the luxuries these can buy, through what is known as *pesos convertibles* (convertible pesos), and those who are paid in *pesos cubanos*. However, most things they need are sold in *pesos convertibles*. This system benefits mostly tourism, the privileged in power, and transactions in international markets. The average salary is very low, the equivalent of ten to fifteen dollars a month, when compared to those received by exiled Cubans living in the United States or elsewhere. Cubans in Cuba have learned to do without basic staples to survive. Individuals living under the peso system receive government subsidies including inadequate housing, insufficient food, health care, and education.

Education and health are generally referred to as the "crown jewels" of the Castro regime. Free health care and education are prerogatives in Cuba, and the country enjoys a good reputation for the medical help it exports to other countries such as to Hugo (a.k.a. Ego) Chavez's Venezuela in return for petroleum. The Castro government claims to have eradicated illiteracy, but what it doesn't tell you is that there is a strict censorship over what is published, including the media. Cubans can read but not to expand their horizons, or to think critically but to receive communist indoctrination.

However, Castro's propaganda works sometimes on public opinion. On one occasion, Elena and Jamie had been invited to celebrate a seder meal during Passover at a friend's home. Among the guests was a wealthy Jewish-American woman whose mother had been born in Cuba. She and her husband were left-wing millionaires who were sometimes blinded by either guilt or by their own perceptions of reality. They had experienced Cuba through books and guided tours, so they had developed a pro-Castro idea of life on the island. Elena was getting fed up with the accolades Castro was receiving from the couple, when she suddenly heard the wife say, "Fidel has been maligned." A friend sitting to Elena's left gave her a squeeze of appreciation for the torture she was experiencing, but Elena had had it and made her point by blurting, "Would you also say Hitler has been maligned?" The conversation switched to golf. Graciously, the host and hostess called Elena that very evening to apologize for the intellectual pretense of their two guests. Elena also expressed her regrets.

Because there is so much need among the people of Cuba for food, medicines, and other staples, Cubans have become very inventive about solving problems. What they call *resolver* (to resolve) makes them find answers to their problems in the most unusual ways. Streets are littered with trash since the collection service is inadequate. Fortune comes out of misfortune for those who are creative, and Cubans fit that bill. There is a character found in the street called *buzo* (scuba diver) who dives through trash bins to find valuables that can be transformed into something useful. These recyclers have become an eyesore to the Castro government, which wants to pretend that life in Cuba is "peaches and cream."

All Cubans have suffered Castro, either through exile or because they stayed. The level of suffering is the same, but the circumstances are quite different. Exiled Cubans have been deprived of seeing their homeland again and reconnecting with their roots. Those who stayed have had to live in misery, barely able to attend to their most basic needs and having to beat the system without being caught. Fear is the common ground between the two groups. For exiles, there is a fear of losing their emotional survival after so many years of being forcibly kept apart from their birthplace. For those who stayed, the fear is more imminent as it has to do with their own physical survival.

Despite the different worldviews, Cubans in exile and in the homeland share an undying love for the island. When Elena went to Guadalajara as an exchange faculty in the 1990s, she stayed at a university lodging shared with five professors who still lived in Cuba. At first, Elena was self-conscious of being considered a *meringue* and feared rejection from her compatriots. That was not the case at all. They embraced Elena, and the group could not wait till the evening gatherings when they would share their very different experiences and laugh, as one people, at the world's foibles. Elena contributed funny anecdotes about her non-English speaking relatives' attempts to communicate in English. She told them about her Uncle Ray who could speak English better than he could comprehend it and his trying to carry out the task his sister had assigned him. Their neighbor was coming over to bring some homemade cookies, but Sara had to run a quick errand. She asked her brother Ray to entertain the neighbor until her return. When Sara came back, she found her neighbor gone and asked Ray what had happened. He casually said, "She came, talked to herself for fifteen minutes, and then left." Much laughter and more stories followed.

In turn, the Cuban professors described conditions in which they lived with such humor that you would think they were telling jokes. When Elena asked about transportation issues, her compatriots told her about the *camellos*, huge red trailers attached to a semi, which could transport three hundred passengers at a time, stopping every fourteen blocks.

A "camello"

Although the situation was far from funny, they described with humor the pushing and shoving to get in and, most importantly, to get out without missing your stop. "If one could laugh at life's vicissitudes the way her people did, surviving would be a cinch," Elena thought. One day, she asked her fellow Cubans if they knew about a bookstore. "Sure, there's one just a few blocks away," said one and proceeded to tell her how to get there. Elena set out for the bookstore, and she walked and walked and walked.

Then it dawned on her that her new friends were used to long-distance walking much better than she was, and that "just a few blocks" was a figure of speech! Elena caught a taxi back.

Life is full of coincidences, and sometimes it seems like everything happens for a reason. One of the Cuban professors happened to teach philosophy at the University of Havana, so Elena asked her if she knew Xenia. To Elena's surprise, the professor responded, "Are you kidding, she was one of the most respected voices of Marxist-Leninist philosophy in Cuba." "What do you mean she was?" Elena asked, afraid to hear the obvious. "She died in an automobile accident in 1985, while preparing to defend her second PhD dissertation at the University of Moscow." Elena was speechless. Her friend and, at a time, member of the Punjab sisterhood was gone. Elena was too stunned to feel the sadness that later invaded her. They had been separated by contradicting ways of life, and now it was too late to reach out for her friend. Elena thought that after more than five decades exposed to such different environments, Cubans could never again be one people. She hoped to be wrong.

CHAPTER 24

Completing the Circle:
A Visit to Castro's Cuba

Always forgive your enemies; nothing annoys them so much.

—*Oscar Wilde*

VISITING CUBA AGAIN was one of Elena's dreams but also one of her worst fears. She had lost her cousin Manuel after his visit with his grandchildren in tow when he suddenly fell ill and had to be transported back to the United States by air ambulance. Although Manuel's illness had nothing to do with the visit, she thought maybe it was a jinx. Stories of petit-harassment by Cuban officials scared her, even if they had been a bit exaggerated. The thought that she could be arrested and never return to her home in the United States had kept her from making travel plans. But her greatest fear of returning to her homeland was the reality of seeing what had happened to Cuba.

Elena knew that the past she remembered had ceased to exist but was afraid to face the storm. She had no one left back in Cuba, only the remains of those who could not leave. Although a stronger force within her was saying it was time to put the past behind, she was fearful of finding that her memories of Cuba had been only an illusion. She told herself many times that everyone's past is gone. What was so different about hers? "The difference is," she thought, "that I have kept it alive through memories I have not completely let go. Most people's past dies a little at a time. Mine will be wiped out all at once." She feared her own reactions. Would she be able to accept her life as it had happened and not the way she had planned it? She had to know.

The time to visit Cuba had arrived. She had to see with her own eyes what had been left of her beloved island after so many years of economic struggle. The U.S. embargo had been in place since late 1960 when Castro's Marxist-Leninist inclination became evident. Despite the lack of trade between the two countries, Cubans on the island had survived shortages of food, medicine, and unsuitable living conditions. Elena decided to join a group of educators who had organized a trip to Cuba. Her first step was to obtain a license to travel from a federal agency in Washington DC, since only specified groups were authorized, including the one she chose: "full-time professionals whose travel transactions are directly related to their research."

Because of travel restrictions imposed by the United States, they had to leave through Canada. Elena was relieved to know they would not be flying in a dilapidated Russian plane, as she had experienced in 2003 on a day trip to Moscow from Saint Petersburg. At the time, Elena and Jamie had been horrified with the condition of the aircraft. There were no seatbelts, and seats would sway back and forth, refusing to stay in their full upright position. At one point, Jamie found a piece of metal lying on the floor and gave it to the unsmiling flight attendant, politely asking, "Is this important?" The flight attendant casually flipped the piece into the overhead compartment, answering Jamie with a cryptic, "No." The experience was a bit frightening but made for a great story later.

Elena and Jamie were actually flying in a modern airbus to Cuba with all the convenience of contemporary travel. When they landed at José Martí International Airport in Havana, Elena could not help but think of Tata and could still see her face on that fateful day of August 20, 1960, when she and Roberto had left Cuba for the last time. Elena was several decades too late for a reunion with Tata, and her heart ached with guilt at the recollection. She suddenly became aware that she had no one to see in Cuba. Her friend Xenia had passed away years before, and Elena thought Sebastián would be too old to still be alive. She wished she could visit Tata'a relatives, but she had left no direct descendants. What a strange feeling to arrive in Cuba and know no one!

Her first impression flying over the island did not prepare her for what she witnessed once on the ground. Even the people who worked at the airport did not look like the fellow Cubans she remembered. Loathing and contempt were palpable from those strangers greeting her to their "new Cuba," a Cuba that clearly did not welcome her with open arms. "Give people a chance," she told herself. "These are hired hands, and they may be running scared." Elena was determined not to give up this soon in her journey. Luckily, things moved faster than expected despite one highly intoxicated traveler that was threatening to delay the process. With minor aggravations, the group was off to their guided tour of Castro's "paradise."

Elena had been told by the travel agency that once in Cuba, she could move around the country unrestricted but, secretly, wondered if this promise was sufficient assurance that there would be no trouble. She realized that to enjoy her visit and attain the sense of closure she was seeking, her attitude had to change. At first, Elena resisted tours of Havana, afraid that they would make her feel more of an outsider. She just wanted to wander down streets she remembered and see for herself what her life would have been like had she stayed.

At her disposal, there were taxis, buses, planes, and rental cars because she had dollars. Her Cuban compatriots had to use slow and infrequent *camellos* to transport themselves from one place to another. These transports, according to the Cuban friends she met in Guadalajara, were called aspirins, one every four hours. However, she just wanted to walk to become reacquainted with the city of her birth. For the first couple of days, that is what Elena and Jamie did. It was a strange feeling not to know where they were or recognize the landmarks she thought she could vividly remember.

During her visit, they were staying at Habana Libre, a four-star hotel she knew as the 1950s Havana Hilton. The hotel had recently been refurbished and included a variety of high-dollar amenities such as an Olympic swimming pool, a solarium, three restaurants, and a number of other services. It was in the heart of the city, a short distance away from her old stomping grounds. She could not fully enjoy the experience, thinking that Cubans on the island could not afford this kind of luxury. In contrast, she knew they lived in crowded and worn-out shacks with little hope for improved housing. The government had failed to fulfill the promise that each Cuban would benefit from home ownership in accordance with their Urban Reform legislation. However, Cubans accepted their destiny with humor and resignation. She had heard about neighbors of a building that had been sinking for the last thirty years, which they had dubbed the Titanic. Elena's mood lightened at the thought that Cubans on the island could still laugh at their fate.

There were parts of Havana that had been restored in preparation for tourism, a capitalist venture the communist government had to entertain in order to survive. This was the irony of ironies, using the maligned capitalism to save their revolution! As a result of the restoration efforts, Old Havana had received a face-lift for outsiders to enjoy. What had happened to "Cuba for Cubans," a favorite Castro slogan in the early days? What had happened to Cuba? to her native city? Havana had been transformed. Living here had to be a nightmare her compatriots suffered on a daily basis. Streets had the look of an air-raid aftermath. She found herself in a crumbling city plagued by old structures with precariously perched balconies airing clean laundry. There was trash, uncollected trash, everywhere. It had been said that Havana was the dirtiest city in Cuba. Elena believed it now.

All Elena could do was to go back in time fifty years, when she and Roberto had left Havana for the last time. She remembered it as a clean, ultramodern metropolis where night lights and traffic made it look like a city that never slept. Elena was thinking of the many times the whole family hopped into Dr. Vidal's blue sedan to watch the night lights along Paseo del Prado, a major artery that ended in the Malecón. She had vivid images of the thrilling neon ads of the time, especially the "Jantzen-wearing" swimmer that dove into a pool over and over again. The neon ad was no longer there. Actually, Elena recalled that eliminating city lights was one of the first actions the revolutionary government had taken. The darkness that engulfed Elena had nothing to do with the artificial lights now gone. It had to do with the death of another memory.

On day 3, Elena and Jamie took a bus to Varadero Beach, a favorite of many Cubans and tourists from around the world. The last time she had been there was during her brief honeymoon in 1960.

Varadero Beach

Elena associated that earlier visit with her youthful hope that her new life with Roberto was an end-all to their troubled experiences with the early days of Castro's regime. Looking back, it had not worked out that way. Elena was thinking of the miles and miles of Varadero's white powdery sand, and the cloudless skies that seamlessly mixed with its translucent blue waters. She thought of the many times she had felt this same ocean caress her, and the memory was so real she could almost taste the salt in the air. Since childhood, she recalled the joy of jumping in the waves, of feeling she was indeed a part of nature. Varadero had been a place to celebrate life at its best. Now, she had the opportunity to savor it again.

It did not surprise her to see that the beach had been converted into a resort with miles and miles of five-star hotels and amenities catering to tourists. Nature was still there showing off its splendor. She ignored all the trappings as she had done during her childhood adventures, when instead of luxury hotels there had been the mansions of those with means to own one of nature's works of art. Varadero Beach was a heavenly experience, a paradise for tourists, and whether she liked it or not, she was one of them by virtue of being able to afford it. The turquoise waters were as beautiful as her memories had portrayed them. She could not get enough of the view. It was almost as if she had never left. Elena ran into the water with the energy and joy of a child and poured its salty contents all over her face, her hair. She wanted to cover herself with magnificence.

After several hours enjoying the beach and eating succulent meals, the women decided to take an early bus back to Havana. They were tired, burned to a crisp, and most definitely, looking like bums. A few minutes into the trip, the bus was stopped, and two *milicianas* (militia women) with rifles entered the vehicle. They made a beeline to where Elena and Jamie were seated and asked to see their travel documents. Elena felt wordless in both languages as a sense of foreboding paralyzed her. Jamie could sense Elena's apprehension, so she collected the passports and other documentation to allow the two women to inspect them. No words were exchanged, and the *milicianas* returned the paperwork with just a nod. They got off the bus, and the trip to Havana continued without further disruption. Elena could feel her rapid heartbeats as if they were inside her head. Her fingers had gone numb from pressing them against her purse. It took her the better part of the 140 kilometer trip back to Havana to collect herself. One of the thoughts that intrigued her was how did the *milicianas* know Jamie and Elena were in that very bus and why they had been singled out. Elena suspected that they had been watched all along, and now they knew not to take any chances during the rest of the visit.

ANDREA BERMÚDEZ

After that incident, Elena refused to put herself through a series of disappointing experiences going down memory lane, but she was curious about the places that had been her old favorites. She wanted to share the family home and her school with Jamie. Not a good idea! Her home in Alturas de Miramar was also crumbling. It had become public housing, having been partitioned for multiple families. The big mango tree that had graced its entrance was no longer there, and the faces that peered out the windows belonged to no one she knew. At this point, Elena suggested that they should not visit her much-loved Ruston Academy campus. She already knew that the facilities had been turned into a training camp for military recruits, so she was not in favor of putting them through another let down.

Jamie understood what Elena was going through in this journey "home" but found words inadequate to express herself. She had never lived through so much loss and admired anyone who would be able to face it seemingly unscathed. Elena decided they had been through enough validation of her past; it was time to see what was here now. She had heard so many times that concentrating on a closed door interfered with finding the promises the future had in store. To be able to move on, it was time to stop letting those closed doors stand in the way.

Elena spent the rest of her time trying to not look back and compare but taking in the new Cuba. However, images of Old Havana kept intruding. She was well aware that the Old Havana (La Habana Vieja) they were seeing now was just a façade, a shell of what it once was. Almost emptied of its former residents, La Habana Vieja had been deprived of its venerable character and turned into a tourist hot spot. It was still thrilling to walk around the Plaza de la Catedral and admire the splendid baroque cathedral with its irregular towers, one taller than the other. Old Havana was the heart of her city, and it made her feel she was indeed in Cuba, even if it was a Hollywood version.

Havana Cathedral Plaza

Watching the traffic of the city was a foreign experience for Elena. Attention-grabbing vehicles made up the sparse but noisy traffic: *fotingos, almendrones, bicitaxis*. Drivers blew the horn (*fotuto*) at one another when passing since there were no rearview mirrors in most vehicles. The *fotingos* —refurbished antique Chevies, Fords, Pontiacs, Cadillacs— majestically rolled down the streets, showing off their multicolor shine and elegance.

Fotingos

The *almendrones* were also old cars, but in a state of disrepair, running with parts conceived only by creative *resolvedores* (problem-solvers). The 1950s had frozen in time. Elena thought that the *bicitaxis*, roofed tricycles for the transport of passengers, were a testament to Cuban inventiveness. Some even exhibited artistic talent and creativity as they appeared in a variety of bright colors, some sporting pictures or symbols of revolutionary heroes. The *bicitaxis* gained notoriety as having been opposed by the government when they first started, seen as a form of capitalism sneaking in.

ANDREA BERMÚDEZ

Bicitaxi

Although considered semilegal, they continued to operate. The government had come up with an alternative, albeit capitalistic as well, a more modern pedaled vehicle. Known as *coco-taxi* for its yellow coconut shape, the vehicles picked up tourists right in front of their five-star hotels.

Public transportation had also failed. Havana, with its more than two million residents, was served by a very infrequent and inadequate bus service. The converted trucks or *camellos* were almost at the point of extinction. Some referred to Fidel in private as the King of the Desert since his policies had made water scarce and introduced camels to Cuba. The *camellos* were being largely replaced by horse-drawn wagons, which also served as a means of transportation. Regular taxis were available only for those who could pay in convertible pesos. Riding the infrequent and crowded *guaguas* (buses) cost about a dollar, a fortune for workers who were paid in Cuban pesos. After forming a long line to board the bus, passengers had to follow a preferential order that had been assigned to determine who actually got to ride on that particular bus or had to wait for the next one. So getting on the public bus successfully was a social test Elena would not pass. The tourists' option was no comparison— spiffy ultramodern buses equipped with video, air-conditioning, and toilets. The cost of a ride was far beyond what a Cuban national could afford. Buses imported from China provided interprovince service, and that was only available in convertible pesos.

A visit to the Vedado District, where Elena spent most of her school days, brought her happy memories. She remembered it as a residential neighborhood that was now transformed into a commercial center. Seeing mansions still standing, bearing the scars of time, she wondered about the fate of owners who had fled. There were no new buildings, no skyscrapers. One of her old favorites, Habana Libre Hotel, where they were staying, was still one of the tallest buildings in the city. With its twenty-seven stories, the hotel's height was hardly remarkable. The hotel was located on Twenty-third Street, known as La Rampa, which was a very popular area for locals as well as tourists. A native would refer to it in lofty terms: "I associate La Rampa with an open space that leads to the sea, as if that space contained all the energy of Havana."

Near La Rampa, and adjacent to the hotel, Elena and Jamie ran into one of Havana's most famous gathering places, the Coppelia Ice Cream Parlour, with long lines to attest to its quality and a wait of forty-five minutes to an hour. The line could be bypassed by tourists who could use a more efficient section and pay in convertible pesos. Elena suggested they stand in line. She wanted to feel she was "one of them." The ice cream parlor was housed in an attractive modern building decorated with a spiral staircase and a stained-glass dome. Jamie and Elena enjoyed the best ice cream they had ever tasted and delighted in the conversations that took place while waiting in line.

This experience called for them to continue the stroll down Twenty-third Street, which took them to the Malecón (boardwalk), the social hub of the city.

ANDREA BERMÚDEZ

Malecón

They could see the old buildings hanging on to vestiges of their past splendor, now en route to restoration, financed in large part by foreign investors. The crashing waves challenged locals attempting to swim or fish, and Elena wondered how many *balseros* had started their journey out of Cuba from this very spot. While gazing at the sea and experiencing the glorious Malecón sunset, Elena made a promise to herself. She needed to find a way to reconnect her children and grandchildren to their Cuban heritage. "Personal identity, much like a tree, needs the benefit of having roots to develop and grow. My children and grandchildren are drifting away from what gave them a beginning. I've got a lot of work to do when I get home," she told Jamie.

Before they left Havana, Elena recorded in her diary the experiences of their week-long visit to Havana. Her demeanor was deliberate, but it failed to conceal the emotions she had been through. No doubt, the visit had been a cathartic experience. Elena felt emotions she had held back for most of her life. Her heart went out to those who had stayed behind. They were a strong and proud people— a different people. She felt very Cuban, but the world she had just experienced was also Cuban. Did she even understand or embrace it as a part of her history? To heal completely, she would have to meld those two worlds into one. That would have to be the next step, and it would have to start by accepting that life never stays the same and that choices make people. Confusing acceptance with approval had been her mistake. She did not have to agree with her countrymen to be saddened by the circumstances of their lives. Sharing their sadness was her first step.

"La Habana se desmorona (Havana is crumbling). The large cracks in the street added to the dilapidated appearance of its buildings, some falling and others propped up to avoid the inevitable, portrayed Havana as a city mistreated by time. Havana had become a chink in Castro's armor.

"La Habana se desmorona" (Havana is crumbling)

A guided tour of the city might not show the realities with which the Cuban people are living. Tourists do not get to see the collapsing infrastructure of broken pipes, water loss, sewage leaks. They don't see the flooded streets that look more like Venice because the drains did not work as they should. Tourists' points of interest, transportation, and meals, however, are another story. Nothing is spared to indulge the whims of visitors from other worlds. Cuba for Cubans? What an irony!" Elena noted in her diary.

She finally understood how Castro explained himself away after so many unsuccessful ventures. The United States is Castro's "*totí*," a small black bird that, according to Cuban lore, is to be blamed for everything. "Yankee Imperialism," the "fall guy," the single big excuse Castro has used time after time to cover up reasons why many of his promises have gone awry. From the beginning, Fidel promised democratic elections within eighteen months but, instead, stayed in power for more than half a century. Various government offices have promised improvements in housing, infrastructure, transportation; but those promises remain unrealized. "How could he blame anyone other than his own arrogance and thirst for power?" Elena realized that it had to be hard for Castro to take a look in the mirror.

"Why don't people rebel?" Elena's friends continuously ask her. "Have you ever lived in fear? Have you ever been stripped of your human rights, of your dignity, to the point that you depend on the government for your daily subsistence?" Elena's questions are answers that underscore the powerlessness and dread of the people living on the island.

After 2006, Fidel's health began to deteriorate, and on early February 2008, he stepped down, transferring power to his brother Raúl. However, the hope of change has not materialized, and life in Cuba is nothing but more of the same. Elena was thinking how the revolution had become a failed experiment. Fidel's words of 1953, while in his first court appearance accused of the Moncada Barrack attack, "History will absolve me," kept coming back to her. Those words had become Castro's mantra as he tried to cover up his failures. After her visit to Cuba, Elena doubted history would be that kind.

EPILOGUE

My dear grandchildren,

Shakespeare, the famous playwright, once said, "Life is a tale told by an idiot." I guess he was referring to how events do not make much sense when retold. I hope that my story does make sense and that you learn to value my life, a life well-lived.

At the time of this writing, I am recently retired and living in Santa Fe, New Mexico, with my life partner, Dr. Jamie Baxter, and two smart and rambunctious dachshunds, Lily and Charlie. Last July, we lost our beloved red miniature dachshund, Libby, a very special soul and, two months later, our princely twenty-year-old cat named DOC.

I have written this book for you. I feel great sadness that you will never have an opportunity to enjoy the Cuba of your ancestry, an island blessed with the beauty of its landscape and its people, but cursed with a tragic history of abuse and neglect. I am proud of my fellow Cubans who have dealt with their destiny with pride and acceptance. The stories I tell you in this book confirm the strength and fortitude of the Cuban people. Like most of my compatriots, I love life, respect hard work, and appreciate God's gifts on a daily basis. Losing one's homeland is a harrowing experience, and earning the "American Dream" requires much sacrifice and determination. There were many tears mourning the loss of the life I knew and understood. Now, as I look back, I am grateful to have been in a country that gave me the opportunity to realize the person I was supposed to become.

The critical events narrated in the book are factual with the exception of names I have changed to respect others' right to tell their own stories. The last chapter describing my return to the island has not happened yet at the time of this writing. I am still fearful of witnessing the Cuba of today after so many decades of neglect and scarcity. However, in my mind and heart I have imagined my return many times, so I have incorporated those feelings and perceptions as well as the experiences of friends who had the courage to visit the island. I am hopeful that when you are all a little older we can visit Cuba together, and only then will I feel that my journey has been completed.

On July 1, 2007, I retired for the third time (from three different States) and decided to go back to New Mexico where I have cultivated an extended family of good friends. I have also been fortunate to reconnect with a few of my good friends from Cuba after many years of separation. I count as special blessings to have all of you in my life.

By the way, of all the titles I have ever earned, my favorite one is Nani.

Con todo mi cariño,

Nani

Santa Fe, New Mexico
September 19, 2010

PHOTO CREDITS

Barroso-Lavín Collection— See pp. 16, 17, 20, 25, 33, 35, 38, 47, 56, 57 68, 69, 74, 93. 96, 101, 108,113, 132, 133, 145, 156, 170, 173, 193, 229 234. Also back page

CanStock Photo— See pp. 23, 27, 28, 48, 88, 97, 98, 99, 100, 102-106, 109-112, 114, 115, 117-127, 130, 131, 134, 135, 137-139, 141, 166, 183, 249, 250, 252, 257, 259-261, 263. Also cover page

IStock Photo— See pp. 90, 107, 160, 204, 217, 264

Miami Dade College— See p 244

Roman Virdi (www.romanvirdi.com)— See pp. 59, 214

Ruston-Baker Foundation— See pp. 75, 76

INDEX

F

Finlay, Carlos, 40, 70
Floridita, 22
fotingos, 260
Fountain of Youth, 110
Freedom Flights, 247
Frente Revolucionario Democrático.
    See Cuban Revolutionary
    Democratic Front
freshwater turtle (*jicotea*), 139, 220
Fusilamiento de los estudiantes, 34

G

García Menocal, Mario. *See* Menocal,
    Mario García
gecko (*salamanquita*), 139
General Weyler, 39
Generation of 1898, 40
Geografía de Cuba, 130, 142
Gómez , José Miguel, 45-46
Gómez, Miguel Mariano, 49
González, Elena, 42
González, Elián, 146
González, Máximo, 38, 41-42
González, Ray, 230, 252
Grafton, Martha, 200
Granma, 51, 157-59
Granma Landing National Park, 127
Grau San Martín, Ramón, 49-50,
    106, 144
guaguas, 261
Guanahaní, 25
Guanahatabeyes, 23-24
guerrilla warfare, 26, 51, 155-56
Guerrita de Color (Little War of
    Color), 34
Guevara, Che, 51, 116, 156, 161, 163

H

Habana Libre, 256, 262
Habana robber frog, 140
Hanes, Fr. John, 80, 228
Hatuey (chieftain), 26, 155
Havana Hurricane, 19
Héctor (Marta's husband), 79, 213,
    219
Hemingway, Ernest, 22
    Old Man and the Sea, The, 22
Hotel Louvre, 111

I

immigration, 247
Independent Black Party. *See* Partido
    Independiente de Color
Independent Party of Color, 46
INRA (National Institute for Agrarian
    Reform), 161
Instituto de Idiomas, 167
Isabela de Sagua, 116
Isle of Pines, 101, 142
Isle of Youth. *See* Isle of Pines

J

Jagüey Grande, 114
Jefferson, Thomas, 204
José Martí International Airport, 170,
    255
José Martí Park, 118
Julia, 230
July 26 Movement, 50, 156-57

K

Katia (Sara's friend), 20

ANDREA BERMÚDEZ

royal palm, 133-34
Rubio, Amaro, 177-78, 182-83
Rubio, Marco, 148
Ruston Academy, 70, 73, 75, 167, 259

S

T

U

V

OKANAGAN UNIV/COLLEGE LIBRARY

02118313

OKANAGAN UNIVERSITY COLLEGE
LIBRARY
BRITISH COLUMBIA

Mental Health Issues & Aging

BUILDING ON THE STRENGTHS OF OLDER PERSONS

Carolyn J. Tice
Ohio University

Kathleen Perkins
Louisiana State University

Brooks/Cole Publishing Company
I(T)P™ An International Thomson Publishing Company

Pacific Grove • Albany • Bonn • Boston • Cincinnati • Detroit • London • Madrid • Melbourne
Mexico City • New York • Paris • San Francisco • Singapore • Tokyo • Toronto • Washington

A CLAIREMONT BOOK

Sponsoring Editor: *Lisa Gebo*
Marketing Team: *Connie Jirovsky, Margaret Parks*
Marketing Representative: *Dianne Lindsay*
Editorial Associate: *Terry Thomas*
Production Coordinator: *Kirk Bomont*
Manuscript Editor: *Sara Shopkow*
Permissions Editor: *Linda Rill*

Interior Design: *Jim Love/Studio Arno*
Cover Design: *Jim Love/Studio Arno*
Cover Illustration: *Margot Koch/Studio Arno*
Indexer: *Elinor Lindheimer*
Typesetting: *Studio Arno*
Cover and Interior Printing and Binding:
 Malloy Lithographing, Inc.

COPYRIGHT © 1996 by Brooks/Cole Publishing Company
A division of International Thomson Publishing Inc.
I(T)P The ITP logo is a trademark under license.

For more information, contact:

BROOKS/COLE PUBLISHING COMPANY
511 Forest Lodge Road
Pacific Grove, CA 93950
USA

International Thomson Publishing Europe
Berkshire House 168–173
High Holborn
London WC1V 7AA
England

Thomas Nelson Australia
102 Dodds Street
South Melbourne, 3205
Victoria, Australia

Nelson Canada
1120 Birchmount Road
Scarborough, Ontario
Canada M1K 5G4

International Thomson Editores
Campos Eliseos 385, Piso 7
Col. Polanco
11560 Méxido D. F. México

International Thomson Publishing GmbH
Königswinterer Strasse 418
53227 Bonn
Germany

International Thomson Publishing Asia
221 Henderson Road
#05-10 Henderson Building
Singapore 0315

International Thomson Publishing Japan
Hirakawacho Kyowa Building, 3F
2-2-1 Hirakawacho
Chiyoda-ku, Tokyo 102
Japan

All rights reserved. No part of this work may be reproduced, stored in a retrieval system, or transcribed, in any form or by any means—electronic, mechanical, photocopying, recording, or otherwise—without the prior written permission of the publisher, Brooks/Cole Publishing Company, Pacific Grove, California 93950

Printed in the United States of America

10 9 8 7 6 5 4 3 2 1

Library of Congress Cataloging-in-Publication Data

Tice, Carolyn J., [date]
  Mental health issues and aging : building on the strengths of
older persons / by Carolyn J. Tice and Kathleen Perkins.
      p. cm.
  Includes bibliographic references and index.
  ISBN 0-534-20754-5
  1. Aged—Mental health. 2. Adjustment (Psychology) in old age.
3. Mental health promotion. 4. Psychiatric social work.
5. Geriatric psychiatry. I. Perkins, Kathleen R. II. Title.
RC451.4.A5 T53   1996
362.2'084'6@ 150dc20   95-43480
                                                          CIP